Being Here

MYLOGS

from:
Beckie
Christmas 2022

Mark Huisenga

ISBN (Print): 1540644529
ISBN (Ebook): 9781540644527

Interior Design by Booknook.biz.

Table of Contents

Preface

AS THE NAME OF THIS book implies, Being Here: *mylogs* is an account—but of what? First, it's not a full account of anything. The word "logs" invokes "entries" and *mylogs* is a collection of entries I've made about various events, experiences, and other matters over the course of many years. Most of these entries were created in the 1980s, except for the chapters Five and Six which describe events between September 24, 2001 and October 2005. However, there are entries as late as the 2010s. Many entries are written in the present tense, though they happened now a long time ago. I've been working on *Being Here*, then, for 30 years. I wouldn't be writing these accounts if I didn't have something that needs relating. Over the years of writing and rewriting, I've changed the tone of the original entries, which are mostly edited out now. Rather than make *Being Here* sequential, I've organized the entries by theme, although these themes tend toward sequential accounts. This approach also suits my personal style.

Who am I writing for? Initially the entries were just for myself, so that one day I might return to the events and ideas of a particular period of my life. There are some experiences that I must recall, experiences that should never be forgotten. However, most of us crave an audience; thus, I'm craven.

My life – in segments – is one theme in *Being Here,* but there are one or two other themes. To the extent that my own life is an extension of human life, there is a larger theme of living. A wise man once said, "to be is to be related," and so another theme of *Being Here* is relatedness—that is, a certain valuing of relationships between each other, the world and the universe. One must approach such valuation cautiously. We humans have a tendency to perceive events a certain way, and that is how they appear to us; what we perceive and what we think we perceive may be very different.

We tend to create narratives about events in our lives, but the narrative we tell ourselves may be just one of many possible narratives. In the following pages is my narrative of certain events. In some cases, I give alternate narratives. An account of events is never simply an account – so many views are possible. We look for a thread, which sometimes unravels and sometimes gets tied into knots to keep it from unravelling. We pin reality down. We impose our narrative on reality. The narrative that follows is my attempt to pin down a version of my life, but there are others.

This paragraph, preface to the second edition: Why a second edition? I was unsatisfied with the first edition's editing. But, more importantly, I have endeavored for greater clarity about certain questions concerning the first edition.

CHAPTER 1

THERE'S A JOKE IN THE Himalaya adventure travel business that there are two kinds of trekkers, those who look up and those who look down. The ones who look up want to see the mountains; those who look down are distracted by the filth and excrement. In Kathmandu, there is not so much looking up as looking down and side to side; there is so much to take in that the senses can quickly be overwhelmed.

Kathmandu's airport portends chaos. Perhaps on the plane's approach to the runway, those passengers with windows facing north get a view of the Himalayas above the smog over Kathmandu Valley. Ganesh, Langtang, Dorjé Lakpa, and mountains with less recognizable names jut into the heavens. Descending into the Valley, passengers can see jumbles of buildings and streets, temples and traffic jams, malls and motorcycles. One used to see paddies and pastures across the Valley floor. These marks of an agricultural economy have given way to the press of humanity that has filled Kathmandu since the Maoist conflict began in the 2000s.

Upon disembarking from the plane, passengers may have to board a bus to be driven 100 meters to the terminal; there are no jet bridges. Buses aren't a certainty though, and sometimes passengers must walk the 100 meters. In the terminal, harried security guards point the way to Immigration. Ramshackle chairs with cracked plastic and ebbing foam padding provide uninviting seats for a new wave of passengers waiting to depart. At Immigration, queues form haphazardly as officials give brusque instructions or stare off into space. They don't inspire confidence in efficiency. Immigration's slowness is more than matched by the speed, or lack thereof, of baggage handlers. Luggage is taken off the plane by hand and piled onto carts, which are then pulled to Baggage Claim by human mules. Typically, just one or two of a half-dozen luggage belts are in working order, so the luggage is brought into Baggage Claim by hand. Ever on the alert for smugglers, Customs officials stop and search Nepali nationals as they try to pass through with their luggage, while foreigners move through quickly.

This situation is an improvement on the past. The first time I arrived in Kathmandu and was clearing Customs, there were dozens of locals grabbing bags, trying to earn a little side money, or baksheesh. As I was picking up one of my bags, a boy ran off with another one. He wasn't stealing it but, without asking if I needed help, took it to the bus that would bring us to our quarters. The scene outside the airport is pandemonium as family, friends, taxis, porters, and hustlers all jostle together to greet the newcomers. Occasionally, a policeman will try to restore some type of order, but usually to no avail. One Indian guide said in the 1970s he went to the airport to greet a group of tourists and noticed a couple of hippies on motorcycles holding welcome signs for Bob Segar. He hadn't heard the song "Katmandu" and didn't know Bob was a rock star. Those were quieter times. Now there are so many people with signs and placards that even Mr. Segar might be missed.

An early tourist stop in Kathmandu is the Thamel district. Thamel is the central location for food and tourist goods, from trekking gear to mountaineering equipment, from Tibetan thaankas (religious paintings) to brass from the Tansen region, from "What a Long Strange Trip It's Been" T-shirts to Nepali shoulder bags (jhollas), from drugs to horoscopes, from Zen bookstores to Buddha Lounge music, it is all there, along with beggars, pushers and thieves. Handcrafted items are abundant, reflecting the aspirations of the culture; some are of exceptionally high quality and some are little better than trash. Newbie tourists typically respond in one of two ways—go on a shopping spree or get completely overwhelmed and duck into a bar or restaurant. Bargains can be had if one's timing is good; the monsoon season, the morning's first customer, or the last customer of a lousy day, can all be to the shopper's advantage. For a time, Thamel had a shockingly overt red-light district, which was not traditional, but has since gone back underground.

If not immediately, then on their first full day in Kathmandu most tourists go sightseeing. Some of the usual stops include Boudhanath Stupa, Pashupatinath, Swyambunath, Durbar Margh, and other places around the Kathmandu Valley. On one guided tour I was leading, the group visited Swyambunath, known also as the Monkey Temple for the obvious reason that monkeys lived in the surrounding woods. A couple of women broke off from the main group to look around, stopping at one of the temple buildings. By the entrance was a small sign that said, "no shorts," and they were both wearing shorts. People in Nepal, and India too for that matter, greet each other and say goodbye with the salutation, "Namaste," a word that has since passed into Western pop culture. The women asked if they could enter the temple and the greeters said "Namaste." So, the women left, believing they had been told, "No more stay."

What often surprises people is the age and diversity of temples. Kathmandu was an Asian crossroad where religions and cultures mingled reaching back to antiquity and was a likely center of esotericism. The temples and arts reflect this history.

After a day or two of sightseeing in the Kathmandu Valley, most guided tours set out to another destination: on a trek, or to a jungle camp, river rafting, a visit to Pokhara or Lumbini. Relatively few tourists have the time to really *explore* Kathmandu and engage with people who have shaped it over the millennia, especially the Newars, but more about Kathmandu later.

The Trekking experience in Nepal can be highly variable; think of it as "you get what you pay for." Everything from the quality of tents to the quality of the food comes down to what one is willing to pay. Some companies sell treks without an English-speaking guide, sometimes led by a Nepali who has a marginal command of the language. This caution applies doubly for trekkers who speak languages other than English. The most expensive treks have the best cooks, guides, and equipment, including medical supplies and even a doctor, sometimes led by a big-name mountaineer. Unfortunately, my experience with mountaineer guides was that most trekkers don't get what they pay for. Mountaineers generally don't speak the language, so can't translate, understand little about the culture except what they've read in books, and aren't attentive to the needs of paying clients. They can regale trekkers with nighttime stories of mountain exploits and recite histories of various attempts on different peaks. For trekkers who enjoy such narratives, a mountaineer can be an interesting guide; otherwise, it's better to join a group whose guide has spent time in the culture, not on a mountain.

Departing Kathmandu trekkers might fly or take a bus, or both, to the trailhead. Just getting there can become its own adventure. Airport scams happened all the time. A common swindle was for some official-looking person to ask to see your ticket and, with sleight of hand, return a ticket – but not your own. No one can be sure they've got an assigned seat until they're sitting in it. Then the plane might fly all the way to its destination but not be able to land because of cloud cover or wind, and then return to try again the next day. Waiting lists can extend to days and gobble up precious vacation time. Busses can start to look positively inviting under such circumstances, unless of course the bus breaks down, the road washes out, there are labor issues, or other nasty problems that can come between a group and their destination. One must hope for the best but plan for the worst. And this point marks the biggest difference between the best trekking companies and the others: the best companies will have a Plan B.

A typical trekking day starts at dawn with a wake-up basin of hot water and tea, delivered to the tent door (assuming you're touring with one of the better companies). Trekkers have half an hour to pack up their bags and get ready for the day ahead before breakfast is served. There is a dining tent, usually with folding stools around a table, and everyone gathers there for the meal. Breakfast might be anything from eggs and toast to cereal to rice or chapattis with curried vegetables. After breakfast people see to their last-minute needs and within 90 minutes after sunrise the group starts off. The porters have already eaten breakfast by the time that the trekkers are just getting started and have a half-hour's lead by the time camp breaks.

PORTER CARRYING DHOKO

Portering is a nondiscriminatory occupation, as well as equal opportunity. Nepalese of various ethnic groups, men and women, even boys and girls, all have an opportunity to be a porter. The main qualification is that they can carry a heavy load on the head, neck, and back; a special basket ("dhoko") with a headband attached to it is slung just above the forehead and the neck carries most of the weight of the load. It is amazing the things that people will bring on a trek, which the porters have to carry. Bottles of liquor are common, along with all kinds of snacks, candies and chocolates, pillows, electric razors (sorry, no outlets), Walkmans (in the 1980s) or smart phones (today) with a library of music, hardcover books, and on and on. Among trekking guides there was legend that a certain rock star and his model wife brought a full-length mirror with them. In the new millennium, besides smart phones, trekkers bring their computers, tablets, and god-knows-whats. Why go if you can't take it with you? Porters who have been at it long enough have cracked and calloused feet with toes that might be splayed six inches across from little toe to big. Sometimes when they get above the snow line, porters risk frostbite and are known to lose some of their toes, if not freeze to death. Porters' behavior was a constant source of aggravation for my friends who ran some of the local trekking companies. They didn't like to get complaints from trekkers about the condition of the porters, nor did they like to see the porters suffer from inclement trekking conditions. Many of them, now successful entrepreneurs, started out as porters themselves. Trekking companies would send shoes and warm clothing for the porters to wear on treks and expeditions. Unfortunately, the porters would sometimes gamble away their shoes and warm clothes in a card game, or simply sell them for cash. The more experienced guides would keep the shoes and clothes until the porters absolutely needed them, and then hand them out.

Some porters had done no other work their whole lives, and it showed; they looked a decade older than their actual age. They often smoked and would sit around campfires every night to cook and keep warm. In the pre-dawn hours, one could hear them hacking, coughing up their lungs. Tuberculosis was endemic. Many porters had higher aspirations and knew that the key for them was to learn English. They would pepper me with questions about how to say various English phrases. The porters could aspire to a job as one of the guide staff because many of them knew people who had done so; it was one means of upward mobility in Nepal's rigid caste society. In his book, *Dark Shadows Falling*, Joe Simpson writes about the plight of porters during a terrible snowstorm in 1984 in the Everest region. While the helicopters came to rescue trekkers, the porters were left behind; some died, others were maimed by frostbite. I was in the region at the time; the deep snow created a lockdown situation. Having experienced hypothermia at altitude, I know how quickly the body's condition can deteriorate. Remote and isolated by the snow, they didn't have a chance.

A cook I worked with once related a story about two porters who froze to death on an attempt of Rupina La pass near Baudha Himal. The weather was bad and the porters ill-prepared. They didn't have their jackets or shoes. The cook, who was the last one to leave camp, came upon them sitting down beside a boulder, complaining of cold. They told him that they would get up in a few minutes and start hiking again. They didn't show up at the campsite that evening. A couple of sherpas returned the next day to find what became of them, and found them there by the boulder, frozen to death. It was an unhappy group of trekkers that continued on. The thought that someone died carrying your load is unpleasant; it is enough that we die carrying our own loads. Loud complaints were heard half a world away.

There are many hazards in the mountains. The cook was a hard worker with laughing eyes, an infectious smile, and quick wit. He later drowned on a trek while attempting to bathe in a river during high runoff.

As morning wears on and trekkers tire, there is a short stop for tea and then later a picnic lunch. How much time is allotted for lunch depends on the distance covered during the morning. After lunch everyone begins walking – inevitably up or down – the trail again. It was hard to comprehend what some people were thinking when they decided to go on a Himalayan trek. They could have the most asinine complaints. "The trail is too steep." "You're making us walk too far." "Doesn't it ever get flat?" They were in the Himalayas for Christ's sake, what did they expect? The world's highest mountains, and they're expecting flat? Up and down is the only way to reach anywhere! The companies that sold them the package sent them glossy brochures with day-to-day descriptions of the trek, how far they would go, and what elevations they would reach; if they thought about it just a bit, they would have realized what they were in for. Of course, some were in no shape to be on a trek, which made matters worse for everyone, but fortunately this was a minority of trekkers.

The guide staff usually made evening camp between 4:00 and 6:00 p.m. If we were near a village, the villagers would gather around to watch us; we were the main event. The cook gets busy with the kitchen right away while the guides set up tents and fetch wood. Some cooks have an awesome talent for culinary innovation using an open fire and a couple of kerosene burners. "Let them eat cake," the cooks could say, because sometimes they would bake a cake for dessert. Trekkers would complain about the food, but then some people will complain about anything. They couldn't appreciate the skill it took to make them their meal nor did they consider that the cook was the first one up in the morning, usually the last to bed at night, and had to carry many of his own pots, pans and utensils. Iron Chef indeed!

After dinner the extroverts stay up and chat while the introverts retreat to their tents. Venturing more than a short distance from the campsite may not be safe. Booze can be a good accompaniment – a favorite is Kukuri Rum. Sometimes harder stuff than booze makes an appearance. Alcohol and altitude don't mix well and are an ill-advised combination over 3,000 meters (10,000 feet). One reason is that it can impair sleep; another reason is that it affects judgment, which could be a problem if one suffers hypobaropathy, or altitude sickness.

After several months of trekking at high altitudes, one longs for a hot shower – but makes do with washbasins and rags. At high altitude, days often end like this: After dinner in the dining tent, or a small trekkers' lodge if available, you climb into your tent. Don't brush against the tent fabric; if you do, you will be showered with ice crystals. Take your boots off if necessary but leave the rest of your clothes on and crawl into your sleeping bag. You will need all of your clothes on inside the bag to avoid freezing during the night. If the altitude is high enough or if the temperature is cold enough, you will be lucky to get even a few hours of sleep. When you wake up in the middle of the night, be careful not to knock the tent walls or ice crystals will shower down on you again. If it's snowing, you don't want to get crushed by the weight of the snow pressing down on the tent roof, so you may have to knock the tent walls and get showered by ice crystals anyway. In really bad conditions, bring a pee cup with you and toss the urine out the tent flap. God forbid you have to take a shit! When the kitchen boy brings you your morning tea, grasp it with both hands until your fingers burn. This will warm up the rest of your body. Don't leave the tent until you have to; once you lose your bodily warmth, you will not feel warm again until after you've been hiking for a while. Pack up your stuff; ignore the ice crystal showers. Now for your boots – damn they are freezing! Yes, you have to put your stocking feet into them or you won't ever leave. Living in a tent surrounded by the world's tallest mountains is not as exotic as it sounds to Western ears. Eventually, I was glad to guide lower elevation treks just for a break.

The flipside of this description is that when you step out of your tent, the Himalayas are towering above, their jagged peaks piercing the sky. As the sun rises, its rays sparkle on the glaciers and make you blink. Diamonds should be so brilliant! The glaciers appear small from a distance, but when seen up close they are as tall as three-story buildings. Sometimes they collapse on themselves into a heap of crumpled ice. The air is thin and pure. Steam rises from the yaks as they are loaded up for the day. On a distant ridge is a Buddhist stupa, prayer flags fluttering in the morning breeze beside it. The moon, still visible in the growing light, passes behind a magnificent peak, its sheer face still cloaked in darkness. Thin wisps of smoke rise from a distant village in the valley somewhere down below. And you, who are you in this grandeur? It doesn't matter.

Being at low elevation usually means a long hike up. Many trekkers are not ready for how unendingly steep the hills are; 3,500 meters from base to top (11,500 feet) is not uncommon. A river valley might be 700 meters' elevation and the hilltop 4,200 meters, passing from Hindu to Buddhist culture during the climb up. Occasionally in the Hindu areas, one finds stone steps on the hillside, put there by someone as penance, thus abetting their karma. Whether the stairs go up or down, or their karma for that matter, is a matter of perspective. Upon reaching such stairs, one first feels relief, but after climbing them long enough, one longs for the rocky uncertainty of a trail. Reaching the summit of some "hills" can take a day and a half. The guide points out the day's hike and, looking up and up and up, beyond view, is the destination. Many hilltops are covered with rhododendron forests—not the small rhododendrons one sees in North America, but Himalayan rhododendron trees, 15 meters tall. These forests are often shrouded in mists and moss hangs from the tree limbs.

RHODODENDRON

Once in springtime, walking through such a forest with several inches of snow still on the ground, we came across an early blossom, flowering bright red against the snowy forest backdrop. We caught our breaths. All thought of the climb vanished in that blossoming moment.

Nepal's most popular trekking regions are Everest and Annapurna, followed by Langtang because of its proximity to Kathmandu. Other regions, such as Rara Lake, Taplejung, and Karnali, are more remote. Even in the popular trekking regions, there are many routes that draw relatively few trekkers. For instance, Base Camp and Kala Patar are the most familiar trekking routes in the Everest region, but there are others – Cho Oyu, Ama Dablam, Gokyo Ri, Lhotse – that make for a better trekking experience. The trek to Gokyo Ri climbs over 5,500 meters (18,000 feet) and offers a commanding view of the region, from Namche Bazaar in the southwest to the Tibetan Plateau to the north, beyond Everest. The elevation is high enough to dissuade trekkers who can't adjust to that altitude, but not so high as to make breathing difficult. People are generally unaware of the Gokyo Ri climb and miss out on a more interesting vantage point, without crowds. From Gokyo Ri, one can view the slow motion of geology; the entire region is caught in an ice flow, glacial though it is. With a little imagination, one can picture how the mighty glaciers of the Pleistocene and other glacial epochs might have appeared.

VIEW FROM GOKYO RI

There are several ways to reach the Everest Region, including by plane to Luk-la. The "Instant Everest" trek sold by one company had as its objective to get its clients a view of Everest from Tengboché Monastery in seven days. This tour required a four-day trek to Tengboché and three days to get back out. My experience was that few people actually managed this feat due to altitude issues, flight cancellations, etc. But if one doesn't fly, the only way into the Region is by foot. The closest road is a couple of weeks away. There is no landing strip like the one in Lukla, gateway to the Everest region. The runway is short and steep, with an approach that forebodes a mountainside plane crash. One plane met that terrible fate. At the runway's end lies a burnt-out fuselage, a grim spectacle for passengers watching the landing approach through the window as the plane screeches to a halt just in front of it.

Leaving the Kathmandu airport to fly to Lukla was a hassle. The flight left shortly after dawn, which meant that travelers would have to get there much earlier. The later a flight departs in the morning, the greater the likelihood that Lukla Airport will be clouded in. This was no small concern as it was not unusual for planes to get within ten minutes of Lukla just to turn back because of cloud cover.

Lukla is no place to be stuck when planes haven't been able to land for a week. People start to behave like animals – no, worse. Desperate to get out, they argue, fight, and offer bribes. The flight out of Lukla is as intense as the flight in. The landing strip falls away to a stony field below. I always felt like the departing plane dropped altitude when its wheels lifted off the runway and then, catching an updraft, would slowly climb skyward. Once I flew out of Lukla in a helicopter – a small Alouette. To say it was a thrill would be an understatement. The flight time to Kathmandu was longer, and more hair-raising, than the twin otter planes. At each ridge we passed over, the wind would gust up from below into the helicopter's blades and blow the small craft up and back; it would quickly right itself and continue onward. Each ridge brought a new panorama of further hills and valleys below trailing up to one mighty Himalayan mountain after another. As on a rollercoaster, my stomach was left somewhere behind. Waiting for me in Kathmandu was my fiancée. I was returning a week later than planned because all of the flights out of Lukla had been cancelled. When she saw me climb out of the helicopter, she ran to greet me and, like in some corny television commercial, jumped into my arms, wrapped her legs around me and kissed me. The surprised soldier standing nearby dropped his rifle, as this display was outside the bounds of Nepalese customs. My friend Gyaljzen, who was there to meet one of the other passengers, couldn't stop laughing.

Another less traveled route to the Region, because of the necessary 24-day time commitment, is the Arun to Everest route, which runs along the Arun River starting near Hilé and venturing due north to the Everest region. The Arun River route passes through a culturally diverse area, peopled by Nepali hill tribes, Rai and Limbu, ending in Sherpa country. One starts in lowland Hindu culture and ends in yak terrain, passing from rice fields to millet, from tropical jungle to alpine forest, from grass to rock and ice. The road now reaches much farther north than it used to, and the trek probably does not take 24 days, but it will still require two to three weeks.

Guided treks of course are for people – customers who paid a lot of money to make this, for many of them, trip of a lifetime. They almost all came to see the mountains; some came to glimpse the culture, and all wanted a memorable experience. Since the 1960s, or maybe since the advent of air travel, people have collected experiences, an iniquity of which I am guiltier than most. A wise man said, "the experiencer always separates [him]self from the experience." The experience that we remember is not the experience that we lived. Travelers come to Nepal, or Africa, the US or anywhere, looking for an experience, paying to have an experience, as if the more they spend the more they will benefit from the occasion. Experience accumulates over time, modifying the future, and we see our lives through the prism of experience.

Trekkers came to Nepal from all walks of life for the walk of their lives. On the treks that I led, the most well represented professions were doctors and lawyers; they could afford the steep prices, in keeping with the steep terrain. Lawyers would listen to what they were told about health and safety risks, but doctors knew better. Before every trek I would do pre-trek briefings, explaining what to expect, the do's, the don'ts, and health and safety precautions. I urged them if they bought any local food or drinks to dry all plates, glasses or utensils since over 90 percent of Nepal's diseases are waterborne. One cannot always be certain that kitchen items are clean, but they can make sure that they are dry. I would discuss altitude sickness, describing symptoms and treatments (go back down), and encouraged them not to take altitude sickness medication unless they were in the direst need. The medicine covers up the symptoms, making it difficult to know how severe a person's case is, until it is too late, and they are already experiencing cerebral edema. Did the doctors listen? No, they were usually the first ones into the medicine kits – they always brought their own. They reminded me of mountaineers' "med kit" stories about their recreational use of prescription drugs during climbs. Doctors make bad patients. More than once, I had to argue with a doctor about going back down and being concerned about the effects of altitude. But one of the symptoms of altitude sickness, like drunkenness, is loss of judgment. They would say "I'm fine" as they stumbled off the trail.

It is said that Nepal is the land of Karma. And there is "something in the air" but it is more akin to a "tendency toward attraction" than karmic cause-and-effect. Many Peace Corps Volunteers (PCVs) noted relevant circumstances. Someone might be thinking about something or some person and then, voila, the event or person would "materialize." We compared notes about such coincidences. In the English language, "coincidence" can often be used interchangeably with "random." Its definition, "circumstances without apparent causal connection," does not suggest meaninglessness, as random events imply. Coincidences may be – in fact often are – highly meaningful. But it is up to the experiencer to realize what that meaning is. In Nepal, the universe has an unusual propensity to attract a person to circumstances involving their fears, expectations, and beliefs. Of course, I might be accused of magical thinking, and I don't have a testable hypothesis for this claim. Still, the following anecdotes may be suggestive.

On one trek was a woman doctor who recently had earned her medical degree. At some point during her studies, she decided that she didn't want to treat sick people; she was more interested in helping healthy people to stay healthy. The trek was a rigorous one over the treacherous Rupina La near Baudha Himal in the region between Pokhara to the west and Kathmandu to the east. This area was exceptionally remote, with few people and fewer visitors; as the 2015 earthquake showed, it is still quite remote 30 years later. Most of the people in the higher altitudes are herders. Those living in the deep river valleys grow rice and potatoes, and raise some animals, as subsistence farmers; in the high hills in between people grow millet. One of the few villages in the region is Barpak. To get to Barpak, one hikes north of Gorkha for several days. It was from Gorkha that Nepal's Shah dynasty originated, conquering their neighbors and establishing the Kingdom. Gorkha, now a synonym for Nepal's British army regiment, is the proper name of the town where it originated. When we arrived in Barpak and set up camp, the usual crowd of onlookers came to watch the show. As in most such isolated areas, there is a dearth of trained medical professionals, even less likely a clinic, and people came to us with their ailments. Guides must follow very strict rules, which I explained in the pre-trek briefing; we would bring a medical kit with us, but the meds were for the trekkers, not people we met along the way. If any trekker wanted to share their own medicine, they were free to do so. These rules didn't usually receive comments, at least until we stopped at some of the villages and the trekkers saw first-hand the dire health care needs. Then there were complaints about the rules' harshness. They had a point; the rules were harsh, for we might have medicine in the kit that could save a life. There was a good reason for the rules, though; not too long before, an American guide had given medicine to a sick villager but later one of the trekkers became severely ill. If they hadn't given their medicine to villagers, it might have saved the trekker's life. In the event, I was later told, the family sued the guide and won their case. This case changed trekking companies' concerns for liability, and guides took greater responsibility for the medical kits in particular, and trekkers' safety and welfare more generally.

The Barpak campsite was set up, including the dining tent. Some villagers came down to enquire about medicine, bringing their sick ones with them. The doctor agreed to examine some of them. One woman brought her young son, maybe a few years old. He was in a bad way, catatonic and unresponsive. He was laid on the table in the dining tent. While she was examining him, he had a seizure and died. The doctor was beside herself. What she hoped to avoid, treating sick people, caught up with her. Later I heard that she gave up medicine. Similarly, on a trek to Annapurna Sanctuary, there was a nurse in the group who wanted a break from work. Camping outside a village one night, a man brought his son to us. This was the first time I saw gangrene, as his ailment was diagnosed. The boy – maybe eleven – had gotten a cut that became badly infected and was now oozing pus and smelled bad. His father had brought him to us looking for help and medicine. In such circumstances, most parents would have brought their child to a doctor, no matter how far the distance. We were several days from Pokhara. I don't know what his circumstances were, but he was not inclined to seek help if it meant going very far. By this time, the boy's leg looked like it would have to be amputated. I wasn't able to give him medicine from the kit, but the nurse, several others, and myself dug into our personal kits and gave the father some medicine for his son and insisted that he take him to a clinic. But, he was a Brahmin and, in my experience, the motivations, whether cultural or religious, of some people in this caste were to accept the hand of fate. Attitudes are cultural. Reincarnation as a world-view can have a de-motivating influence.

On another trek, a Brooklynite with a pessimistic turn of mind – what could go wrong, would –complained frequently about his shoes and how sore his feet were; so, what should happen? In the middle of the night on the outskirts of a small hamlet, someone reached into his tent and stole… his shoes. All he had left to walk in was a pair of sneakers and flip flops. For him and his wife, the trekking route changed. He would be unable to continue on that particularly ambitious trek. They broke off from the group to rejoin later. This incident caused me to modify where I put personal effects inside my tent. Items that I could least afford to lose I would put in the middle of the tent, next to me. Less important items, I put on the periphery. Crime was becoming more frequent along some routes; trekkers sometimes awoke to find that their tent had been cut open and items taken.

On several occasions, the strongest, most physically fit men, who had braggadocio to spare, were rushed to lower elevations because of altitude sickness; one loudmouth was carried down on a yak's back in the middle of the night to save his life. One never knows how they will react to altitude, and one and the same person can be fine one time but suffer severe affects another. There was the actress, used to getting her man, but found herself unable. Bankers and lawyers on very tight schedules – for whom time was money – got stuck for days waiting for planes. There was the chef who couldn't eat because he was sick to his stomach, and lovelorn strangers who met their match (this happened often) on the trek. We attract what most concerns us or, put differently, you get what you focus on.

Of all the groups that I led, one trekker stands out for his obduracy—"Ralph." Ralph was a retiree who had been on a couple of treks already, a decade earlier. This trek was to be, and deserved to be, Ralph's last. Ralph had had a quadruple bypass a couple of years before and had no business going on a trek. Two family members, who mostly left the guide staff to keep an eye on him, accompanied him. Ralph knew everything. He thought he could speak Nepali, but the Nepalese couldn't understand what he said, and yet he would correct me. My command of the language was far from perfect, but I'd been speaking it for several years and could at least hear a conversation and understand what was being said and be understood.

The trekking group was large, with more than a dozen people. Ralph continuously fell behind, as might be expected, and because of his health issues was often found panting on the trailside near the rear of the procession. The Sherpa guide, Dorjé, and I were concerned that Ralph wouldn't make it all the way to the Everest Region; I found myself spending much of my time monitoring him. This situation was unfortunate for the other trekkers since they didn't get as much of my time as they might have liked and had paid for. I tried to divide my time between clients to answer their questions and address any concerns. With Ralph on the trek, this wasn't possible. I admired Ralph's dogged tenaciousness but feared that he would kill himself as a matter of principle.

The entire group came to appreciate the conundrum, which came to a head when we reached the base of Kala Patar. Ralph was in a bad way; his family members urged him to remain at Gorak Shep, the last small outpost, but he stubbornly refused. Instead, he pushed himself steadily up, imagining perhaps that he was in better condition than was the case. He became gradually paler, started to lose his coordination and would have to stop occasionally to prevent himself from keeling over; he gasped for air like a fish out of water. I tried to get him to stop out of concern for his health, but he would have none of it. The other trekkers held back, sharing my concern. Finally, as a party, they confronted him, individually expressing their concern and begging him to stop. He again refused, at which point the group, spontaneously, all agreed that if Ralph would continue up, they would not, and he would be the cause of their not reaching Kala Patar's summit. With this entreaty, Ralph finally relented. He agreed to hike up to a small flat spot a short distance away and wait there for the rest of the group. Ralph finished the trek without further incident and seemed much humbled by the group's *espirit de corps* in its concern for him.

Guides aren't immune to circumstances either. Treks could be as hazardous for guides as for trekkers and cooks. While guiding a trek near Baudha Himal, I had a severe case of hypothermia. There were a dozen trekkers, all from the US. This trek was not easy, lasting several weeks including crossing a high – over 5,500 meters – pass. About a week into the trek, we started at low elevation to begin an all-day climb– and this was just a hill! By day's end, we had climbed from 600 meters to 3,600 meters. The weather changed as we ascended the last 500 meters, first getting cold, then starting to drizzle, which became rain, which soon changed to snow, and then became a squall. The paying clients were our main concern; camp was set up quickly and we made sure they were able to get inside their tents and change into warm, dry clothes as soon as possible. As we were attending to them, I didn't notice how much my own body temperature had dropped. When everyone was getting comfortable and assembling around a crackling fire, I noticed that I was shivering. The shivers turned to shakes, becoming quite uncontrollable, to the point where I could no longer stand. A couple of the other experienced guides noticed my condition. By the time they sat me in front of the fire and covered me with sleeping bags to warm me up, I was pretty far-gone. Then the strange sensations began; first I noticed a general numbness but accompanied by unusual mental clarity. I knew what was happening and why it was happening and that I had no control over my deteriorating condition. For a brief time, I'm not sure how long, I felt as though I was having an out-of-body experience, my consciousness drifting. It was indescribable then, and it's less describable now. Many hot water bottles, hot almost to the boiling point, had been packed around me to bring my body temperature up, yet I couldn't feel them. This condition lasted over an hour. Intermittently I was talking to my companions, but the whole time I was aware of the unusual state of mind brought on by the hypothermia. Eventually I warmed up and could eat some hot soup. The next morning, we summited the hill and continued down to the river valley below, at 1,500 meters, and the storm the night before became a distant memory as we went to bed, sweating in our tents.

Inevitably, we all carry our own baggage; it is a load that no porter can carry for us. It is best to travel light.

SHERPA MEMORIAL

CHAPTER 2

PLANES ARE HARBINGERS OF ADVENTURE, beckoning the new and unknown. A change in place means a change in circumstances, if just temporarily. The journey of a lifetime might take a day, so much has the world shrunk. So, we fly and time flies with us.

Eventually the passengers find their way through the airport doors, past burly baggage handlers and surly gate agents; they've run the security gauntlet, having been dispossessed of their goods, stripped of their metals, deprived of liquids, exposed to god-knows-what ranges of infrared or ultraviolet particles, patted down, and finally turned loose into the terminal. The plane, hopefully, sits at the gate while passengers gather outside, hoping departure will be on time. They've been told to arrive two hours before departure, with no assurances of an actual departure time, and must now pass the time. Some solemnly read their papers, books, and magazines, others quench their hunger or thirst; many straggle from store to store, a few make small talk, and there are a typical, obnoxious few who talk loudly on their cell phones. What could possibly motivate them? Are they so loud because they think that they can't be heard or are they having trouble hearing?

Are they self-important, wanting others to hear what they have to say? Or are they just oblivious and always loud? Or does their sense of etiquette fly out the window when they are getting ready to board a plane? Airlines have come to epitomize the phrase "hurry up and wait." Yet we, the public, put ourselves through this torture to the tune of millions of passengers a day. Then there are the complaints: Why don't airlines install seats that are a little bit bigger than the ones in most Economy classes but smaller than the seats in business class? Would this really be so difficult or cost that much? As passengers queue onto the plane, the overhead bins fill up and the last to board may find that there is no room for bags. Some people who are seated in the back of the plane like to place their carry-ons toward the front for rapid retrieval and deplaning, leaving the people sitting in front bereft of space. Perhaps airlines should reward considerate passengers with frequent flyer miles.

The first time I saw the Himalayas! After assembling in Chicago, the Peace Corps Volunteers (or PCVs) I was entering service with left for Nepal, flying from Chicago to Hong Kong, Hong Kong to Dhaka, and from Dhaka to Kathmandu. In Hong Kong, most of the group spent the night in their hotel rooms. But four of us decided that after 14 hours on an airplane, we had to see Hong Kong, not being sure if we would have the chance again. We dined at an authentic Chinese restaurant – a first for me. The waiter gave us some tips on what to eat. His suggestions were so good that we tipped him back, quite a lot as it turned out. He followed us outside the restaurant to bow his thanks, an Asian custom that took some getting used to. Hong Kong in 1983 wasn't pricey like it is today. After dinner, we explored Hong Kong's streets, checking out everything that looked remotely interesting. Retail shops spilled out onto the sidewalks and streets, where people milled around colorful displays until the shopkeepers turned them out to pack up in the wee hours. There were all manner of gadgets for sale on the streets and down the alleys. Eels and countless other foods were being hawked by street vendors—edible for the locals but not so appealing to uninitiated Western palettes. By the time we returned to the hotel, it was nearly morning. We were on the plane to Dhaka, Bangladesh a few hours later.

The flight to Dhaka was uneventful, except that the plane was stranded on the airport tarmac after landing. The Royal Nepal Air Corporation plane sat there for several hours in the sweltering Dhaka heat and humidity. The plane reeked. By the time a couple of hours had passed, you wouldn't want to go near the rear of the plane because the toilets had overflowed. Nepalese are squatters, Westerners are sitters; plane toilets are made for sitting and many squatters had missed their target.

Although the plane door was open, there were armed guards with machine guns standing at the bottom of the rolling stairs, and they refused to let us so much as venture beyond the threshold, so we stayed on the plane. Fortunately, the flight attendants kept the liquor cabinet open. We drank more Carlsberg beer than was good for us as we passed the hours. When the plane took off from Dhaka to Kathmandu, all faces were plastered against the windows. Everyone was trying to catch a glimpse of the Himalayas. I caught a glimpse of a few remote peaks, rising loftily above a sea of September clouds, as we approached Kathmandu. Unfortunately, we were arriving during the monsoon and the clouds were piled on top of each other, loftier than the mountains. This would be the only tantalizing glimpse we would have of the peaks for the next month.

When we got off the plane in Kathmandu Airport, the scene at Customs was total chaos. Luggage took forever to get off-loaded onto a short trolley and pulled (by hand) to Baggage Claim. Then our bags were moved from place to place in Baggage Claim, rifled through in Customs, while each of us was "processed" separately. When I finally made it out of Customs, some little kid grabbed my bag and ran off with it, me chasing after him and the Peace Corps staff person who was sent to fetch us chasing me and the kid, attempting to corral everyone together. The kid was looking to earn some "baksheesh" by being "helpful" – help that I didn't want. "Baksheesh," I would learn, greases every skid on the Subcontinent. It essentially means "tip" but beggars will hit you up for "baksheesh" without doing anything to earn it. Bureaucrats will stall the processing of an application if they aren't given a little extra "baksheesh" for their help. This was my first lesson in baksheesh; there would be many more.

Following hard on the night out in Hong Kong, too much beer on the tarmac in Dhaka, and then the crazy scene at Customs, my head was spinning. One of the lingering memories from that day was Nepal's unfamiliar smell, the smell of

South Asia; I had noticed it in Hong Kong but in Nepal it bludgeoned my nose. Years later when I returned to Nepal after an absence, I realized that I didn't notice the smell—a mix of raw sewage, smoke, spices, unfamiliar plants, lead from car exhaust, and god knows what else.

The caravan of Peace Corps jeeps that met us at the airport now brought us to the Embassy clinic, where, before we had the opportunity to get near any food or water, the doctor and nurse put the fear of God into us. We were lectured that we would die if we weren't careful. We were issued our medical kits and then packed off to High-Intensity Language Training.

This training was outside of Kathmandu, but still in the Valley, in a town called Godavari. Godavari lies southeast of Kathmandu, nestled close to the hills that ring the Valley. Godavari commands a view across the expanse of the Valley and is situated near a Jesuit school and botanical gardens. According to some travel books at that time, it was an area suspected of having ritual human sacrifices to Shiva, although Nepalese said that was all in the distant past. On later visits to Godavari, I found it to be a very pleasant place, now with a high-end hotel and Tibetan monastery nearby. However, it rained almost continuously the whole time we were there for language training. To just say it rained is to understate. The monsoon rains can only be appreciated by someone who has been in South Asia during that season. Everything that gets wet doesn't dry. Clothes and shoes are perpetually damp. Mold is ever encroaching on the weary attentions of householders and contributes a sense of dankness. Then, towards the middle of October after several days of nearly continuous rain, one brilliant morning we woke up to crystalline air. The sky was a brilliant blue and there were – the Himalayas! No site on earth compares to the enormity of those mountains. From Ganesh Himal in the west to Langtang and Dorjé Lakpa directly to the north of Kathmandu to the Jugal Himal in the east, we had an unobstructed view of the range across the valley from Godavari. It would be another nine months before I had a chance to venture into them. The mountains exerted a powerful magnetic pull on me then, and still do so now. Their grandeur continues to stand sentinel to my mind. Years later, I feel exhilarated when I wake in the morning after dreaming about them the night before. They came to represent for me the ethereal and eternal. Coming from Montana and its pristine summits, the Himalayas are beyond any possible comparison.

My first trek was the Annapurna Circuit, my first break since arriving in Nepal ten months earlier. Completing the Circuit took three weeks, which was respectable timing, if one's objective is speed. Starting at a friend's post on the southern flanks of Annapurna IV, we began the trek during the monsoon. My companion, Dale, was a Mormon Buddhist, not a common confluence of interests; about 12 years my senior, he was in much better physical condition for the trek because he lived in the hills, where of necessity he got to exercise. I was a Terai wallah. The Terai is the northern extension of the Gangetic Plains into southern Nepal, terminating at the foothills. I had had little physical conditioning that might have helped me to prepare for the altitude or level of exertion.

One very foggy morning on the second day, while the mists clung desperately to the air, we stopped briefly at a small teashop along the trail. Such intra-monsoon mornings aren't unusual in Nepal's steeply closed-in hills, where vapors from the rice paddies and forests hang over the lands. Finishing our tea, we continued up the trail a short way to the bridge that fords the wild Marsyandi River. Through the mists, a woman approached us; she wasn't dressed like a local woman. She was wearing tight Capri pants and had on a sheer cotton shirt with folded-up sleeves, unbuttoned halfway down the front. The shape of her breasts was pronounced, and we could see her nipples distinctly. In an uptight Hindu culture, such attire was unusual. She walked straight up to us and motioned for food, putting her hand to her mouth and then to her stomach. We tried communicating with her in Nepali, I tried speaking some Hindi, Dale tried German, but she didn't understand anything we said, in any of those languages. She talked, but we couldn't understand her; by appearance, she looked to be from the Near East. After we gave her some food, we continued on our way. She followed behind us at a distance, until we got to Baundada, "Hill of the Brahman," where she disappeared from view. Sometime later, I asked a volunteer who lived in Baundada, but who wasn't there when we passed through, if she knew anything about this woman. The volunteer said the woman had been in the area for some months and had no idea where she was from; she was raped and died during childbirth. When we met her, she showed no sign of being pregnant. In Nepal's hills, such incidents were not unheard of. Other volunteers had similarly strange stories. One told of a guy, apparently European, who showed up on the outskirts of a village and just stayed. After some weeks there he eventually died, probably of starvation but no one was sure. The villagers were very poor and didn't have resources to care for themselves and were hard-pressed to aid this unwanted stranger.

The Thorong La ("La" meaning "Pass") is the high point of the Annapurna Circuit, in more ways than one. From the top on a clear day one can see 360 degrees of Himalayan peaks, many over 7,000 meters, in Tibet within eyesight to the north, Tukché Peak and its neighbors in the distant west intimating Dolpa and snow leopards. To the immediate south stands Annapurna I, and to its near western slope is Dhaulagiri. The day we crossed the La, though the middle of the monsoon, the sky was clear and bright. Monsoon clouds were gathering in the southern distance and some stray ones were attempting the Himalayan summits, only to vaporize in the high-altitude sunlight. The La crossing is not without danger. Once in Kathmandu, I met a trekker who faced amputation of both of his feet because the weather turned on him and his companions when they attempted it. He struggled to walk with crutches, on feet that were little more than clubs – deadweight. At least one of his companions fared worse and didn't make it at all.

The trail descends down a very steep, long path to the holy temple of Muktinath in Buddhist Northern Nepal. Muktinath is both a Hindu and Buddhist pilgrimage site; Hindus come there from all over South Asia to worship believing that by bathing in each of the temple fountains one will not reincarnate. These 108 fountains are in the outer courtyard, decorated with bull faces through which the freezing water is piped, 108 being a sacred number for Shaiva, Vaishnava, and Buddhist (and baseball) adherents. Muktinath means "place of liberation." Inside the temple is a gold statue that is supposed to be the size of a man. By the time we reached Muktinath after crossing the Thorong La we were so trail-wary that the fountains looked quite refreshing. We attempted to abrogate our future incarnations: The icy water from the fountains quickly convinced us that bathing in one fountain would be quite enough and that we would be fated to reincarnate.

We stayed the night in Muktinath and witnessed a show of local horsemanship. The Tibetans are cousins of the Mongols, famous horsemen in their time, and the riders clearly prided themselves on their skills. The next morning, we continued on our way from Muktinath north to Kag Beni. Kag Beni was at that time the last trekkers' outpost before reaching the then restricted zone of Mustang. In that far region, the landscape changes. Departing from Muktinath, Tukché Peak, a darkly imposing mountain, stands sentinel to the remote wilderness beyond. The trail divides north and south at the Kali Gandaki River in a narrow and windswept valley with steep ascents on either side. Even in the wet monsoon season, this dry place lies in a rain shadow and receives little precipitation. The wind was constant, dancing with the river's waves, blowing their crests upstream while gravity pulls the great volume of water ever down. Farther downriver in Marpa the winds power generators that electrify the community. But en route to Kag Beni the fields, marked by stone fences, and houses, also made of stone, look distinctly Tibetan. Cliffs rising to the east reminded me of a moonscape, their foreboding spires looming over hikers walking up the valley floor. We reached Kag Beni by mid-afternoon.

None of the trekkers' lodges seemed ready for guests at that time of year, as most of them were closed. It took some searching, but we finally found an inn that was willing to take us for the night. Most lodges were really people's homes, where a spare room or two furnished with a few beds could bring some extra income. That day a group of monks from the Mustang Monastery were also guests at the home. But they were special guests. As we learned, there is a custom that on one day every year, the monks stay with each family in the community to pray, chant, and ask for blessings upon their homes. Our fortune was to be guests at this lodge on that day. For a while, we listened to the monks chant, then we set out to explore the small town and its surroundings for the rest of the afternoon.

After dinner, some of the monks took a break from their chanting and prayers. We started up a conversation with one of the monks. Despite their Buddhist asceticism, most Tibetan monks have very nice watches and shoes, which look out of place with their red robes and golden silk belts. This monk spoke Nepali, so we were able to learn about some of the customs of the region and a bit about Mustang. Our conversation eventually turned to the Buddhism in Mustang. At the time, I understood that there were two branches of Buddhism, Mahayana and Pali. I was not aware that Mahayana Buddhism of the Tibetan variety had quite so many sects. We learned that many of these sects exist because they adhere to a certain number of sutras – sayings attributed to the Buddha. One sect accepts 108 sutras while another sect subscribes to 112, and another sect attributes some other number. As we discussed these differences, I began to appreciate that Buddhism is as fragmented as Christianity, although historical similarities can be pushed just so far. Buddhist sects do not share Christianity's history of bloodletting. However, both religions have disagreements that have amplified over time. One or two sutras can mark substantial differences in belief. Buddhists historically have been more tolerant of such doctrinal differences than have Christians. After this conversation with the monk, we wondered about the odds that we, with our shared interest in Tibetan Buddhism, would have a solitary opportunity to learn about doctrinal variations from a monk from the enigmatic Mustang Monastery – that we would be housemates for an evening? We are each drawn to the circumstances in which we find ourselves—attracted individually and, where there is affinity, those we share.

People associate pictures of starving children with distended tummies with Africa, but hunger haunts many parts of the world. Many trekkers hike the Annapurna Circuit each year. They spend a lot of money along the way. Nonetheless, many villages remain desperately poor: "too many cameras and not enough food," to quote a Police song. The sight of one famished boy still haunts me. Dressed in shorts and a T-shirt, his skin was drawn thinly over his bones, accentuating the curves and inflections of the skeleton beneath. He had suffered from long malnutrition. His gaunt, vacant look marked his hunger-compromised intelligence. Pictures of blank faces of starving children staring out from the television screen do not capture the immediacy of their deprivation. Their need is perpetually urgent, but hidden under the eaves of thatched roofs. I shuddered and continued on up the trail, what could I do? The Nepalese have a saying, "Ke garné?" which translates "what to do?" the implication being that there is nothing that can be done. "Ke garné?" is a philosophy of life, an outlook that pervades the culture. In conversations one hears "ke garné?" frequently, conveying its implied sense of hopelessness, even despair. The flipside of "ke garné?" is a humored acceptance of things outside of one's control, over which one cannot be, for which maybe no one can be, responsible. We're hungry, "ke garné?" we're poor, "ke garné?" our lot in life is what it is, "ke garné?" The boy is, like millions of children, starving to death – "ke garné?"

When food, as in basic calories, is sufficient, people turn their attention to its quality and flavor. In South Asia one curries flavor, or the main flavor is curry. Curries are as varied as the many spices available. Buying spices can be intimidating as one is confronted with tins upon tins of spices of ever greater degrees of potency: black pepper, cardamom, cinnamon, clove, coriander, cumin, fennel, garlic, ginger, marjoram, paprika, saffron, turmeric, and, the most potent of all, chili.

Growing up in Montana, there weren't many hot foods, so my taste buds had a very low tolerance for spicy foods of any kind. But living in Nepal, this changed. The Nepali word for hot-spicy is "piro," similar to the English "pyro" and "pyre," evocative of fire and death. Fortunately, a Nepali family took me in while I lived in the village, inviting me to share their meals. After living there for a year, I still had not adjusted to the spicy local cuisine. Then they went to Kathmandu to vacation for a couple of weeks. I arranged to take my meals with the neighbor across the street while they were away. Radasham graciously offered to feed me twice a day. Radasham was of northern Indian descent, Madeshi. The language they spoke was a Hindi dialect referred to as "dehaati," a local language unique to that location, only distantly resembling Nepali (dehaati means "local"). He had a sarcastic sense of humor and could crack a joke with straight face, so that you might think he was serious or ignorant. Radasham majored in English, a completely useless degree in that time and place; he was like so many of his countrymen, graduating high school and college to return to the village whence they came, and back to the family farm as their main source of income. He was a little bitter in his lack of opportunity.

In that part of Northern India and Southern Nepal, people love to eat really hot, really spicy foods; Radasham's family was no exception. The first morning I went to his house to have my first meal with him – actually it was closer to noon and I was getting very hungry – Radasham told me that he had asked his wife to keep the heat to a minimum. Because I was a foreigner and not a Hindu, he politely had me eat in the front room of his house, rather than in the dining area with the rest of the family. The meal was traditional – dal bhat. Dal is lentils and bhat is rice. Dal bhat is usually eaten twice a day at meal times, every day of the year. Growing up I always liked rice, and initially I liked dal bhat. This lasted for about a week after coming to Nepal. Eating the same meal twice a day every day quickly grew tiresome. Eventually most PCVs adjusted to the diet and acquired a taste for it, appreciating the subtle nuances of flavors. It took me longer than most; I didn't adjust to the diet until well into my second year. Since it isn't possible to avoid hot foods, one must adapt to them. Dal bhat is typically served with spicy curried meat and vegetables, and hot peppers on the plate; chilies are the one spice that is guaranteed to flavor any meal. The custom is to eat dal bhat with one's hands, without utensils. The heat from the chilies can linger on one's finger. Rubbing one's eyes during or after a meal will cause them to burn fiercely and tear, and the consequences of masturbating after meals featuring strong chilies is not a laughing matter.

With my fingers, I scooped a bite of Radasham's wife's dal bhat and immediately felt intense pain, but I was really hungry and didn't want to offend my host, so I took another bite and another. The burning sharply increased until my whole mouth was aflame. Each new bite amplified the pain of the preceding bite. At the same time there were other unpleasant sensations; my nose started running like a river, I began to sweat profusely out of every pore, tears flowed down my cheeks and, most unusually, I heard my sinuses draining inside my ears. Radasham, courteous host that he was, could see my discomfort, but he really wasn't able to do anything for me other than bring me more water, which I didn't drink anyway since it wasn't treated or filtered. My hunger drove me to eat about half the meal before I couldn't take anymore. After the meal, I was committed to not having a repeat, and suspected that his wife couldn't pull off a bland meal. I had to leave.

I cooked up a story about needing to go to the fish farm near Bhairahawa, where I shared a small flat with three other PCVs. We often had business there, so it wasn't unusual for me to leave for a few days at a time. It took that many days before I could eat anything without a burning sensation. If I drank water, my mouth burned; everything I ate burned except for yogurt and chai. That episode changed my taste buds, though. Since then I actually prefer hot and spicy foods. Whether this is because the chilies permanently damaged my mouth's pain nerves, I can't say.

North of Bhairahawa, at the confluence of the first row of hills that mark the end of the Gangetic Plain is the town of Butwal. Butwal has two sections, old Butwal to the west and new Butwal to the east. Old Butwal had the charm of a Nepali hill town; new Butwal was an industrial, trade, and transportation center serving as the gateway from the Terai to Pokhara to the north and Kathmandu to the northeast. For nine months of the year (this was before the new bridge over the Kali Gandaki River was completed) one had to cross the river over a footbridge. Old Butwal was a pleasant place to stop for chai. In the 1960s, Butwal was on the Hippie Trail, receiving its share of freaky travelers as a gateway to the north. Some hippies stopped there because the town had character, and also because about 5 km north of Butwal there is a little enclave called Bhut Khola. "Bhut" means "ghost" and "khola" means river – Ghost River. And indeed, the locals tell stories of ghosts that haunted this little corner of semi-tropical Paradise. The River, really it was not much more than a stream, except during the monsoon, plummeted into a small round pool from unseen heights in the towering hills above. The pool was simultaneously turgid and clear: turgid where the waterfall plunged into it, and clear along the pool's rounded edge. One could not see the pool or the waterfall from the road, half a kilometer away. An old PCV who had married a Nepali and still lived in Kathmandu said that the hippies "discovered" the pool and made it a regular stop *en route* to the Himalayas. Since those days, Bhut Khola has fallen into obscurity, no longer frequented by travelers and mostly shunned by the locals. PCVs knew about it and would visit on occasion. In fact, a PCV had died there when he dived into the pool, too near to the rocky edge where the falls cascaded onto jagged rocks. Presumably his was one of the resident ghosts.

Pokhara is the only location on Earth where one can enjoy a rooftop breakfast at 600 meters (2,000 feet) elevation with a view of mountains rising to 8,000 meters, a 7,400 meters relief from valley floor to mountaintop. Dhaulagiri, Annapurna, Machhaphuchhare and Manasulu border the valley to the north, to name a few legendary peaks; peaks famous in the annals of mountaineering. But Pokhara's valley at their base is an attraction in its own right. In the heart of the valley is Tal Lake ("Lake" Lake). Though not a pristine alpine lake – the elevation is too low – it beautifully reflects the mountains in calm waters. Vendors rent small rowboats, for an hour or a day, to tourists. Because of Pokhara's location, it is a kicking-off and termination point for mountaineering expeditions and for trekking groups going to Annapurna Sanctuary or the Annapurna Circuit. Life along the lakefront is laid-back. Morning starts whenever one cares to get up. There are many tourist restaurants, most of them offering fixed breakfasts for a good price, with a view, and the food is generally decent. There is something in Pokhara for everyone: boating on the lake, bicycling, shopping, hiking, meditating, dallying with drink and drugs, or just soaking it all in. The tempo is reminiscent of island life. Cows wander lazily across streets that have moderate traffic, occasionally wandering onto the airport runway to be shooed off before a plane lands; drug pushers really don't push, and hawkers really don't hawk. The weather is pleasant for seven or eight months of the year with very rainy monsoon days. Many Hindu pilgrims pass through Pokhara on their way north to Muktinath, where they will wash away the sins of this and past lives. Caravans of donkeys and yaks, harkening back through long ages of trade, still move in and out of Pokhara, bringing in goods from Tibet and then returning. Yaks don't actually come as far south as Pokhara since the elevation is too low for them, but they ply trade in the surrounding high hills and Tibet. (A Sherpa once explained that when yaks reach lower elevations their tongues swell, and they can choke to death.) With the advent of Nepal's Maoist insurgency, Pokhara fell on harder times.

In contrast to Nepal, India is a difficult place for travelers to enjoy since Indians won't let them; yet India is always fascinating and even the dull moments aren't so dull because India is, well, India. Hawkers, vendors, and hustlers shape the landscape for foreign travelers. Seldom does a foreigner venture anywhere without being assailed. I made several excursions to India while living in Nepal. On one, I went to Rajasthan via Lucknow, Kanpur and Delhi. My first stop was Jaipur, the 'Pink City' in the desert. The City's old walls do have a pinkish hue, and treasures within – the museum for one. In the mid-1980s it was dilapidated and falling apart in places, yet held beautiful artworks, trinkets, gems, pictures, and old manuscripts that were well worth the price of entry, which was only a few dollars. The Hawa Mahal, Palace of the Winds, is a fine and delicate structure, crowded amongst a ramshackle assortment of buildings. It is written that the architect who designed it and the Raja who hired him were "Adepts," a peculiar term connoting religious accomplishment. A short distance from Jaipur is Amer. Once the heart of the ancient kingdom, this old Raj fort dwarfs similar structures in Europe, and makes Dubrovnik seem scant by comparison. The Hall of Mirrors and bedchamber of the King house thousands of tiny mirrors and miniature gemstones that capture light and reflect it in every direction to be re-reflected forever unto eternity. One candle can light up the hall. Rajasthan's cultural motif of tiny mirrors adorns local apparel and accessories and, so far as I know, may very well originate from Amer Fort. From Jaipur I went to Pushkar to see the only temple to Brahma in India, Brahma being chief of the godhead with Vishnu and Shiva. The temple stands atop a hill on the town's outskirts. God the Father, God the Son, and God the Holy Spirit, echo Brahma, Vishnu and Shiva. No writings with which I'm familiar explain why there is just one temple to Brahma in India, nor do the Indians whom I've consulted know. Pushkar has the feel of a desert oasis. In the midst of the dry landscape, the city wells up next to a small lake, which it surrounds. The state-run hash shop was then on a main street near many dining establishments, for those who got the munchies. The whole place had an aura of the 1960s. One could imagine Jerry Garcia and a caravan of deadheads settling there for a long, strange trip. The broken path up the hill to Brahma's temple made for a slow climb. Gradually gaining altitude one can see on the expanding horizon distant sand dunes that are loosely anchored by a covering of dry vegetation. The temple is not one of India's most spectacular, but the location is unlike any other. I thanked Brahma and continued on my way to Agra to see the Taj Mahal. Volumes have been written about the Taj, yet I find that it is beyond any words I might use to describe it; the Taj must speak to one itself. It speaks in shouts and in whispers, in one and in many a voice.

Young tourists, complete strangers, will gravitate toward each other in locations such as Rajasthan. *En route* from Delhi to Jaipur, a French woman and I made small talk on the bus. Upon arrival in Jaipur I went to a hotel that I had already staked out. She suggested that we share a room. I wasn't sure why she would want this arrangement but agreed to it. Was she interested in a fling, or did she feel a margin of safety, was she lonely? Attractive and lithesome with long dark hair, her English was not so good and my French non-existent. Nevertheless, we were companions for several days in Jaipur. When we got to Pushkar I ditched her, not wanting to be subject to another person's program, and she was somewhat dependent on me in a way that made me uncomfortable. Also, at that point in my life I wasn't interested in the complications of an intimate relationship, no matter how brief. While in Pushkar, I met a Swedish guy who was a companion on several daytrips around the town's environs. It was my first friendship with a Scandinavian, who I found had many similar perspectives but also wholly unfamiliar ones. What is it that draws such strangers together? We are drawn to some and repelled by others. There is a calculation that we make almost instantaneously, if we like someone or not. Yet I've found in life that the people to whom I'm closest are not those to whom I was most immediately drawn.

On other trips to India, I visited Darjeeling and Varanasi. Darjeeling is a former British hill outpost, famous for its tea, huddled under the mighty eaves of Kanchenjunga, the largest mountain on Earth by mass. Most tourists visit Darjeeling in the fall or spring; I went during the monsoon. I stayed at the house of a Tibetan lady, Dawa, who was recommended by other PCVs. Each morning she brought a cup of Darjeeling's finest to my bedroom before making breakfast. In the market, she introduced me to the various classes of tea; the highest class was reserved for British royalty, she observed, and was well beyond the meager sum in my pocketbook. The tea gardens in the monsoon are mystical; clouds drift up from the valley below, slowly wafting their way through the plantations to the ridge, mingling there to continue in ascent up Kanchenjunga's remote slopes. Is it any wonder that the tea tastes so good?

Varanasi could hardly be more different. Loud and rambunctious, seething with a humanity desperate for salvation. They come to submerse themselves in the Ganges, and wash away their earthly dross. Most disadvantageously, in my view, for the dross in the Ganges might be much worse. Varanasi has little mystical character but a too-human holiness that speaks more of mammon than of God. The religious center of India, Varanasi attracts pilgrims from all over the Subcontinent. Sometimes these pilgrimages take on a comic-tragic dimension. Many Indians are superstitious, consulting their horoscopes and astrologers for decisions large and small. The village mayor where I lived related a story about some guy who consulted his astrologer and was told that he faced grave danger on a certain date in the near future. The astrologer advised him to go to Varanasi to purify himself in the holy Ganges, so to bravely face the approaching danger with the assurance of salvation. Being terrified by his prospects, the man went to Varanasi and did as the astrologer had recommended and "cleansed" himself in the Ganges. The weather, unfortunately, was unseasonably cold when he did his oblations, and he caught pneumonia and died soon after. So, the astrologer's prediction proved accurate in the end.

Sitting at the Ganges' edge watching the water flow, the carcass of a cow floated by, along with every color of polyurethane bags, plastic bottles and all manner of trash, rising above and falling below the surface; yet this water purifies. Less reifying than the water, Varanasi's monkeys are nuisances. People can't leave anything out where the monkeys can get it. In fact, it is hard for people to keep anything out at all because the monkeys are known to walk inside dwellings and take what they want. One man described how a monkey walked into his kitchen and grabbed food right out of the refrigerator. In Varanasi the monkeys have learned how to forage as well as the other dominant biped. The hotel where I stayed had a rooftop garden with some tables and chairs, and it would have been nice but for the monkeys, which had scattered the furniture everywhere. Though sacred, these relatives of Hanuman the Monkey God, rescuer of Parvati, Varanasi would be a nicer place if they were better controlled.

What possessed me to go to Tioman Island in Malaysia, I don't know. Someone I met on the road suggested going there and it seemed like a good idea. For travelers who have time, flexibility, and are minded to talk to other travelers, new adventures and diversions are always just a conversation away. Through swapping information with others, one hears of good places to eat and to avoid, deals on hotels, interesting temples or events. I've rearranged whole itineraries because a conversation on the road led me to a new interest.

Perhaps I heard about Tioman while I was stuck in Singapore waiting for a money transfer. The 1980s were a different banking era than the 21st Century, when ATMs instantly dispense cash almost anywhere in the world. Back then, transferring money could take days or even weeks. And so I spent several weeks in Singapore waiting on money. The departure point for Tioman was several hours' drive up Malaysia's east coast, north of Singapore, a drive dominated by monotonous oil palm plantations. From the port at Mersing we took a high-speed hydrofoil to the Island. When we got there, the Island was more or less empty of tourists and we had our choice of bungalows. On the downside, it was Ramadan and, on our first morning there when we showed up for breakfast after sunrise, we found there was nothing to eat until after sunset. Such was my ignorance of Muslim culture then. My companion departing sooner, I stayed in Tioman for a week, taking time to explore. Most people go to Tioman for the beaches, scuba diving, and snorkeling, but its natural beauty should be the main attraction. Tioman separated from the Malaysian mainland some tens of millions of years ago and has a distinctive animal, notably reptilian, life. The most interesting trail, to the Island's summit, passes through fairly dense jungle, past some small waterfalls and swimming holes, to a lightly forested plateau. There are large snakes, the biggest I have seen outside of captivity. They were indifferent as I passed them by, slowly slithering about their business. There was a plethora of lizards, the most unexpected of which was a population of stumpy four-legged, long-necked reptiles that reminds one of pygmy Diplodocuses. While watching them from the brush, I decided to experiment and see how they would react to music. I sang, why I don't know, "Mull of Kintyre" a

Paul McCartney ditty. They became interested, coming closer and closer, standing, listening, as if spellbound. When I tired of singing and stood up they quickly darted into the underbrush, out of sight. Biological relics, still alive in this mammalian age, I don't know what species they are.

Tioman became an intermission during a long stay in Singapore. Singapore was then and remains a shopper's paradise, among other things. When I first visited in 1986 I hadn't been in air conditioning for several years. Walking in and out of Singapore's icy shopping malls caused an awful headache; the temperature changes varied drastically from the chill inside to the steamy outside. There were steamy places in the City, too. One night by happenstance I ventured into Singapore's red-light district near the docks, away from the usual tourist areas. The prostitutes I saw would have had to drive a hard bargain. Having recently arrived from Thailand, I thought these girls - and not all of them were girls - had some catching up to do. Not everything in Singapore is as it appears. Some years later on a return trip to Singapore, my wife and I with a couple of friends, both gay, wanted to visit this red-light district that I told them about; they had to see it. I led them to where I guessed the red-light district was, from my hazy memory. At the entrance is a Chinese gate similar to the gates one sees in Chinatowns around the world: dragon-covered posts on both sides of the street with an ornate dragon-themed arch above. Unlike US Chinatowns, this entrance featured two fashionable, slender young things – an improvement on my last visit. As we passed by one of them said, "Oh, you lucky girl!" Our friends busted out laughing; I was clueless, but they explained the girls weren't girls at all but transvestites. A friend who had moved to Singapore to work on an oil rig told me about one of his dates: He was a big guy, muscular and tall, a Vietnam Vet who found a home in Asia. He was taking out a beautiful Chinese girl. Things got hot. He reached under her skirt and "grabbed a handful" of something he didn't expect. Shocked, he kicked her out of the car, regretting later that he didn't punch "it" out. Singapore is the only place where strange men in bars bought me beers. I thanked them and let them know I had no interest.

Soon after the start of the hot season, roughly March in South Asia but varying by latitude and lasting until the monsoon rains bring relief (usually in June/July), the hot winds start. They blow in from the west, beginning in mid-morning and lasting until late afternoon, ratcheting up the heat and bringing a daily coating of fine dust particles. The winds can be more than just hot – at times they are scorching. A person can be out in the winds and quickly get dehydrated without realizing it because, first, the temperature is high anyway and, second, because the winds rapidly wick any moisture from the skin. Once I came close to a heat stroke during this season while visiting farmers. Mornings were the best times to make visits, but I could seldom meet more than a couple of farmers because they liked to chatter. Frequently, I would return in the heat of the day. This particular day was hotter and windier than usual and at mid-day, I was still on my bicycle. When I reached the village, I felt nauseated and faint. It didn't dawn on me that I was dehydrated. I sat in the shade of a teashop and drank a glass of water, and immediately began to perspire. All the moisture had been sapped from my pores and partially re-hydrating them was enough to make the sweat start again. A friend stopped to chat with me and could tell I wasn't feeling well and was steadily getting worse. He quickly prescribed a homeopathic remedy; procuring a pomegranate, he had the teashop proprietor mash it up in a glass, and add a bit of lemon, sugar and water. The drink proved an effective remedy, helping to ease the nausea and increase my body's water retention. I had an awful headache for the rest of the day but learned my lesson and did all my farmer visits in the morning and evening hours during this season. When the winds die down in the evening, the night sky is notably hazier, increasing day-by-day, week-by-week until the monsoon rains start and clear the air. The winds blow strong; any unbolted doors facing the windward direction will fly open or slam shut. In the evenings, people inevitably have to search the neighboring fields for items the winds carried off. If caught in the winds' direct onslaught, one will have to shake their clothes to be rid of the dust. The winds' loud and endless droning makes it hard to hear and be heard, and even at short distance conversations must be shouted.

A similar wind cycle whips Africa's Western Sahel, though with some seasonal differences. There, by the end of December through the start of February, the air gets thicker and thicker. Infinite tiny specks of dust are suspended in the air, especially around the cities where vehicle exhaust throws even more particulates into the air. This dense air then just hangs around, literally, for weeks. There might be occasional breaks in the smog when the mercilessly hot sun beats down on the land, but by evening the dense, foggy air settles back in. Respiratory diseases flare up. By February, earlier than South Asia, the hot winds start to blow. They begin in the morning and blow right through the day and into the evening. In the Sahel, the winds have an ameliorating effect of clearing the air, dispersing the thick, hard-to-breathe smog. Over the course of a few weeks, the difference in air density changes notably. Once when working in Kano, Nigeria and points to the northeast, including Borno, Jigawa and Yobé states, the air was so thick that breathing was difficult. Returning a couple of weeks later, the winds had driven the stagnant air to some less fortunate place. Still, this dispersion of stagnant air was the only palpable benefit of the wind; as in South Asia, the wind is hot, uncomfortable, and covers everything in fine layers of soot by the time it dies down at the end of the day.

On both continents, the winds are harbingers of the rains. To say the rains are welcome would be an understatement. During my first monsoon in Nepal, when the rains started, the villagers ran out into the torrential downpour and danced. Children stripped off their clothes and ran naked onto the streets yelling and clapping. They know the rains are life giving. To show how torrential the rains can be, I once got the notion to attempt a shower during a typical downpour. Going to the rooftop in my shorts, I was able to soap up and rinse off. In South Asia, people wash themselves while wearing a cotton cloth; bathing is an art. The women, with their long, flowing hair must manage to soap, rinse and dry without flashing too much skin. Gracefully they lather up and rinse off one limb, one stretch of skin at a time while wearing a lungi, adjusting it around their privates as needed, until clean. I preferred a pair of loose gym shorts; this was much easier than bathing the traditional way. Someone told me to bring lots of books to the village because when the monsoon started there would be plenty of time for reading. This was sage advice. I read for days on end because the rain fell for days on end, taking periodic breaks to work and socialize. I came to appreciate Alexander the Great's discouragement at the endless monsoon rain. However, for farmers and laborers, the monsoon is a time to get busy since there is much to be done. Fields must be plowed, rice must be planted, and fishponds must be stocked. Early in the morning near the fields, the workers would sit on their haunches in the rain and mud, getting stoned before falling behind their oxen to plow the paddies. The monsoon also brings a change in diet. As the rains continue, fewer and fewer vegetables are available; there is too much water and not enough sun for many types of vegetable to ripen. The main vegetables are eggplant and snake gourd. Snake gourd is an irredeemably bitter plant and one that is unlikely to ever appeal to Western palates. Eggplant became my main vegetable, but I ate so much of it during two monsoons in the village that now I find it hard to swallow. Jackfruit is a seasonally available fruit, though before ripening it can be prepared like a vegetable. Traditionally cooked in a hot curry sauce, it is served with rice – of course. Unripe jackfruit has a fatty texture that was hard to get used to, although many of my friends found delicious. Occasional breaks between rains during the monsoon are most unpleasant, with the sun's rays boring through scattered clouds like lasers. Sometimes there are extended, rainless breaks. Then the heat AND humidity are stifling. Walking between rice paddies filled with shallow water in the unpitying sun, one can see, quite visibly, the moisture rising into the air as it evaporates. A person on the other side of a paddy will appear wavy as the humidity distorts their image. Then the clouds come, and the rains start again, interminably, and the hot inter-monsoon dry-spell is over.

Relief from the Terai heat would come from trips to Kathmandu. The relative ease of travel to Kathmandu was one of the few advantages of being posted in the Terai. These trips weren't as often as I would have liked; PCVs were encouraged to stay at their posts, but when a good excuse afforded itself we would hop a night bus to the capitol. While planes flew from Bhairahawa to Kathmandu daily, airplane tickets were outside of our budgets. During my service I took just one, memorable, round-trip flight from the Terai. Having taken off, the plane looped to the north and then turned east, providing an expansive view of the Himalayan front from Annapurna to Dorjé Lakpa. The flight was short – less than half an hour. Nearing sunset, the moon was rising above the mountains, which stood towering above the plane at over 7,600 meters. The memory is of a half-moon, shining through the plane window with the Himalayas at eye-level glowing orange in the distant sunset.

Buses were, and still are, the main means of transportation in Nepal. Occasionally someone was able to bum a ride in a private car or truck, which I managed just a couple of times. A bus ride to Kathmandu could take anywhere from 8 to 12 hours, depending on how many stops the bus made, how long the drivers stopped during breaks, how much the driver had to eat (and sometimes drink), how much traffic was on the roads, how many people and animals crossed it, and the condition of the bus (if it broke down). Most buses were night buses, departing anytime between 5-9 p.m. and arriving 3-9 a.m. The innovation at that time was video-equipped buses, nowadays undoubtedly there are DVDs. These were the best buses to catch a ride on because they usually had better quality seats, stopped less often – sometimes just once – though for a premium price. The only catch was the videos. Bollywood movies are meant to be played loud. To the uninitiated, they resemble tawdry Broadway musicals, with lots of singing, dancing and gratuitous violence. And the bus employees and passengers loved it best when the volume was high – distortingly loud. The tradeoff was to take a quieter bus, which would most likely be local, stopping more frequently. At some point during my stay, I discovered Valium. At that time, local pharmacies sold prescription drugs without the need of a prescription. This was very convenient if one had a gut problem or was running a fever and their medical kit was depleted. It was also convenient if one needed a sleep remedy. Timing was everything. One had to take a 10 mg pill about halfway between Butwal and Chitwan and then one could sleep nearly the entire rest of the trip, waking upon arrival in Kathmandu and ready to go. The one obligatory stop on every bus driver's route was the town of Mugling. This custom probably started because Mugling is where the roads to Kathmandu and Pokhara fork. Although just a bus stop, Mugling was famous for the quality of its dal bhat. (It was also infamous with the many people who picked up Giardia or worse from eating there.) Drivers, we guessed, were given baksheesh by restaurateurs to stop their buses at particular eating establishments. No doubt the drivers got free food too. Most passengers, in various states of alertness or apoplexy depending on the video they'd been watching, piled in to pile it in. Stuffed with food, everyone would return to the bus to continue the journey, and another movie. The only thing that seemed to keep the drivers from dozing off afterwards was the harrowing road, which took every bit of their concentration to maneuver over.

The road to Kathmandu cannot adequately be described without photos. The terrain is so steep it defies imagination that a road could have been cut through it and that buses, trucks, and every other manner of motor vehicle traverse it. Crawling up the road, one can fully appreciate why Kathmandu was isolated from much of the world until the 19th Century. The journey to the Capitol without this road was grueling, not the preserve of diplomats, with the exception of Maharajas who could afford the luxury of being carried. One also gets a sense of the precariousness of the city's population – an earthquake, a flood, a war, a diplomatic tiff with India, could completely cut Kathmandu off from the world except for airlift. Going up, though slow isn't as hair-raising as the trip down. The buses' bumpers are suspended over the road's edge, which drops hundreds of feet to the Trisuli River below. Sometimes the buses aren't maintained well; brakes give out and they and all their passengers plunge into the river. Once such a plunge made international news by claiming the lives of an estimated 200 people. How do that many people lose their lives in a single bus's fall? Let's see: there are 24 rows of seats, 2 benches to a row, 3 people squeezed onto a bench; the aisles are crammed full of standing passengers, from the rear to the front stairwell, maybe 50 standing in all, plus another dozen or so on the roof, with assorted livestock. Sometimes the crushing weight of so many passengers and freight cause buses to blow a tire. No, it is much better to go up than to go down, the actual direction presupposing the metaphorical if one doesn't survive.

To reach Bhairahawa from India, one travels through the grimy city of Gorakpur, where my luggage was stolen while I was waiting for the train. A guy – he looked Bihari – offered me a cigarette. I was not in the habit of smoking, but at that time, I occasionally had a cigarette to pass the time. We chatted for a few minutes and he moved on; I didn't think anything more of it. About a half an hour later I got on the train, feeling unusually lightheaded. A man on the bench across from me started up a conversation in very good English. The man who gave me the cigarette (he didn't speak English) joined us, sitting on the bench next to me. My bag was beneath my legs under the bench. After waiting some time for the train to get underway I realized that my bag was missing, and the guy who gave me the cigarette was gone too. The English-speaking gentleman had completely succeeded in distracting my attention. I jumped up and ran off the train just as it was starting to leave. I found a policeman, and then began the interminable process of filing a police report. At the same time, I realized that I must have been drugged. My lightheadedness had now descended into a funk, and I was straining to keep awake as the report, the policeman, the night clerk and a detective kept badgering me with questions.

During the ordeal an MP (Member of Parliament for those of non-parliamentary persuasions) walked in; everyone in the station stood to attention except me, I was too out of it. He was clearly offended by this indignity. I listened to him complain about my lack of respect, though feigned to not understand Hindi. The others excused my behavior by explaining that I was an ignorant foreigner, which was true enough. Eight p.m. became 3 a.m., and somehow, I managed to stay conscious throughout, but I realized that I wasn't going to get my bag back and that I would have to find a hotel for what was left of the night. In the following days, after relating my adventure to friends and acquaintances, I learned that this was a typical set up, and that similar crimes had been reported by other people who they knew. The M.O. was just as happened to me; two guys working together would target a traveler for a sting. They would drug then distract them and steal their luggage. The next time I went to India, I didn't accept smokes and didn't let my bag out of my grip.

Gorakpur isn't the sole place where I've been robbed; I was also mugged in Maputo, Mozambique's capitol. This mugging happened on a bright and sunny Sunday afternoon, just around the corner from the main thoroughfare and Avenida Hotel, in front of a church. A friend and I were walking to a nearby restaurant for lunch when he noticed two guys approaching us. My antennas were down because it didn't seem like the time or place for a mugging. My friend diverted across the street with me following, but after just a short distance the men accosted us. Each one of them tried ripping off each one of us; I lost a little bit of money, he lost a $500 cell phone. Reflecting on the incident afterwards, it seemed to me that the thieves were poorer for the incident and we had just lost some stuff. They lost their humanity.

Notwithstanding these muggings, my crime fighting credentials were tested in Providence, Rhode Island, on a trip for a job interview. While sitting in the airport waiting for my return flight to Washington, DC, I noticed a film crew nearby setting up their cameras but didn't pay them much attention. As I sat reading, an attractive woman asked if I would watch her suitcase. I told her that I would and continued to read. Soon after, a guy came along and grabbed her bag. I stopped him from taking it and we got into an argument; he told me that the bag belonged to his sister and she had asked him to get it for her and he made a few other excuses for taking the bag. Many onlookers who were waiting for the flight got involved and encouraged me not to let him take the bag. Following a few minutes of argument, he gave up and went away. When he left the others assured me that I had done the right thing. A few minutes later the woman returned with a microphone in her hand. I noticed the film crew and camera were pointed at us. She explained that the event had been staged to see how people would react in a situation when they were entrusted with the care of a stranger's goods. I was the third dupe that day and was the only one to protect the bag – the "only hero." Someone later mentioned seeing the piece on the evening news – my five minutes of fame.

CHAPTER 3

THE PEACE CORPS JEEP DROVE away after dropping me off in the village where I would be posted for the next two-years. I felt utterly thrown back on my own resources. A couple of months before I had visited the village with another, experienced, volunteer, and we both agreed it looked like a decent place, which turned out to be right. My immediate problem was that no one in the village expected me, nor did anyone expect me in the regional Agriculture District Office where my supposed boss was located. When I was dropped off that fine January afternoon, I had no place to stay and no defined job to do. We had been trained in fisheries and agriculture extension for several months and had received extensive language training. However, the village where I landed, Bahadurgunj, was situated so close to the Indian border that most people spoke Hindi, very few spoke Nepali. As I watched the jeep drive away, I said something in Nepali to those crowded around me, which no one seemed to understand. I suspected poor pronunciation, but when I repeated it, someone understood and said, "yes, that's how you say that in Nepali." My stomach sank. That was the nadir; from there things improved. Most PCVs share similar experiences, to one degree or other, when the cord to headquarters is finally cut. Many Nepal volunteers had to trek to their posts, sometimes for days or even weeks. They would show up unexpectedly in a village without a word of introduction, which I at least had. With tentative grasp of the language they would have to organize their lives and work. One or two had been robbed and killed on the way to their post. As my stomach sank, the local School Headmaster, who spoke English very well, showed up and rescued me from the situation. I felt relieved then and feel gratitude even now for his kindness. Mr. Gupta had spent seven months touring the US a decade earlier in an exchange program. He introduced me to the people who would become my "family." The villagers found me a temporary place in the Krishi Upkendra (agriculture sub-station). In the guestroom upstairs there was a (bedbug-ridden) bed and I would use it until permanent quarters could be found for me.

As I came to learn, I wasn't the first volunteer to have lived in Bahadurgunj. One "Mr. Peter" had lived there for five years! Seldom do Volunteers extend their stay in the Terai, but he had. He lived with the Pradhan Paanch who, resembling Groucho Marx, was the local mayor and who, as a result, was very positively disposed toward PCVs. There had been another volunteer in Bahadurgunj since Mr. Peter, but he was medi-vacced (evacuated for medical reasons) before his service was completed. He too was remembered fondly. People in this town knew how to look after a PCV. Because the Headmaster spoke English and Mr. Peter had taught English in the local school for so long, there were a fair number of young people, in their twenties, who spoke English and I had no problems getting around in their company.

I decided to apply to Peace Corps during my tenure at the City County Planning Office in Livingston, Montana. I had considered joining Peace Corps since my freshman college year but didn't seriously pursue the possibility until the year I graduated – skiing extended my education by a year. Wanting to experience life in another culture, I was young and altruistic, and volunteer service appealed to me. I really didn't care where I would be assigned, except small islands and large urban areas. Small islands – limited to going around in circles, was uninteresting; urban areas – too oppressive. Joining Peace Corps was a game of roulette; you submit your application and wait to see what country you land in. In my case, the marble landed in "Nepal," and so I was bound for the Himalayas, or close anyway.

My adopted family was one of the few families in town whose mother tongue was Nepali, and I quickly befriended one of the two brothers. Krishna, the elder, was the manager of the local agriculture cooperative; Bhuvan, the younger, had recently finished his education and was going into business. He became my closest friend. Parvati, Krishna's wife, was a teacher and they had two girls, aged two and five, and soon they would have a son. When in town, I dined with them twice a day and would drop by whenever, just to hang out, and was always welcome. I found a second-floor flat right across the street from the Upkendra, with windows overlooking the town's main street. Mostly Hindus populated the town, although there was a sizeable Muslim population in the area. The Indian border was just 8 kilometers away and we would often cross the border to shop. The border guards recognized me and would let me pass, so India was quite accessible; I didn't need a passport. Bahadurgunj was otherwise unremarkable. One could look across the vast planes and imagine the halcyon days of ancient Indian civilization and the Ashvamedha, the horse sacrifices, which were once common. After all, this was Kapilavastu, the ancient capital of Lord Siddhartha, the Buddha, whose father was King Śuddhodana. Now, peopled with the Saakya clan's remote descendants, one can yet feel those bygone days in the characters of the villagers.

My flat was two front rooms on the second floor of a two-story building, the main front room being considerably exposed to the elements. There were two windows that took up most of the front wall, overlooking the street below. When the wind drove the monsoon rains, water would sometimes soak the first meter of the room and everything in it, though generally the elements were more welcome than unwelcome. There was a third room behind the two I rented, which the landlord occasionally leased out to students at exam time or was used to store supplies. Thank God there was a ceiling fan in the room, for in the hot season (which in the Terai lasts about nine months) a fan was the difference between comfort and considerable discomfort. Unfortunately, the electricity worked about half the time, usually being out on the hottest days, because of "load shedding," when a fan would have been most useful. "Load shedding" is a pejorative term, but sounds better than "cut the power," which is what the utilities do after all. The water supply was a downstairs hand pump, in the rear of the building near the bull stalls. One of the landlord's hired hands slept in the front room on the main level. Keeping the bulls in an adjacent shelter is a long-standing tradition on the Subcontinent, probably for fear of thieves. The bulls were hard working animals, though the workers who took care of them worked harder and looked less well kept. One bull was very large with long protruding horns - a real Brahma bull. He didn't like me, and let me know, shaking his mighty horns whenever he saw me, though I never did anything to him and went out of my way to keep out of his way.

On several occasions, this bull and I crossed paths at the building's entrance and he threatened me: all the more reason to avoid any encounter with him. One afternoon I came down the stairs, turning the corner at the bottom and entered the front room on my way outside. Just as I turned the corner and stepped into the room the bull walked through the door and came straight at me. I had nowhere to go. In the room's corner were a chair and a chest. I quickly stepped onto the chair to the chest's top, trying to get as high as I could and as far out of the animal's reach as possible. It was no use. He quickly cornered me and pushed me with brute force. His high head and huge horns were leveled at my chest. He thrust his head straight at me. I grabbed the horns. I knew at any moment I would be gored. Then, for no apparent reason he turned and walked away. I stood there relieved and trembling, thanking Providence. I made sure that we did not cross paths again. The risk of being gored by a bull or buffalo is a hazard of rural life, and not at all uncommon. I've been on buses when goring victims, in various degrees of dismemberment, were being taken to a hospital or clinic. Neighbors would discuss how one animal or another had done this or that to someone. Domestic animals are often a source of tension in society: whose property they are, whose property they are on, their behavior and how that reflects on the owners. These problems are age old and may be the original impetus, along with agricultural produce and tools, for the recognition of "rights" to "ownership" and the need to exert one's rights and protect their ownership.

There were two powerful political families in western Kapilavastu, and I got to know the patriarchs of both clans. The Shah family owned lots of land and a small palace on the south side of town. The patriarch's stables were filled to the ceiling with bags of "complexal," an inorganic fertilizer, a lot of it passed the "use-by" date. Of course, this fertilizer would be leaked into the market over time. The other family, the Rajuriyas, had a large spread in a small town 4 km south of Bahadurgunj. These two families were both from the traditional zamindar class of Northern Indian large landholders, however they were Nepali. Mr. Rajuriya was an important man, a Secretary in the government, and Mr. Shah had previously been a Secretary.

The Rajuriyas had a large fishpond and as the local extension agent, I would visit occasionally to check on how the fish were doing. His son, in his mid-teens, befriended me and I was always welcome. Per custom, they would serve tea and have me stay for lunch. One day after checking the fishpond, there was a small crowd waiting at the entrance to Mr. Rajuriya's house. Since he spent most of his time in Kathmandu, his days in the village were taken up with affairs of his estate. Many of those waiting to see him were peasant farmers or workers, hoping for favors rather than to conduct business. I had heard that in this part of Nepal indentured servitude still existed, people became slaves to pay off family or other debts. One petitioner, an old 'musselman' (Muslim) in a full-length gown and scraggly gray beard, entered the room and bowed down on his hands and knees then crawled to my host with his face to the floor. When the old man reached Rajuriya he stopped and kissed his feet, over and over. I'm not sure what his petition was for, but the Secretary granted it. Later in Bahadurgunj I asked about this display, wanting to understand the old man's motivation. Nepalese traditionally limit such displays to family or to royalty. My friends explained that the old man is "Rajuriya's man." "What do you mean 'his man'?" "Like a cow belongs to someone, the old man belongs to him."

My neighbor, Radasham, taught me an important lesson about "international development." Development, in an international context, refers generally to the process of countries moving from unindustrialized, mostly agrarian, societies to more sophisticated, industrialized economies. Economically this transition tends to lift people out of absolute poverty, where they cannot meet even basic needs, to relative affluence, though they may still be poor. Whether this transition can happen for nine or ten billion people without ruining the environment remains to be seen. It is the custom in rural India to do oblations in the fields first thing in the morning, usually just outside the village. Consequently, one can find shit everywhere alongside the skinny paths that lead from the village to the surrounding rice paddies. Radasham wasn't a poor, simple farmer; he had a university education, having majored in English. He spoke English well enough to converse intelligently about many subjects. He understood health care and kept a copy of the book "*Where there is No Doctor*." Yet, like his fellow villagers, he went to the fields every morning for oblations. One day I asked him why he did this when he knew how unhealthy it was for those living nearby. "Radasham, you see the flies land on the shit, and you know those same flies are there when you eat and sometimes land on the food. You know that this spreads disease. So why don't you use the latrine? There are many close by. Why do you go to the fields?" His answer: "Because it's my habit. I like to watch the sunrise over the fields in the morning while I'm taking a shit. This is how I like to start my day." It struck me then that development involves attitudes as much as education.

But culture weighs heavily on peoples' attitudes. The town's mayor once told me: "Ganges' water is the purest water. Three years ago, I collected a jar of Ganges water and brought it home. To this day it still has no smell. Water from other sources would start to smell bad after so much time in a jar but not Ganges water." Meanwhile the Ganges must be one of the world's most polluted rivers.

Rickshaw drivers in South Asia are often targets of abuse. They earn a pittance for grueling work. Yet many rickshaw drivers take great pride in their occupation. Most drivers (known locally as "rickshaw wallahs") accessorize their rickshaws with dual mirrors on the handlebars (pointed toward themselves), tassels, horns and bells, religious iconography and tinsel. There is no limit to what they will haul on their rickshaws -- so long as someone pays. PCVs used to joke, "How do you make a pig bark like a dog? Strap it to a rickshaw on its back." This particular rickshaw must have belonged to an "untouchable." A Brahmin would never (knowingly) ride in a rickshaw that had been used to haul pigs. For wallahs who can afford to buy them, a rickshaw can be a decent investment. One friend owned three rickshaws, which he leased to several drivers. There are rickshaw syndicates where one owner will have hundreds of rickshaws and hire drivers for them. The syndicates are run with mafia-style efficiency and brutality. It is an accomplishment when a driver can command the resources to buy his own rickshaw; inevitably rickshaw wallahs are men, though occasionally one finds women drivers.

In Bahadurgunj's local Development Bank, I met the family of one proud owner of a new rickshaw. They were agitated, grief stricken. The banker was a genuinely concerned man who made the driver a loan for his rickshaw. The family was trying to settle the driver's account, with difficulty. As the banker later explained, the driver could no longer settle the account himself: The town had an ordinance that all vehicles, rickshaws included, had to have headlights or lanterns lighted after dark. At dusk the driver was just returning to town, wrapping up his day, with the last light fading from the sky. A tollgate policeman stopped him, assessing a "fine" for driving his rickshaw after dark without a light. Apparently, the rickshaw wallah argued that it wasn't yet dark, and he was driving straight home. For his impertinence, the policeman beat him to death with a bamboo nightstick. The rickshaw wallah perished but left his family with a rickshaw and a debt that they could not afford to repay. They were seeking relief from the bank. Police brutality is universal – remember Rodney King? However, victimization fluctuates with income.

Whole penal systems can be criminal. One political agitator I met was incarcerated after a demonstration; he was thrown into a cellblock with other prisoners who had been there for a long time. He was soon released but while in the cellblock had learned about the "leper block," where really (politically) dangerous criminals were sent. One of his fellow prison mates, sentenced to five years, was held in the leper cellblock for a time and had contracted the disease.

There was one man in the village who completely annoyed me, and whenever I saw him I went in the opposite direction. The first time we met he was drunk, or rather he was a drunk. He had certainly been drinking and was carrying a live cobra. Some friends and I were in a bus stop teashop when he approached us, swinging the cobra. Slurring in two languages he pushed the cobra in my face: "Are you afraid of snakes?" "No," I replied, "but I don't like cobras." Pushing the cobra closer: "You're not afraid of snakes?" He could see that I was getting upset: "He won't hurt you - I pulled out his fangs." Well, maybe, but snakes' fangs grow back. Then he started taunting me with it, enjoying my discomfort. The shopkeeper intervened and made the guy leave, but he was always on the lookout for me. He caught snakes for a living; it was his 'jyatti'. Jyatti is a Hindi word that signifies one's caste or place in life. Whether this was his best or only source of income I didn't learn. To me, drinking, or being a drunk, and catching cobras seemed to be a formula for early, permanent, retirement, but he was well into his 50s. Students sometimes found cobras in the school latrines and he was the guy who was called in to catch and dispose of them, a kind of "cobra-rooter." Unshaven and scraggly, he seemed very reckless; how could he specialize in catching cobras, especially considering the margin of error cannot be very high? Not a snake charmer, I never met anyone else from his jyatti, and I doubt there is an over-supply. At least the pay seemed adequate to his drinking needs. In South Asia there are jobs, many hereditary, that don't exist elsewhere. The intense competition for resources means that people find very creative ways to make money.

Particularly in India, if there is a way to make money someone will figure it out, ingenuity never being in short supply. One Indian newspaper ran an interesting story about a guy who found an unusual way to make money. The story began in one of the home ministries where a bureaucrat was going through pension records and discovered the account of a pensioner who had been collecting payments for so long that he was the world's oldest man. So the ministry set out to find him. India's long-standing practice until recently is for employees to use their thumbprints as identification when claiming payments. Thumbprints are used because of the low level of literacy and because they are unique identifiers. The thumbprints thus served a dual purpose as proof of identity and proof of payment. As it happened, when the ministry officials found the pensioner, instead of the world's oldest living man they discovered a house full of thumbs nicely preserved in jars of formaldehyde. The jars' well-preserved thumbs were blackened with ink from long years of use. Apparently, the scam artist who owned the thumbs was so successful that he employed a team of people to help him collect pension money on payday. How he got all of these thumbs was an open question. Some of them he bought from the families of dead pensioners, other thumbs were thought to have been acquired by less pleasant means.

Bhairahawa (officially Mahendranagar) could be a rough place. Situated just north of Nepal's border with India, Bhairahawa is a thoroughfare for trucks and buses in-bound from Gorakpur, crossing the border just to the south in Sunauli and then passing through the city. Many overland tourists enter Nepal via this crossing and transit through Bhairahawa on their way to Pokhara or Kathmandu. Besides being a transportation and distribution center, Bhairahawa has a small but thriving agro-processing industry. As a transit point, the city attracts certain types of people and business. Being a large town close to the border, Bhairahawa also has a vibrant retail sector. When I was there, Bhairahawa had the best food in that part of the Terai, with several decent restaurants, or so it seemed. One restaurant had the best yogurt, so thick that it stood up on a plate, resembling a piece of cake. It was made with water buffalo milk, rich and sweet. The same restaurant had superb puri for breakfast. Puri is a greasy but tasty delicacy of the region, and is served in the morning with curried vegetables, called sambar. Mostly Nepalese populated Bhairahawa but there was also a sizable population of Madeshis, Nepalese of Indian descent who live in the Terai, are descended from the Saakyas. Ganja could be procured in town for a few rupees at many local kiosks, and rickshaw wallahs were famous imbibers. There was also a local distillery churning out rum and anise-flavored liquor – Dudhiya – "dudh" being the word for milk; like ouzo, one adds water to dilute it, turning it white. Since the mid-1980s the Madeshis have been advocating their rights of citizenship, to the point of violent demonstrations and killings. Madeshis have been a marginalized group, often ridiculed though seeming to suffer no systematic discrimination, until the 2015 constitution. But as more and more Nepalese relocated from the hills to the Terai, marginalization turned into discrimination, such is the role of immigration in politics and power.

Some years earlier a fisheries PCV lived in the area, posted about five kilometers northwest of Bhairahawa. He had apparently been in the village for quite a while and had little contact with other PCVs or Westerners. There weren't many Nepalese in the village where he was posted; most of the inhabitants were Taru, the original indigenous people, pre-dating even the Madeshis. Very few Taru spoke Nepali at that time. Communication was certainly an issue. Several people relayed this Volunteer's story, including one Peace Corps staff who was directly involved. He was observed wading into a fishpond with his net, emerging a few minutes later with a large carp and, to the amazement of onlookers, totally naked. Not stopping, he walked down the dirt road to the point where it met the paved road, then caught a bus to Bhairahawa, still naked, and disappeared into the city. Eventually, word reached Peace Corps headquarters in Kathmandu that this volunteer had gone AWOL and some staff were sent to find him. By the time they started looking, several weeks had gone by. Eventually, after some inquiries, they learned of his strange behavior and discovered that he had checked into one of the local hotels. They found him there in a room, in bed, with the fish, now badly decayed. He was "psycho-vacced" to the US where he spent some time in a mental ward re-adjusting. I never learned if he recovered. Some people don't do well in social isolation, if in fact this is what brought on his condition. Some PCVs in Nepal lived in very isolated, remote areas, not days but weeks from a major center; nevertheless, they did not suffer mental breakdowns.

This wasn't the only incident of a PCV from this area being evacuated. A Peace Corps supervisor told of an incident when a volunteer who had gone "saddhu." "Saddhus," or fakirs, are India's famous mendicants, often followers of Shiva, who have sworn oaths of renunciation. This Supervisor told me that one-day while driving to Bhairahawa on business he thought he recognized a PCV who was posted nearby sitting in the local market under a Pipal tree, dressed as a saddhu. The Supervisor couldn't believe it at first but, after pondering for a few kilometers, decided to return and look again. Sure enough, the saddhu was this PCV. He was quite off his rocker and had to be psycho-vacced. In yet another incident, a PCV posted in the area was psycho-vacced for enjoying too much of a good thing. During the holiday of Holi it is common for everyone to inhale, drink, or otherwise consume large quantities of ganja. For the uninitiated, it is possible to overdose on THC, marijuana's active chemical ingredient. This PCV passed the point of overdose, reportedly consuming so much that he was barely coherent weeks later. In one more incident, a PCV posted near Bhairahawa was psycho-vacced, in his case because no good joke goes unpunished. PCVs are issued medical kits; these kits include small cartons for stool samples, malaria prophylaxis, anti-diarrheal medicine and similar treats. The kits also include a health questionnaire that Embassy doctors use to check the status of a PCVs' health. One of the last questions on the form was: "Is there anything else that you need?" As relayed to me, thinking he was funny, this volunteer answered: "a plastic blowup doll." The doctor didn't like his sense of humor (or lacked one herself). She sent for him to come to Kathmandu, after which he was soon returned to the US.

Besides PCVs, there were volunteers from other countries based near Bhairahawa. One, Marco, a Swiss volunteer, had a project to disseminate improved potato varieties to small land-holding (smallholder) farmers. Occasionally we met for comradery and drinks. He was fortunate that he had his own vehicle; Peace Corps only issued bicycles. One day Marco had to go to Kathmandu and we decided to go along. We left in the afternoon and figured that the trip would take about five hours in a four-wheeler, versus the usual eight to ten hours on the bus. We were cruising on the road from Bhairahawa to Butwal, going pretty fast but no faster than the other vehicles on the road. Anyone who has been in a village market in South Asia during a "haat bazaar," the main market day of the week, expects there to be lots of people milling around. We were driving through a village where there was a "haat bazaar" that day. People crowded on both sides of the road but not on the road. An oncoming local bus stopped to let some passengers off and pick up some new ones. Marco had no way of seeing that some passengers who had just disembarked passed behind the bus to cross the road. I caught a quick glance of a woman's smiling face peering from behind the bus to check for oncoming traffic. Suddenly, several people darted across the road, two young men and the woman. They must have seen us because we were approaching fast, but they seemed to calculate that they could run across safely. The two young men crossed quickly; the woman started across but then turned to face the jeep as we raced toward her. She froze there in the middle of the road like a deer caught in the headlights. Marco slammed on the brakes but there wasn't much he could do. If he veered to the right he would crash into the bus and if he veered to the left, he would run into the crowded marketplace. As the Jeep screeched to a halt the big front grill hit her, sending her hard to the pavement. We all jumped out of the jeep to where she lay. The two young men reached her first crying "Amaah, Amaah," – "Mother, Mother." She was unconscious but there was no evidence of external trauma.

The people in the market crowded around to gape; everyone is fascinated by an accident. Some people who had seen the incident reassured Marco that the accident was not his fault and they would be willing to provide witness. We didn't stand around to talk; we carefully picked up the woman and put her in the back of the jeep with the help of some bystanders; her sons climbed in too, along with a couple of men who pitched in to help. Marco drove as quickly as he could to Butwal Hospital. We immediately sent for a doctor, meanwhile the police caught up with us. The doctor did not come for a very long time and from his mode of questioning and the statements that he made it was clear that he wasn't terribly concerned about the welfare of a low-caste village woman. Marco was in a dreadful state, however, and was prepared to throw money at the doctor if it meant that she would get help. The police questioned us all and were sympathetic in light of the circumstances. However, they had to abide the law, which meant that they would hold Marco until their investigation was complete. After taking statements from my companion and I they gave us permission to leave. We were reluctant to leave Marco but under the circumstances there wasn't much else we could do. Later we learned that the police let him spend the night in a hotel rather than in prison.

Marco was a sensitive person and this incident crushed him, but he remained in Nepal. The woman lingered in unconsciousness for several days before passing away. According to Nepalese law Marco had to pay the family restitution, which I remember as being 6,000 rupees. In the event, Marco doubled the amount. Sad to say but the family probably had never been so well-off financially; this was a considerable amount of money in Nepal. There was no insurance to pay compensation. Tellingly, compensation for killing a cow with a vehicle was 10,000 rupees.

Not long after this incident I was mildly injured. The villagers packed me off in a jeep to see a doctor in India where better medical help could be found than in Bahadurgunj. Long waits for doctors are a sad fact of life in many poor rural areas. Eventually we gave up when we learned that the wait would be really long. A woman had doused herself with kerosene and set herself on fire. Her burns were extensive and that would keep the doctor busy for the rest of the night. I never learned whether this was a case of "bride burning." Once I visited a village where a burning bride had set many homes ablaze while trying to extinguish the flames.

Uneducated people commonly think they need medical help when really all they need are cheap, over-the-counter supplements. During the dry season especially, one sees desperate mothers on buses carrying emaciated babies to the nearest clinic. Such is the price of their ignorance of basic hygiene, sanitation, diarrhea and rehydration. A small packet of rehydration salts in a bottle of water can save a life. The salts were very affordable. But then, the poorest families can't afford hygienic bottles. What might be a five-cent cure becomes a very expensive visit to the clinic relative to a family's income. Marketers have helped raise awareness of diarrhea and cleverly named the rehydration salts "jivaan jel," which translates loosely to "elixir of life."

After I had been in Nepal for just a few weeks I knew that I would want to stay longer than my Peace Corps service, but that lay in the future. Nepal was one of the most requested Peace Corps destinations, though I never asked to go there. I was a "Fisheries" volunteer but ended up doing mostly agricultural extension work since my post didn't have many fishponds nearby; in the dry season most ponds dried up. The farmers were great, and generous to a fault, even though most of them had but little. An interest in markets took root; I would find out what goods were selling for in the local markets and learn how much they would cost to produce. Pineapples were an especially good bet. A farmer could intercrop them with pulses and maximize their land use. Returns were over 100 percent per fruit. Usually after considering the math, the farmers were convinced. Their reaction to seeing the math (sales price − costs) convinced me to buy a small, solar-powered calculator, which I carried with me on farmer visits. The work was the least part of the experience, though eventually it would be a catalyst for my career. Relationships were paramount. The main "opportunity cost" of being in Peace Corps in Nepal was remoteness of a relationship, physical or otherwise, with the opposite sex. Posted where I was in the Terai, there was an uptight Hindu culture and the largest Muslim population in

Nepal. Rarely was I able to interact with women. The Country's culture seemed to influence the Volunteers' culture and, while volunteers of both sexes shared great camaraderie, there weren't many love relationships. During the time of my service, I had one misguided fling. It would be four years until I had a love interest.

During my leaves I made three treks – Everest, the Annapurna Circuit and Langtang, and visited Darjeeling, Agra, Delhi and other places in Uttar Pradesh, West Bengal and Rajasthan. Volunteers had a certain number of vacation days, but Nepal has so many holidays that there many opportunities for travel – one-week trips to near destinations. When my service was over I traveled to Burma (now Myanmar), Thailand, Malaysia, Singapore and Indonesia. My urge was to see new places. I re-entered the US in San Francisco, staying a week in Berkeley. This was a strategic entry point, easing transition from the streets of Kathmandu to Planet Berkeley, and thence home to Montana; I called my sisters ahead of my arrival and arranged to surprise my parents. When I met them at the door my Mom cried. No sooner was I in Montana than I decided that I had to get back to Nepal, but how to get there? I called trekking agencies and lined up work. One agency was desperate for an American who knew the main treks and could speak the language. They made me a pittance of an offer but agreed to give me a round-trip ticket – I accepted. We agreed that I could take odd trekking jobs so long as it didn't interfere greatly with the needs of their clients. The arrangement would last from fall to spring, after that I was on my own, which worked out well since by spring I had become known in guide circles and was turning away work.

CHAPTER 4

IN MY DREAMS IS A bay of calm water, twilit, the ground white from a dusting of snow, cold though not freezing, under the eaves of high, snowy peaks encircling it. When I reach this place, I am at peace. It was a place that I visited sometimes – before. I don't know if a physical equivalent exists to this dream landscape. Perhaps I saw the picture in a magazine; it could be somewhere in Nepal or Montana. Montana. How remote this tranquil dreamscape seems now.

My family moved to the Treasure State, when I was eleven. We vacationed there the summer before, in 1970, and visited Yellowstone Park. My parents fell in love with the area and bought the Ninth Street Island Drive Resort. Just as its name suggests, the island is an extension of Ninth Street where it crosses the Yellowstone River. The island is hardly an island anymore. For many years on the upstream side of the island there was a cement operation. Through constant dredging for raw materials the east channel of the river was made to flow. Once the operation closed nature took its course and that channel slowly silted in. The Yellowstone is one of the finest blue-ribbon trout streams in the US, inhabited by rainbow, cutthroat and brook trout. Fishermen were among the Resort's many occupants. Soon after moving I bought a rod and with the help of an occasional fisher took up fly-fishing. Looking back, and through the movie sensation of "A River Runs Through It," which was filmed nearby, my circumstances were privileged, though at the time I was just a kid and didn't consider myself fortunate. The river was a few hundred feet from our front door and town was not very far away. Such were the days in rural America when grocers were local and scale economies hadn't yet impinged on a sense of community. Town kids could safely ride their bikes to schools, which were just a few minutes away, and without parental supervision.

Livingston is remarkably located on the northward slopes of the Gallatin and Absaroka Mountains. Purportedly Livingston is the third windiest location in the continental US for a town of its size, and if not must be in the top ten. Winds sometimes blow through town with hurricane force at upwards of 80 mph. Due to its geophysical location, the Livingston valley has occasional "Chinook" winds – a word deriving from the Salish tribe of the Pacific Northwest. Not many English words have their origins in Native American vocabulary, place names aside, unlike Hindi whose Indians give English speakers "avatar," "bangle," and "cheetah," just to start with the ABCs. The local Chinook winds are driven by air pressure differences between Yellowstone Park, to the south dominated by a low-pressure air mass in the higher elevations, and the high-pressure air mass in the vast plains to the North. The differences in pressure gradient from south to north are sufficient to cause major atmospheric displacements, i.e. strong winds. The Yellowstone River Valley is a funnel for the wind. When the winds reach the Gallatin and Absaroka Mountains as they pinch together in the northernmost part of Paradise Valley they are forced to higher elevation, compressing the air and heating it, and then rip down the north slopes, their temperature rising considerably. Standing outside of school during lunch hour in a Chinook, the temperature rose 20° in a matter of minutes, as if someone turned on a heater. Chinooks may be warm, but the winds can be vicious. Interstate 90, crossing the plateau south of town, is occasionally forced-closed by the wind and traffic diverted through town. Tractor-trailers have been blown over. Not all winds are warm Chinooks, however. One of my "when I was a kid" stories is about walking the mile to school along the river on a winter morning when the temperature was 30° (F) below zero in sustained winds of 40 mph. The wind chill temperature was minus 70° (F) below zero. And the Federal Government shuts down when Washington, DC has a few inches of snow.

Montana's cold has its upsides. Snow, skiing…learning to ski – though slowly – was all downhill, and an up. Looking back, face covered with powder, notwithstanding the spills and chills, some of my pleasantest moments were on the slopes, though skiing has been my nemesis: broken leg, busted knee, cracked ribs, shoulder dislocations, surgery. Dodging trees and cliffs, we searched for powder wherever it might be found. I learned to ski with my sister, who eventually quit because she disliked cold. Bridger Bowl, the local ski area, could be brutal. The chairlift *en route* to the top occasionally stopped, and then the chair would swing interminably in icy wind. When stopped at an exposed place high above ground, windy drafts battled woolen layers until eventually even the innermost layer couldn't retain warmth. She started skiing again as an adult, regretting the lost years in between. I have no such regrets. During college I arranged my classes so that I was free to ski on afternoons. We would hit the slopes as soon as we got out of class, studying at night. Bridger's chair-accessible trails were a teaser for the best skiing, above the chairlift on the upper slopes via the "Stairway to Heaven." The most intrepid skiers might get four runs a day if they stuck to the Stairway. Ski boots aren't made for climbing; the hike up is steep in spots requiring strenuous effort with skis in one hand, poles in the other, but the pay-off is the "cold smoke" powder at the top. Big Sky Ski Resort was not a strong draw for poor students, though this has changed since the Lone Peak tram to the summit was installed. One of Montana's great scenic places: Lone Peak's summit views include Yellowstone Park to the south, the Tobacco Roots and Spanish Peaks to the north, the Gallatins and the Absarokas to the east, covered in cloaks of snowy white in wintertime. However, Bridger is close to Bozeman, and is much cheaper. To the east of Absoroka Range that runs through Yellowstone, the Beartooth Mountains, made of complex Precambrian metamorphic rocks, are a different geological formation. Big, broad, atop a very high plateau, the Beartooth's keep their snow until mid-summer. Snowplows often cannot clear the Beartooth Pass until Memorial Day. In June and July, weekend thrill-seekers might grab their skis and head up to the headwall just north of Red Lodge. The best plan is to take two cars: park one car at the bottom of the headwall, then drive the second car to the top and ski down to the first. Passing vacationers stop to take photos. One group got such a kick out of seeing us skiing in July that they left a six-pack. There are risks, besides the obvious ones; summer thunderstorms and lightning make a hazard of aluminum ski poles, chasing us back to the safety of our car on one occasion, the hair on our bodies standing up from the static in the air.

Livingston, Montana – and the broader Yellowstone Park region – is dominated by a mountainous landscape. Besides the Gallatin and the Absaroka Mountain ranges lie the Bridger Mountains to the northwest and the Crazy Mountains to the northeast. Farther south are the Tetons and to the southeast the Beartooth Mountains. Some of these ranges are familiar, others remote, visited mostly by backcountry enthusiasts. On one of the more heavily traveled routes is a hidden gem, known locally as the "Hot Pots." This natural formation lies on the 45th parallel in Yellowstone Park; most vacationers pass it by without a second glance. There is a small parking lot next to a sign that says "45th Parallel" and no obvious reason to stop. A trail from the parking lot follows the Gardiner River upstream to a point where boiling hot springs emerge from the ground flowing into the River. Here the boiling and icy waters mingle, as do the people who come there to soak. It had been a great place for skinny-dipping and, less fortunately, partying. On weekend nights, or any summer night, locals from Gardiner, Livingston and Bozeman came there. Usually they relaxed in the waters, minding their own business. Lovers embraced in the thick steam hanging thickly over the water. During peak runoff the River can rise dangerously, and some people drowned. The Park authorities eventually closed the area to visitors after 6 p.m. – there were liability issues. Soaking in the boiling waters on a full moon night, the mountains starkly lit against the starry backdrop, elk or buffalo can be seen grazing across the shore. Many nights we stayed until sunrise. These were essential moments, creating so strong an impression that even now I vividly recall the swirling heavens, splashing water, sweat mixed with steam, and faint smell of sulfur. No time of year was off limits. We would sometime go in the dead of winter in temperatures of minus twenty degrees. The trick was to take clothes off the lower half of the body first, then the upper half, piling them on the ground in that order then slipping quickly into the water afterwards. The bitter cold discouraged us from getting out but eventually the time would come and, dressing hurriedly, we would dash back to the car with heads steaming and hair freezing, while the car heater seemed to take forever to warm up the frozen vinyl seats.

Pine Creek Falls lies in the shadow of Black Mountain in Paradise Valley. It's a popular local attraction for day-trippers who like to be in the mountains but aren't up for a strenuous hike. Take old Route 89 to get there. Old 89 flanks the western Absaroka Mountains; it winds through ranch country, passing through cattle pastures, tumble-down barns and occasional derelict houses, aspen groves and pine forests. At Pine Creek there's a small store and café, an old Methodist church and a few houses – a dot on the map. East towards the Yellowstone River is a KOA Campground. A short distance passed the Church is the road to Luckock Park, along which there is a summer church camp. Continuing beyond the camp is a campground. Black Peak dominates the view from the campground. Many people bring trailers there on weekends. Occasionally, high-schoolers from

Livingston have keggers there. Campers share the area with deer, moose, bears and other wildlife. To the south there is an old logging road that almost reaches the mountaintop. At the end of the track a summer pasture and a ramshackle ruins of an old camp house are the evidence of long-vanished inhabitants. I wonder at the constitution of the person who lived there, far removed from any neighbors, surrounded by the stunning backdrop of mountain tops against sky.

The hike to the falls is a pleasant mile, moderately uphill. On either side of the falls, the terrain inclines steeply; to the east the trail ascends in long switchbacks. To the west are cliffs. As a teen I attempted to climb the cliffs freestyle, in tennis shoes, not realizing how stupid that idea was. I found myself in a place where going down was no longer an option; I tentatively stepped down, slipped but quickly caught a handhold. The only way out was up. I began to panic, pouring sweat and losing my judgment. If I had continued down I probably would have slid and fell. Somehow, I clawed my way up the slippery rocks and scrambled to a place where I could negotiate sideways to the creek above the falls, eventually reaching safety.

The stream flows fast above the falls and splits into two channels midway down. At the top there is a water-worn rock face on which one can lay back and bask in the sun. On nice weekend days it's possible to meet any number of people on their way up or down. One surprising time a friend and I reached the top to find a topless woman and her boyfriend, both looking flushed. Clearly, they just had sex. She was beautiful, and I thought the man very lucky. Many years later, I was camping at Luckock Park and met an ageing woman who was staying in the campsite next to mine. We started a conversation; she told me how she used to raise horses and compete in shows. She had been in a bad accident and had to give this life up. She never found an occupation to replace the one she had lost and had turned itinerant, going where there were people she knew, finding work and then moving on. There was one special man in her life. He had "taken her" at the top of Pine Creek Falls once; it was the best sexual experience she had. Her boyfriend moved to San Francisco some year before; she had hooked up with him a couple of times, but he had too negative an attitude for her. She had taken to studying Buddhism and was dabbling in meditation. She showed me a book she was reading on different techniques. I didn't pursue this conversation very far – my experience of Buddhism being too intimate. She had talked to her old boyfriend recently and they wanted to get together again, and he promised not to be so negative. Memory brought her to Pine Creek, as if she might recapture that magic afternoon when she was young. She showed me a picture of her younger self, and I recalled that beautiful, flushed woman we chanced upon years earlier. Her beauty was gone, and she looked aged beyond her years, and it seemed she felt this loss more keenly than her other losses. Hope may spring eternal, but the well from which it floods in youth becomes a trickle with age.

Mountain waterfalls are not spectacular in the same way as thunderous river waterfalls – think of Niagara or Victoria Falls. They emanate a different enchantment. In folklore such places are populated with sprites, water elves, fairies, devas. In the Himalayas small shrines may sanctify them. And mountain waterfalls often are alive, with swirling water droplets blowing in the air, refracting and reflecting light and forests and pools. Such places can inspire a unique consciousness. One loses oneself.

Continuing a couple of hours up the trail above the falls one reaches Pine Creek Lake. The trail to the lake ascends steeply – a local rancher counted 32 switchbacks – through ruggedly beautiful terrain with wide views across Paradise Valley to the west, with the Hylight Mountains south of Bozeman in the distance. Nestled under Black Mountain's jagged peaks, pristine water, the lake is large for its elevation. Twice I've backpacked there in July, each time waking up inside tents that were sagging under the burden of wet, heavy snow. Just the day before the sky was clear and the temperature hot. The weather forecast was fine. We had not packed for winter but, as the locals say, weather in Montana isn't anything if not unpredictable. Pine Creek Lake trail also makes for an energetic day hike. I was once fortunate to walk it with a companion, who would one-day attempt Everest.

For a century, Chico Hot Springs has been a health tourism – now healthy lifestyle tourism – destination. It is a favorite place of kids in Park County. Hot springs flow into Chico's pools from the hills above. The mineral spring waters flow into the pools at a very hot temperature. Since fresh water circulates through the pools constantly, chlorine isn't necessary. There are two pools; one large swimming pool and another hot soaking pool. The pools have been restored several times over the years. The old lodges are built of fir and pine, creating a rustic atmosphere. The main restaurant is gourmet, the bar fun, and the surroundings majestic. Behind Chico, a steep trail leads to a small pond from where the hot spring water is piped down. Local high school kids sometimes go there to party, occasionally partying too hard, a number having died in car crashes on the long straight road that verges from old Route 89, as evidenced by roadside crosses. Chico Hot Springs is a Montana Historic Site. Its location in the heart of Paradise Valley, just north of Yellowstone Park near Emigrant Peak and the Yellowstone River, brings an adventurous clientele whose interests range from fly fishing to mountain biking, pursuing favorite activities during the day and soaking the day's adventures away at night.

Continuing on the gravel road past Chico, one eventually reaches the "town" of Old Chico. From Old Chico's crossroads, turning east one reaches the old mines, going straight one reaches the base of Emigrant Peak, and turning west brings one to… "the Dredge." The Dredge punctuates my psychological landscape much as Emigrant dominates the physical landscape. The Dredge is a giant hole, an old mining scar that once was home to one of the world's largest dredges. It was a substantial operation. All that's left now is a marvelous hole. The Dredge is about the size of a city block, with cliffs on three sides and mine tailings on the near side. Since the dredging equipment was packed off to South America many years ago, the sand from the tailings has silted down to the water's edge creating a small beach on that side. The Dredge water is deep. One need venture just a few meters from shore to reach deep water. The water is cold, too. The only time for swimming is a warm summer day. Opposite from the beach side is a 40-foot cliff. This measurement is certain since we once brought a long rope to determine the cliffs' height. Dangling the rope from the cliff top to the water's surface, pulling it taut for accuracy, we made a mark and later measured the segment's length – 40 feet. Jumping was a cheap thrill, and one didn't have to jump far from the ledge to splash safely. A first-time jumper, unnerved at the prospect of landing too close to shore, leaped as far from the cliff's edge as he could. In his stretch for distance, he forgot to bring his legs straight together with his arms tight against his side; the water hit his soft parts full force: arms, legs and balls. With diving, as with life, watching isn't the same as taking the plunge.

Once in a vivid dream, I found myself on the road between Old Chico and Chico Hot Springs, except there wasn't a road, nor were there houses, telephone poles or electric lines. I was the first human in Paradise Valley, and have no idea how I would know this: I enter the Valley from Chico Canyon, stepping into a Pleistocene panorama of grass, mountains, sparse trees and wildlife. The dream has a powerful emotional impact. I am walking under the night sky with stars blazing above and no lights to dim the view. Animals graze undisturbed by sight of a man, and the mountains, most especially Emigrant Peak, rise skyward. Then a couple of drunken college chums burst into the room and woke everyone up. The dream was shattered but its influence continues to give a certain sense of direction. Humans dismiss dreams too readily. In pre-modern societies, dreams could signify portentous events; Native Americans' dreams played a crucial role in tribal affairs, for instance leading to the Ghost Dance. Yet in the modern and post-modern eras dreams are dismissed as the products of randomly firing neurons or symptoms of sexual tension. I am not so dismissive of dreams; many are random and symptomatic, but some unfold life's mysteries. In one such "random" dream I found myself with high school classmates: my best friend and two other people with whom neither of us would have socialized. This dream was memorable because it was both unlikely yet somehow real. Many years later, at our 20-year high school reunion, I found myself living this dream, as though I had pushed "Rewind" and then "Play" buttons: not déjà vu but seemingly I tuned into the future. The scene lasted maybe ten minutes, down to the finest details, including the dim-witted young man working the cash register at the 7-11 where we stopped to pick up some items.

South of Chico is Yankee Jim Canyon, the most intense rapids on the Upper Yellowstone River, just below Devil's Slide and Yellowstone Park. To the west of the Canyon is Tom Miner Basin. I don't know if Tom Miner was the guy's name or if Tom was a miner. There used to be pictures of old Tom in Livingston's museum. The basin itself is a large drainage that feeds into the Yellowstone River. There is a petrified forest on the upper reaches of the basin; hiking through wood-turned-to-stone is a geological rarity, if one reaches this remote destination. Many such treasures in the Greater Yellowstone region can only be reached on foot. Yankee Jim Canyon's rapids swell and crash, particularly during spring's high run-off. Nearly every year white water rafters have accidents, and sometimes drown in the raging river. Trout fishing by raft in this stretch is risky but trophy catches may be snared in deep pools. Farther downstream, at "Carter's Bridge" where old Route 89 crosses the Yellowstone River, inner-tubers set float, riding the river to Livingston's old radio station five miles to the north, floating passed cattle, houses tucked into groves of trees, occasional wildlife, then wending through town. Over the course of many years some thoughtless jerk decided the river would be a good place to dump old cars; at that river bend one had to paddle out from shore or risk shearing their tube on rusting metal. Rapids near the golf course get sketchy: I've seen people get sucked through their tubes. The Yellowstone River can be dangerous just about anywhere. One high school classmate drowned, right in town, shortly after graduation; eddies and undercurrents dragged him to an untimely death. The day of his funeral bore witness to the misfortune – all hell broke loose as lightning and thunder and tearing rain raged in advance of his pending internment. Floating a river in an inner-tube – for a thrill – is uniquely modern. Rafts have been around for ages, but only in the last century could one grab an inner-tube, drive to a casting-off point to spend a summer afternoon idly floating downstream.

In 2000, I spent 10 days backpacking across the Hylight, Gallatin and Absaroka Mountains. I brought little food; the wild beauty of the mountains was sustenance enough. Gross food doesn't sate a fine appetite. Setting out south of Bozeman, I passed by Mystic Lake, Hylight Lake, and then traversed Hylight Peak, eventually descending into Paradise Valley, crossing over to Emigrant Peak and Old Chico, reversing the course of my long-ago dream. I camped above the Dredge. That evening as the sun was setting behind Hylight Peak to the west, the valley was enveloped in silence, captured forever in that moment. Every sound, the birds chirping, the distant engine, the light breeze blowing through the tall grass, all were part of that silence. Sounds emerged from the silence. Silence is not empty – it is full. In the middle of the night, a pick-up truck accosted my camp. I could hear it coming – windows down, music blaring, loud voices. The bar must have just closed. The driver, presumably a drunken redneck, made as though he intended to run over my tent, no doubt aware that someone was inside of it, and that this could be good fun. I didn't leave the tent, anticipating that this might be what they wanted. The truck would have to run over the tent to get me out of it. After what may have been 10 – very long – minutes of the truck creeping ever closer with engine gunning, the driver changed course and drove away. Why? And so this incident ended much as my dream of Old Chico so many years before, serenity shattered by numbskulls. The Buddhist ideal of detachment from circumstances eludes me.

Most poignant of backcountry wildlife, seen only at high altitude, is mountain goats. Brilliant, snowy white they stand out from the snowless terrain of Rocky Mountain summer. Clambering beyond the slopes of Hylight Peak, I've encountered them traversing the Bridger Mountains from Sacajawea Peak to the "M," and deep in the Crazy Mountains, where I almost walked into one. He was walking down slope on one side of a low ridge and I was on the other; the rock wall between us dropped suddenly away and there we stood, looking each other in the eyes for a moment. In a twinkling, he disappeared from the rocky outcrop, recalling unicorns of legend. Other backcountry wildlife I've encountered are bighorn sheep, black bear, cinnamon bear, deer, elk, antelope, coyotes, rattlesnakes and innumerable birds, but not a wolf or a mountain lion. In Yellowstone, a grizzly bear nearly ripped out our car's window sniffing for food. A much closer grizzly encounter happened near Mystic Lake, in an area frequented by fishers, mountain bikers and day hikers. Venturing off-trail to cut short the distance to a nearby ridge, not more than a quarter-mile, I came on a huge grizzly ripping apart a log where, presumably, it had found a buggy trove. It looked up at me. I froze. It went back to its log. I diverted to the far ridge, not the near one to which I was heading. Heart pounding, I hurried on, stories of grizzly encounters racing through my mind. After a distance I came to a trail heading toward the ridge. 'What good fortune,' I thought; the trail would allow me to get through the brush more quickly. Forging quickly on, I noticed signs of more traffic along the trail, and then saw a huge paw print and a large bear scat. Here I concluded that I was heading directly to the bear's den. With no option left, I went straight up the ridge ahead, losing my time and my way.

The Absaroka Mountain Range is a perfect hydrological system: a '10' on the hydrology scale, precipitation eventually finding its way unobstructed to the lower valleys. The mountains that shape Paradise Valley stand sentinels to the wilderness beyond. Ranging from Livingston at its northern terminus to the Tetons to the south, the Absaroka Range is one of the Rocky Mountains' longest. Atop Emigrant Peak on a clear day, the mountain-scape disappears into the distant east and south. At the heart of the Absarokas *en route* to Hell Roaring is Thompson Lake. Eight miles into the wilderness area from the trailhead, the path drops steeply at first only to rise again until reaching the lake. Rugged, packhorses are recommended for a prolonged stay; a rubber raft is a fine addition to the kit. A weeklong high-school camping venture brought us one summer. Early mornings were glorious! The most ambitious of us would rise well before the sun, grab fishing poles and raft to try our luck. Breakfast of fresh-caught trout with eggs and pancakes, cooked over an open fire, can satisfy the hardiest appetite. Thompson Lake is large, and the surrounding mountains geologically active. At nighttime rocks are heard crashing down from grey heights and occasionally landslides nearby, recalling the giants in the Narnia Chronicles. Our would-be adventures were drowned by rains that started every morning and lasted through nightfall, until dispirited we returned home after five soggy days. As Theseus saved the boys and girls of Crete from the Minotaur, so our guides brought us through the labyrinthine mountain forests, if not to Athens, home at last.

North of the Absarokas, northeast of Livingston, the Crazy Mountains belie their volcanic origin. A lonely outpost of a range, they survey the Beartooths, Little Belts and Bridgers in the distance. One seldom meets other hikers in the Crazies, having hiked them from the west going east and the east going west I never encountered more than a few individuals. Cottonwood Lake is a little gem under mountains' eaves, just north of Crazy Peak, near Grasshopper Glacier. The glacier lies in a north-facing cirque just above the lake. There are different explanations of how the grasshoppers were frozen into the glacier, most likely they were blown in; whichever theory is right, they froze quickly. Some of the species are now extinct. Granite Lake is about a day's hike into the Crazies from the east.

This lake lies under jagged, lightly forested peaks overhanging the river valley down below. Perched above Granite Lake beneath large cirques are two smaller lakes, adjacent but separated by a high ridge, Druckmiller Lake and Pear Lake. Having scrambled this ridge, I looked down and spotted a log floating near the shore of Druckmiller Lake. The log caught my attention because the lake was in the alpine zone above the tree line, and a log seemed out of place. The stunted pines and scrub surrounding the lake were spindlier than the log floating just beneath the surface. As I stood there puzzling the log swiftly darted away. The only fish species in the Crazy's rivers are native cutthroat trout. As I was hundreds of feet above the lake, I guess I saw one very big fish, and that's no fish story. Continuing up the trail that passes Granite Lake, one finds an old quarry site where someone went to immense trouble to build a short stretch of railroad track that ran from higher up the mountain to a small cabin below. Askew from the track lay a small, heavy iron car that the miner must have used to move loads of ore. By the time of my visit, part of the cabin had collapsed, and the tracks were in disrepair, but once the mine must have been a going concern. The miner probably had mules or horses pull the empty load car up to the mine and gravity carried it back down. This enterprise, which, when in operation, must have been an eyesore amidst the grandeur, now, fifty or a hundred years later, appeared deeply mysterious. One wonders: What happened to the miner? Did he strike it rich or go broke? Did he die there, or did he leave while life was left in him? What was he like? As there weren't answers, the mystery deepened. With the distance of time such aging relics as lay around this old mine become interesting and, maybe eventually, worth preserving.

The Tetons and the Gros Ventre ranges begin at the southern terminus of the Absarokas, just beyond the Yellowstone's southern boundary. Reaching the Tetons from Bozeman is a five-hour drive through West Yellowstone and passed the site of Old Faithful geyser; but reaching them from Livingston via the Park's north entrance can take several hours longer, traffic being the unnatural constraint. My college roommate was from Jackson Hole, the town nearest to the Tetons. Summer was a great time for a road trip to visit him. Now populated by high-income individuals, in August Jackson is a meeting site for the world's central bankers and other powerful money people. In the 1970s, though, it was a quaint, backwater Wyoming cowboy town. I've often thought that Jackson would be a wonderful retirement location, but real estate prices have gotten too high for my income. The Grand Teton is a grand mountain, on any scale, and would make a fine view every day. On one trip my friend's father offered to take us fishing. He drove to a heli-pad where a helicopter awaited us. This was my first chopper ride; I never caught my breath. The pilot flew us across the Teton front and then east to the Gros Ventres Range, passing over the Elk Refuge. He flew into the heart of the mountains where we landed at a small lake, shimmering in the morning sunlight. The lake is on an island of privately-owned land, surrounded by national forest.

My friend had brought me there previously; driving to the lake took several hours in a sturdy four-wheeler. It took us a mere 30 minutes to get there by helicopter. A small boat with an outboard motor was tied to a makeshift dock, and we commandeered it for the day. The fish were biting and beer abundant; as we depleted the cooler of one we filled it with the other. The trout were all natives – cutthroat to the uninitiated, with a few brookies thrown in. Some would jump high into the air, wrenching the line in mid-flight, so that they got away. But this was not a good day for the fish as we departed with our legal limit, and memories with no limit. The helicopter returned in the afternoon, flying us back to Jackson triumphant. That night we cranked up the barbeque and feasted on fresh fish. Fishing is lyrical and epic. Many are the paeans to fishing, metaphorical and literal, and I desist from writing another. I've known many serious, recreational, fishermen, who always take from the water more than the fish they have caught.

We, each of us, create our own realities, though we do not necessarily create our circumstances. Our lives are the canvases upon which we paint, though condition and quality of the canvases and brushes vary. The metaphor can be pushed too far but it is apt – and not original. The intensity of our desire, how hard we drive ourselves to our destinations, sets in motion the events that culminate in our individual circumstances.

Sometimes these destinations take years to be realized. For example, as a young boy, I dreamed of being a paleontologist. Dinosaurs fascinated me, more than anyone else I knew. When my Mom went to the bookstore, all I wanted were books on dinosaurs and extinct mammals. I would imagine them and how they might have lived, getting lost in prehistoric worlds. Jump ahead to my junior year in college: I was enrolled in a summer study program that didn't pan out, but at the last minute a small team from the Museum of the Rockies, in need of another pair of hands, requested a summer intern. They were going to excavate a dinosaur quarry in Eastern Montana that had been found by a local rancher on Department of Fish and Wildlife land. Very little was known about the specimen except that it was probably a Tyrannosaurus rex and had been slightly exposed to the elements. The rancher who found it some months before covered the exposed bones with plastic to keep them from further damage. The initial team comprised three people, the Museum's Director, a recent graduate of the School of Film and Television to document life on a dig, and me.

Eastern Montana is a little-known, seldom-visited corner of the world. The Badlands there are in fact quite bad, meaning that the land is dry and desolate. If a person got lost in them they might not find a way out. There is an Old West legend of a miner who struck it rich in one of the Western Montana mines who got lost in these badlands, never to be seen again, and the gold is still there, waiting to be found. In summertime, the temperature can be as hot as the edge of the Sahara and in wintertime it can be as cold as the Arctic. Winds sweep this vast expanse of emptiness. Populated largely by rattlesnakes and antelope, the ranchers who make their living here have learned to accept the vagaries of nature. Most Americans can hardly conceive of the Badlands' extent. They stretch across the southeastern third of Montana into western North Dakota, Wyoming and northwestern South Dakota, an area bigger than many states. The land is rich in fossils, particularly from the Cretaceous period. Unless one spends time in them, it is hard to appreciate their subtle beauty. Like the Grand Canyon, they are a testament to the power of water.

Over tens of millions of years, water has carved out the land, exposing layer upon layer of sediment, which by their weight crushes the sediments beneath. And the colors! Browns, tans, beiges, oranges, reds, and blacks, all layered one on top of the other. The oranges and reds were once seams of black coal that caught fire, perhaps from a lightning strike, which then smoldered through the seams over many hundreds or thousands of years. By moonlight the Badlands appear utterly fractured and forsaken.

Up to the time of this dig, just four complete T. Rex fossils had been found. Our hope was to find a fifth. We stopped in the small western town of Jordan and bought some provisions. From Jordan we drove east about 20 miles and then turned north into a maze of dirt roads. We stayed in a small cabin that had a kitchen and a living area with three small cots. The only luxury was a radio, sorry no bathroom, just an open-air outhouse facing the prairie. In the few driving rains that blew through while we were there, the raindrops hit with such force that they pierced the cabin's front door, soaking the entrance. Giant anthills dot the landscape, their high mounds topping the sagebrush. The dig site itself was a half-hour's treacherous drive along narrow ridges between sedimentary hills leading to the edge of the Fort Peck Reservoir. It's been said that the Fort Peck Reservoir has more feet of shoreline than any lake in the world, and I can well believe it. Little fingers of the lake infiltrate small narrow canyons between the hills. A slight green fringe of grass and sedge borders the lake. It was at just such a location where we found the site, about five meters above the lake waters on the edge of the grassy fringe. When we got there and began to remove the plastic we scared off a rattlesnake that had made it a home. This site and the dig would be our avocation for the next six weeks.

We started excavation by removing piles of sediment that lay on top of the fossils. This was brute work, taking off the top layers, shovel, pick and ply bar. Of the fossils themselves, we saw a few pieces of rocky bone sticking ever so slightly out of the dirt. In less than a day we had removed a ton of sediment and reached the quarry site. When we got to the bones we dispensed with picks and shovels in favor of trowels, awls, dustpans and brushes. Then we started the slow, painstaking work of little by little exposing the fossils that lay in their Cretaceous grave. Since this specimen could become a museum exhibit we dug carefully. As the fossils emerged a story also began to unfold. The Museum Director, a Ph.D. paleontologist, attempted to piece together the puzzle. In the quarry site with all of the fossils were many sheathes of tree bark, ancient strips from cedar trees.

It appeared that the Tyrannosaur might have fallen into an ancient streambed, its frame possibly caught by a cedar log that spanned the stream. This scenario was suggested because all of the bones were jumbled together, and we never found the skull, much to our disappointment. The skull, the heaviest part of the animal, would have been weighed down against the water's flow; the body would have tumbled downstream, but one could only guess at the stream's direction.

The animal itself was a juvenile. The slow emergence of the fossil from the dirt was filmed. We had company while we were there. Some fossil prospectors who maintained relationships with the Museum would seize any interesting opportunity to be part of an excavation; since we were unearthing a T. Rex there was particular interest. A reporter from the local Jordan newspaper joined us one afternoon. She interviewed us and took some pictures. Later she sent a copy of her article; in it she said we were "digging in earnest;" hence, the specimen was named "Ernest." When we had uncovered all of the bones we put plaster casts on them. Some of the bones were so heavy that they could not be hauled out on the pickup truck. These bones were eventually flown out by helicopter. It was an interesting time in paleontology to be working at this site in the so-called "Hell Creek Formation." Half a day's drive from our site a team from UC Berkeley was also doing some excavations and explorations, led by Professor Bill Clemons. It was fascinating to learn about the controversies raging in the profession at that time. This was a time when the giant meteor extinction theory was first proposed as an explanation for why the dinosaurs died out. This theory may be accepted wisdom now but was novel then.

Since initial burial and unearthing, "Ernest" never saw the light of day or, rather, he's been re-buried in a box somewhere in the Museum's storage. When I last checked, around the turn of the century, he still sat in a crate in the basement of the Museum of the Rockies along with the film footage. Oh well, he was in the ground for 65 million years, so what if he spends the next 100 in a box? Since there wasn't a skull, the fossil undoubtedly would be of less interest to the public. Nevertheless, I'd had an opportunity to dabble in paleontology, fulfilling my childhood dream.

The Tyrannosaur excavation kindled an interest in earth science and geography. As a kid I always loved maps and the excavation gave this interest a new twist. I started exploring maps of Cretaceous North America, looking at the ancient boundaries of the Tethys Sea and how the land had changed over the millennia. I took a couple of geography classes, deciding afterwards to become an Earth Science major. I hoped to get experience applying geographical planning concepts to the real world. Within a year I had that opportunity. Desire set in motion the chain of events, such is the universal calculus of our lives: opportunity knocks. Probabilities – probable events – are realized or become "might-have-beens." My Dad, who was on the City County Planning Board of Park County, Montana, learned of a part-time Assistant Planner position, which he told me about; I jumped at the opportunity. The County's development and planning issues proved useful training for later work. Less than half the land in Park County was privately owned; the rest belonged either to Yellowstone National Park, the Bureau of Land Management, the Forest Service, or some other Federal or State entity. Much of the time I spent drawing maps of different sections of the County, although my drafting skills were just okay.

One pressing issue that the city and county were wrestling with at that time was how to zone for renewable energies, particularly wind turbines. These were the early days of wind power generation and Park County is one of the windier places in the US, being located on the eastern front of the Rockies, with the Yellowstone Valley a natural wind funnel. In fact, the winds around Livingston proved too strong and in a couple of cases blew the blades off the rotors. One of these locations was on the edge of town, where the population density was too high to allow someone to put up experimental technology. People were concerned about a blade flying loose and causing serious damage, or death. In those days many people didn't trust the technology. One early wind technology pioneer, then based in Boulder, Colorado, related a story of a trade show that he attended in Cheyenne, Wyoming. He put a small wind generator on display to show off his company's technology. During the show an elderly couple came and looked at the display, the old woman, baffled, asked her husband, "Earl, why would we need more wind in Wyoming?" There were other issues that came up in the Planning Office, some that were to set the tone of debate between naturalists and ranchers for the next decades. These issues included rights of access to lands both public and private, land exchanges between private interests and public interests, and – eventually – reintroduction of wolves.

One bleak winter, Bozeman was blanketed in a dense fog that lasted for weeks; fog so thick that drivers had to use their car headlights every time they ventured out. It sapped the will. By the first week's end, I felt so gloomy and depressed that I lacked the energy to ski. Anyway, skiing in fog isn't much fun. Each day the fog seemed to get thicker and my mood became correspondingly worse; weather plays no minor role in our attitudes. My temper grew short and I grew listless, all signs of "cabin fever." Finally, I reached my limit and had to get out of town. I drove south towards the Hyalite Mountains. A few miles outside Bozeman the fog lessened, by five miles I was blinking in bright sunlight. I got out of the car and looked back at the city, shrouded in fog just a short distance away. Here, in every direction, there was bright, blue sky. The fog was entirely localized and struck me as a metaphor of life. We live in a fog of meandering thoughts that seemingly come from nowhere and swirl around our minds; our brains fire neurons that take us from one association to the next. Yet clarity is just a short space away, bringing whole new possibilities to life.

There is no pot of gold at the end of a rainbow, or rather not the gold most often associated with rainbows. Driving on Highway 90 from Belgrade to Livingston one afternoon I was caught in a thunder-burst. As the clouds broke a very high, arching rainbow appeared that spanned the eastern edge of Gallatin Valley. As I drove closer, instead of receding the rainbow remained stationary. Crossing under Bozeman's Seventh Avenue overpass the end of the rainbow appeared to be on the road straight ahead, getting closer and closer until, unexpectedly, I was driving through the rainbow. All the colors of the rainbow shimmered intensely, their light refracting in every direction: sparkling, tiny drops of water like so many billions of yellow, orange, purple, red and green stars. The car passed through it in seconds, seconds that seemed suspended in eternity. My body was tingling, and the magnetic sensation lingered afterwards. Fortune found me—and finds me still—in the pursuit of a higher understanding of the "meaning of life." Grappling with this fundamental concern has ever been a pursuit of serious people, but the challenge is compounded in today's fog of information and a serious inquirer has no idea about where to start and how to proceed. Fortune, or fate, guides us.

Exploring Montana's terrain and the forbidding Himalayas seems small labor next to the terrain that awaits exploration within. One must look for landmarks: People don't know how to think. We inherently assume that because we are born with the ability to think we know how to think. No one taught me how to think! I was born with a functioning human brain that started to think automatically, representing to myself the world around me, filtering impressions as they pass through the senses; yet no one ever instructed me properly how to think. Because of such almost criminal neglect, I've spent nearly my whole adult life un-learning what I mis-learned when I was young. Worse, I'm not alone and most of humanity shares this same sorry state; what's more, humanity has no concept of its dire situation, and so we are on the brink. The brink? The malaise of our era – "I Know." This attitude – "I KNOW" – all possible perspectives essential for a balanced mental life, dissipate, like fog in the light of the morning Sun, so certain we are of our sole point of view.

"Ask, and it will be given you. Seek, and you will find. Knock and it will be opened for you. For everyone who asks receives. He who seeks shall find. To him who knocks it will be opened." These words are as true today as they were two millennia ago. The last century has brought new formulations, but their meaning is the same: "you create your own reality;" "you get what you focus on;" "thoughts' representations affect perception;" "If you believe a thing is so, is not that thing really so – to you?"

As fish swim in water and may not be consciously aware of water except in its absence, humans inhabit a world of thought, an idea passed down through the ages. Yet, this metaphor is an almost exact depiction of our situation. Our world is populated with incipient thoughts, concepts and ideas, representing objective phenomenon such as "rocks" and "trees", and less obvious concepts such as "value" and "fairness". We are immersed in a world of thoughts. We fail, as a species, to appreciate that our brains *amplify* thoughts. Think about what this means! So many of our circumstances can be understood through this fact.

What I now KNOW is that thought – our thinking – is the lens through which we view our world; and, we do get what we focus on. We paint our reality into existence every moment by our thoughts, or more accurately: what we think is real. Sound simple? The fact is simple the process is not. During childhood, through adolescence and continuing on into adulthood to old age, we build up a system of mental reflexes, without an awareness of them. The mechanism for this system is similar to the physiological reflexes of our bodies; our thoughts have a neuro-physiological base. These reflexes aren't inherently bad, and they can be advantageous when trained appropriately, such as for sport or chores or other repetitive tasks. However, with just a few repetitions, behaviors can become habitual – reflexes. The essence of our condition is that the thought process divides "I," which observes what's happening inside, from "me" to which things happen. So that, "I'm stressed out, but I need to be Zen;" "I'm angry but shouldn't be angry;" "my heart is broken, and I must stop the pain;" exemplify our condition. One part of our psyche set against another part of our psyche. But this division isn't real: it is all one process. "I am this, but I should be that," the basis of so-called 'self-improvement.' The brain is one and the process is one. This separation of the thinker from the thought is one of our earliest and strongest reflexes. As others have noted and here is repeated: "thought creates the thinker;" it's not the other way around – the "I" who I believe I am is a product of the thought that created it. Neural reflexes dominate and distort our views, falsely informing our perceptions of the outside world and the world within. By being aware of these reflexes and habits of thought, we may begin to see more clearly. Reflexes can weaken; they can lose their force. The Treasure State is here.

CHAPTER 5

MY PARENTS' HOUSE FACED THE Bridger Mountains, of which Sacajawea is the highest peak and Fairy Lake lies in its shadow. Looking east from the Bridger Mountains one can see the Crazy Mountains cresting over the start of the vast plains that continue to the Mississippi River. There are trails up Sacajawea and nearby peaks, and a long trail traversing the Bridgers' ridgeline from the Bozeman 'M' to Bridger Bowl and on to Sacajawea. Fairy Lake is the site where the ashes of Lynn Henneman, my sister, mingle with the winter snows and the wildflowers that spring and summer colorfully sprinkle among the rocks.

When one of my parents call me at work, it usually means something is wrong. Such calls have been the harbinger of bad news in the past. My Mom called once to tell me that Dad had a heart attack and was in the hospital. Another time Mom called to say that Dad was in the hospital, this time with a ruptured intestine. His intestine lining was weakened after he over-medicated on aspirin several years after his heart attack. This call came on 9/11, and when most Americans were apprehensively watching the twin towers burn and crash, we were anxiously awaiting news of Dad's condition. My Dad made this call; he said that Lynn was missing. So began hell.

First was confused silence, then I asked, "what do you mean she's missing?"

"She's missing," Dad said. "This morning she wasn't in her hotel room."

My sister was a Flight Attendant for United Airlines. She was on a layover in Boise, Idaho and didn't show up for work that morning. On layovers, airplane crews typically meet in their hotel lobby to catch a shuttle to the airport. The crew had waited for Lynn to join them and then the Pilot went to check her room. He could hear the TV on inside and knocked on the door, but no answer came. He got a hotel staff to open the door to see if she was there, and if everything was all right. She wasn't there, the bed was still made, and her uniform and other personal items were unpacked, with stockings hung to dry on the shower rod. She obviously had not spent the night there. The hotel's computer logged in that she left the room around 3:45 the afternoon before, September 24, and never re-entered. The Pilot called the Garden City Police immediately. The hotel is located on the river in Garden City, near the bridge that crosses the Boise River to Boise proper. After the Pilot made a statement to the police, the crew went to the airport, but United had to cancel the flight that day because there weren't enough crewmembers to legally fly the plane. When my Dad called, this was as much as anyone knew. He called Laura, my youngest sister, and then called me. Laura lived in Idaho Falls; she and her husband drove straight to Boise. Dad said that he and Mom would soon go there.

I waited further news, which came in bits and pieces. I stayed at work; I don't know why since I couldn't concentrate. I called my wife and told her the news. Within hours, the press was on to the story. Some of the events and their order are blurred by time and emotion; others are stark. When I got home, my parents called from Boise. Laura was there and Lynn's husband, Walter, was on his way from Sag Harbor, New York where he and Lynn lived. The hotel where Lynn stayed gave them rooms. Lynn's ex-husband and still good friend, John, had also arrived from Bozeman. This was Monday. My parents asked me to come to Boise; I was needed there. I wanted to leave immediately but had to make some arrangements first. My wife wanted to join me, she and Lynn were close, but we needed someone to take care of our kids.

We were all emotionally distraught. That night I broke down; I felt that Lynn was no longer alive and that I would not see her again in this life's cycle. I sat at the kitchen table and sobbed. I tried hiding my concern from my kids but hearing me cry they came to see what the matter was. I told them that Aunt Lynn was missing and we didn't know where she was. They seemed unable to register why their Dad would be in such despair or comprehend the situation's dreadfulness. My wife urged me to get a hold of myself, which wasn't possible. She took the kids upstairs.

More than a sister, Lynn was my closest confidant. We were 20 months apart in age and shared the same interests. She was concerned about life's deep questions. She was also a part of our household. Since moving to the East Coast to be with Walt, she came often to visit. My wife, a Flight Attendant for American Airlines, inspired Lynn to seek employment as a Flight Attendant, too. If my wife had to fly a trip, my sister often covered for her, staying with us to watch the kids while I worked or when I was traveling. She was our kids' second mom.

That night we learned that Lynn was last seen on the "Boise Greenbelt." The place-name "Greenbelt" struck me as oddly coincidental, as we lived in Greenbelt, Maryland. The next day the police launched a massive manhunt for Lynn or any trace of her. There was a helicopter flyover of the river using infrared technology; bloodhounds were set loose and the police conducted visual inspection of the shrubs and grasses on the river's banks. Given where Lynn's stuff was eventually found, I questioned how well the police conducted their search and learned that no one kept precise records of where the search was actually conducted. The news of Lynn's disappearance was not treated as a missing person case right away. The police left open the possibility that she had just run off. Lynn had circled in her wallet calendar the date September 24. They soon discovered that the date was circled because it was the anniversary of her first marriage. The young detective assigned to the case called me on Tuesday night. He asked a lot of questions, many of which didn't seem particularly relevant. On Tuesday, I took care of my affairs at work so that I could go to Boise on Wednesday, if Lynn hadn't turned up by then. Friends offered to watch our kids, so my wife came with me. My parents and Laura had not ventured from the police station or hotel since they got to Boise, but the press was eager to speak to them. One friend, a photographer for the Washington Times, encouraged us to convince my parents to hold a press conference, urging us to take advantage of their interest in order to find Lynn; we had a window of opportunity that would slip away with the next major news event.

Meanwhile events in Boise were moving fast. Lynn had been in Boise on a previous layover, so she was familiar with the town. On Tuesday, my parents and Laura printed a pile of "missing person" flyers with pictures of Lynn on them that they began to distribute. My wife e-mailed some pictures of Lynn to Laura. They were posting these flyers around town. At one restaurant Walt and John stopped to show the flyer to the staff. While the police seemed unable to make any headway on the case, they found some important leads. Walt knew that Lynn was going to shop for a gift for our niece; he guessed that Lynn visited the Boise Museum and shopped at the Museum Store. When they checked the Museum, this turned out to be the case. Lynn had also told Walt about a salad she ate at one of Boise's restaurants. An excellent cook, Lynn liked the recipe so much that she experimented with making the salad at home but couldn't get it quite right. Walt guessed that Lynn would eat again at that restaurant to find out what ingredients she was missing. Walt and John began canvassing the local food establishments to search for the salad and word of Lynn. One of the guys they questioned said that he saw Lynn on the Greenbelt the evening she disappeared. He would later be a witness during the trial.

Eventually, Walt and John found their way to the Table Rock Brew Pub. The waitress there remembered Lynn from the Sunday night before, that she had eaten the salad and had a beer and found Lynn's dinner receipt. The salad would become evidence, as would the waitress and the receipt. Lynn left the Brew Pub around 7:15. We now knew that Lynn had been to the Museum, the restaurant and was seen on the Greenbelt before 8 p.m.; it would be another week before we knew anything more.

The local TV and print journalists meanwhile were chasing down their own leads, few of which had any basis in reality. One media source came up with a story from an "eyewitness" that had seen Lynn with some guy in a local comedy club. There were stories linking Lynn's disappearance to other local disappearances. In retrospect, and having seen cable TV shows of less dramatic disappearances, the story and circumstances were bound to fuel morbid interest: Flight Attendant disappears without a trace on layover in humdrum Boise, Idaho.

My wife and I reached Boise on Wednesday night. Mom and Dad were devastated. We sat at the dinner table discussing the events, reviewing details of what the police had told us, and going over and over again what we knew and what we didn't know. After dinner, we went out to continue searching, not far from the hotel. This was my first time in Boise and the Greenbelt looked rather sinister to me, especially in the fading evening light. Derelicts could be seen hanging around. There were areas of thick brush close to the walkway. We passed the run-down Shiloh Inn and a seedy bar, and some creepy-looking characters passed by. During the ensuing weeks there was an emerging consensus from Boise's citizens that the Greenbelt did appear to be a dangerous place and there was a need to cut back the scrub brush from the banks, if not the derelicts.

The next day we split into groups and searched along the riverbanks, in the park, in town anywhere within a few blocks of the river, and we posted missing person notices in heavily trafficked locations. The human mind has a tendency to fantasize, to imagine things that aren't real and even can't be real. At a time like this, the mind can go in so many different directions and think so many unrealistic thoughts that the rational and the irrational blur, the rational mind even being overwhelmed by irrationality. But then, nothing about this situation was rational. My mind will sometimes slip into fantasy and imagination and I have to be ever vigilant to guard against unreality. My Mom has this tendency, and is not vigilant, and her mind eventually was consumed by the most negative fantasies and imaginings. On the other hand, her psychic faculty is sharp; many times, she told us that she saw an image of a trailer and that Lynn had something to do with it. As so happened the man who killed Lynn was living in a trailer park at the time, about a quarter mile from the hotel where we were staying, next to the river. The Boise River is linked to a whole network of irrigation canals, many of which we explored.

At one point, Dad, Walt and I explored the underbrush in some of these places more thoroughly. What I describe as underbrush was more like the underbelly of the city. In this "underbrush" were vagrants' camps scattered everywhere, piles of shit where people didn't use toilets, junkies' used syringes and low-life trash. I was reminded of the worst conditions in low-income countries where I often work. On Thursday my wife and I were walking on the Greenbelt and I saw a guy who obviously was wasted out of his mind and looked like he was recovering from a drug hangover. His sight made me shudder. At that moment, I thought to myself "I wonder if this is the guy?" I was sure we were looking for a murderer. Once when we just crossed the Garden City Bridge to the hotel my wife noticed a small path leading along the bridge's foundation down to the river below. She suggested that we go down there and take a look around. I told her that I didn't see the point since this is one of the areas that the police told us they had explored extensively. If I had followed her suggestion, we would have found Lynn's stuff then. But we continued on to the hotel.

Press interest in the story was growing; at least to the extent that it was getting regional coverage and coverage in New York. The story was so bizarre that it might have gotten national coverage. At press conferences I was the family spokesperson and made public pleas for any information on Lynn. Afterwards I got calls of condolence from friends elsewhere in the US who had seen the press conferences. Between searches and flyer posting Dad and Walt were able to arrange a reward for information that would lead us to Lynn. United Airlines contributed half of the reward money. United wasn't entirely cooperative through these events. They resisted giving tickets to my wife and me to fly to Boise, and later for me to fly to the trial. They were generous with their reward, however, and for this we were grateful. Information accompanying the reward was:

LYNN HENNEMAN

Reward Offered for Flight Attendant

September 29, 2000, 05:15 PM, PST

The family of Lynn Henneman, a missing flight attendant, has made another plea for her safe return. They are offering a $10,000 reward. Her employer, United Airlines, is also offering $10,000.

Henneman disappeared Sunday after a dinner at Table Rock Brew Pub.

Searchers took to the water for a more detailed search of the Boise River, looking for clues. "You have to start to consider foul play and part of that consideration is that her body might have been dumped," Lt. Jim Tibbs, of the Boise Police Department, said.

The search was focused on the edges of the river, where clues may be hung up in the branches. But it isn't easy because the water is low this time of year, and it's a challenge to get watercraft downstream.

Searchers were able to make it about 10 miles west of Veterans Memorial Park.

Henneman, a flight attendant from New York, has been missing since Sunday. The search has been made by air and land in the past five days.

If you have seen Henneman or have any information, call Boise dispatch.

On Sunday, Diane and I returned to Greenbelt, Maryland. I had no hope of finding Lynn when we went to Boise, and by the time we left the other family members had lost theirs. John left the day before as did Laura and Mark. My parents and Walt stayed a couple more days and then they left. Soon after they left, Lynn's stuff was found along the riverside, near the bridge where my wife suggested we look, in an area supposedly searched already by the Garden City Police. Unfortunately, the whole crime scene investigation was broadcast on live television and all of the items that were found were beamed through television screens across Idaho. The "breaking news" interrupted an after-school television show that my nieces and nephews were watching in Idaho Falls. Lynn's torn clothing, underwear, and other personal items were given close-up shots. One can imagine the effect that this scene had on the children. Among the items was a copy of the New York Times dated 24

September, an unusual small backpack that I had described to the police, and the book that she had been reading, "Conversations with God."

On October 10, the news we had been dreading finally came. A fisherman found Lynn's body in the river. It was a strange twist of fate that the man who found her would eventually move to Bozeman, Montana, where he would one day by chance install a hot tub for my parents and answer some of their questions about the body's discovery that the police wouldn't discuss with them. An autopsy was done on the body and a couple of weeks later we learned some of the results. Walt and my parents agreed that the body would be cremated, and we flew to Bozeman for the memorial service. I accompanied Walt to the funeral home to collect the ashes, which were turned over to us with all solemnity in a large, vacuum-sealed, plastic bag.

The police filled us in on the story they had pieced together from the crime scene, the autopsy and other detective work. Lynn was last seen walking on the Greenbelt from the restaurant to the hotel. At least two witnesses had come forward with accounts of meeting her on the path. Their information put her within a quarter of a mile from the hotel near 8:00 p.m., just as it was getting dark. At some point she was abducted, raped, and murdered. She sustained serious head wounds though the cause of death was strangling, near the Garden City Bridge. What the police didn't say is that while she died of strangulation, she was probably being brutalized and in searing pain from the head wounds, but she continued a struggle, which the murderer ended by killing her. Remarkably, the autopsy salvaged enough semen from the body for a DNA sample. The cold river water preserved the semen even though her body was in the water for ten days. They would eventually have a DNA profile of the killer, but over the next two and a half years, they couldn't come up with a match. So we waited. Because the body was recovered on the Boise side of the river, jurisdiction over the case was transferred from the Garden City Police to the Boise Police, which we welcomed. The detective now in charge of the case would work it hard without letting it go completely cold. As proof, the police took 156 DNA swabs from potential suspects in the case. These were the most DNA swabs the State of Idaho had ever processed in one case up to then.

At the memorial service Walt, Laura, and I each gave eulogies for Lynn. My eulogy, desperate to find some meaning, some value, in Lynn's tragedy, was:

October 21, 2000

Thank you for coming here today to support us at this most difficult time. Lynn generally did not like ceremonies, but Memorials are for the living and this Memorial service is an opportunity for us to fix our memories of Lynn.

An author once wrote: "There is no permanence in earth life, and no real meaning, except in the contact of personalities, and in the effort of growth. What are called events and circumstances and are supposed to be the realities of life are merely conditions which produce these contacts and allow this growth." This Memorial and these circumstances are an opportunity for our growth.

In the events and circumstances of Lynn's life, her contact with us encouraged her growth. We, who are assembled here today, were the persons with whom she had contact: her family and her friends gathered here from Illinois, Montana, Massachusetts, and New York. It is through her contact with us that she grew into the person that we love and who loved us.

We each have talents that, as in the parable, are ours to make the most of. Lynn was blessed with many talents.

Lynn was a gifted singer, she sang at her wedding, at my wedding, and at the weddings of friends. She and her husband, Walt, would play guitar and sing with their friends in New York.

She was a superb chef, as some of you who are here and had a chance to taste her cooking will attest. It amazes me that Walt is not fat.

Lynn was a talented seamstress, having sewn wedding dresses and bridal gowns, and providing advice to others on their sewing projects.

But, Lynn's most endearing, though often unnoticed, talent was her ability to listen. Lynn would listen to us with attention, care, and interest. Didn't she make each of us feel special?

Talents can be cultivated, but we each have qualities that are innate, that make us who we are – that are our being. Paraphrasing another author, "a person's talents and being are two quite different things, and the use we make of our talents always depends upon our being."

What were the qualities that made Lynn who we remember her to be?

Lynn had a kindness that was unpretentious and that knew humility.

She had graciousness; she was not judgmental, and she accepted each person for themselves.

Lynn had a thirst for knowledge and was comfortable with herself.

As Lynn grew through her contact with us, these qualities took root in the fertile soil that is her soul. When we were young, Lynn would sometimes describe the person that she hoped she would become when she grew up. Looking now at her life, she became that person who she always imagined. Her being was like a gentle perfume, which those around her scented.

Lynn's life can be an example to us here today. If we each can listen to each other with the same care and attention that Lynn demonstrated, this will be a better world to live in – starting today.

After the eulogy, we brought Lynn's ashes to Fairy Lake, one of her most loved places, on a beautiful, crisp autumn day with patches of snow on the ground. On the trail around the lake Mom and Dad stopped to pray. My Mom held the plastic bag; all that was left of Lynn. She broke down, crying "my baby, my baby." It was all too much for my son, who seemed to emotionally disconnect. We walked to the rocks above the Lake's far shore on the mountain's side. There, Walt, talking to her, to us, to the mountain, scattered her ashes. These moments are recalled with difficulty, with feelings of intense loss and grief. After scattering her ashes, we climbed back down to the trail, stopping to take a few pictures. These pictures have a surreal quality to them; people have commented on their otherworldliness – as though Lynn was with us. We returned to my parent's house, where we were met by reporters.

Some hard months followed. My Mom's mental condition deteriorated, and my Dad's physical condition declined. At the end of November my Grandmother died; she was old – 90. I traveled to Chicago for her funeral. It would be 2 1/2 years before Lynn's killer was found, and then only after he had raped and murdered another woman.

In Greenbelt, Maryland, there is a King Hawthorne tree with a memorial plaque at its base, which reads:

May this tree bloom
And grow with joy
In every branch
As Lynn did in her life.

Friends of ours who knew Lynn arranged to plant this tree. I penned the inscription. The tree with this plaque had been ready for months, but because of bad weather and other snags the city landscapers had not been able to plant it. The landscapers finally called to tell us that the tree would be ready to plant over the weekend, but I was leaving for Bangladesh that day. I asked them if they would wait until I returned. They said they couldn't, that the tree had to be planted before then. I explained the situation, why the tree was significant and the meaning of the plaque. The man sympathetically understood and offered to plant the tree that day, before I left to catch my flight. Quickly we called our friends to let them know and a small group met at Greenbelt Lake to watch the planting. As soon as the tree was in the ground I left for the airport. The date was April 12, Lynn's birthday.

The place-name – Boise's Greenbelt – the fishermen who found her body, her disappearance on the date of her anniversary, the tree planted on her birthday, her negative vibes about going to Boise, her mystical leanings, her yearning to see behind life's veil, and some other small coincidences have left some of us feeling that unconsciously Lynn played a part in orchestrating the events surrounding her death. It is a reality that she stepped into. Now I look back and remember her as a little girl, so shy and fearful, her lack of desire for children, though she loved her nieces and nephews, and her strong interest in mysteries of life and of death. It's as if she had a life-long presentiment of her violent passing. In light of events on Boise's Greenbelt, that night if Lynn wasn't killed maybe someone else would have been. From this perspective, unconsciously, Lynn sacrificed herself. Why would Lynn have walked into such an end? We each choose our circumstances. She was murdered just a few weeks after marrying Walt, who she left her first husband for while still married. This decision left Lynn with a sense of guilt, particularly given our strict Christian upbringing. Though Lynn's relationship with Walt started seven years earlier, being now newlywed, she may have been facing this guilt afresh. On her way back to the hotel, she told a guy who stopped to talk to her "marriage is the only way to go." Since we were kids, our parents linked guilt with punishment. As sex was one reason that influenced Lynn's divorce, what punishment was more fitting than this act of sexual aggression against her? But, this is speculation that makes certain assumptions about life and fate.

People across the US knew and loved Lynn, in southwestern Montana, in Sag Harbor, New York, in Greenbelt, Maryland. Lynn had many gifts; she especially knew how to listen sympathetically so that others felt that they mattered. Lynn was murdered by a serial rapist, who was freed by the penal system just nine months earlier.

The Internet is at once highly useful and destructive. After Lynn disappeared and before her killer was found, there were many pieces – articles, blogs, reports – that appeared about her case. I was able to track some of these items on Google. When news broke about the case, I could gather information from many sources, which taught me to be very discerning about information on the Internet. Some of the pieces that appeared may have been well meaning but had no basis in any reality and amounted to on-line speculation. People believe in what they believe. This isn't a tautology. If I believe that something is a certain way, then that belief makes it so – for me. One example of such speculations, taken from an Internet site:

> "The police reluctance to release even the barest of details may be due to their suspicion that the Henneman murder could shed light on two other previously unsolved homicides in the area. Several hundred yards from where cops believe Henneman was murdered 22-year-old Kay Lynn Jackson, was raped and murdered on April 5, 1998 - Palm Sunday - while walking to church. Ada County Sheriff's detectives are also probing the unsolved homicide of another young woman, Cassandra Ann Yeager, who was found June 27, 1999, at a local reservoir. She had been shot with a single bullet to the head."

Of these earlier murders, one had already been solved and the case was on appeal, the other case hadn't been solved but there were suspects. There were no connections between the cases. The one helpful speculation might have been that the

Greenbelt appeared to be unsafe and that women who ventured there ought to be on the alert. Several attempted rapes (and one prank cry for help) after Lynn's murder should have further borne out this conclusion. Then there were the downright demented Internet entries. One guy, writing from somewhere in Idaho, blogged stuff that implied he knew something about Lynn's murder. The blog was so twisted that I copied it and sent it to the Crime Victims Unit to turn over to the police should they think it of interest. In fact, the police did follow up and brought the blogger in; he was apparently someone with a sick mind and checkered past. Who are these people? Where do they come from and why would they get a thrill from such dementia? Do they really crave attention so badly that this is what they resort to? We all crave an audience. Much of the time, people behave the way that they do with the notion that someone might be watching. What we do, we do to impress, which then feeds our sense of self. We act to impress, but in doing so lose ourselves. Our center moves outside; the audience – real or imagined – becomes our motivator. Some people spend their entire lives ever playing to an audience, even if just in their imaginations. This need for audience can drive some, if they don't get the attention, to ever more bizarre behaviors. These people – what audience do they imagine they are playing to? One example from a website, gives an idea of what I mean:

> "Help me with a story idea by writing to Dateline TV at NBC News. It's of a kinky sex life and love relationship to a women (sic) named Lynn Henneman in Garden City, Idaho."

What???!!!

Cheryl Ann Hanlon was murdered on March 1, 2003. Erick Virgil Hall was arrested shortly after for her murder. Police took a DNA sample from Hall and ran it against the foreign DNA taken from Lynn. The samples matched. The police now had Lynn's killer; next came the detective work to link him more closely to the crime, though it would be circumstantial. The Crime Victims Unit called with the news. The counselors there had kept in contact with my family to give periodic updates of how the case was going; it had seemed like some constant chase up blind alleys. Then there began the long period of procedural stops-and-starts as the legal system ground its way, eventually, to the trial. Nearly a year-and-a-half after Hall's capture, we finally had our day in court.

After Lynn's murder but before Hall was captured, I became involved in a project in Bosnia. Working in Bosnia helped to keep my perspective on what our family had been through. The tales I heard and the tragedies I saw in Bosnia, and the fortitude of the people, were of a magnitude that I could scarcely comprehend but related to. The project started seven years after the war ended, but the drive from Sarajevo Airport to the old Center still looked like a war zone. This impression was reinforced by various meetings around the city where we passed through former checkpoints, cased in barbed wire. One disconcerting debriefing was on the dangers of lurking landmines. This presentation drove home the need to stay on tarmac surfaces and not venture off into fields, and to stay out of vacant buildings that might be booby-trapped. "War-torn" hardly begins to describe Sarajevo, or much else in Bosnia, at that time. "War-shredded" would be a nearer description. The extent of damage caused by various sizes of ammunition belied the circumstances of its use. Sarajevo's buildings are pock-marked with shell impacts; small divots in walls showed where sniper fire was aimed at hapless passers-by, larger divots within a narrow range indicated machine gun blasts, while holes blown through buildings came from mortar or tank rounds fired from positions somewhere in the surrounding hills. Some buildings had gaping holes, with easily imaginable impacts. The impacts were stamped in walkways too. In places, the holes were patched with red cement, showing where a shell had hit its mark. It was hard stepping on these patches, knowing that someone died there.

I stayed at the Holiday Inn, infamously the place where the first shots of the war were fired. There, snipers assassinated a young schoolgirl walking on a nearby bridge, where there is now a small memorial. Bosnia is a place of memorials harkening to an Islamic aesthete, Austrian sturdiness, two World Wars, Olympic glory, failed socialism, ethnic cleansing and indomitable spirit. The Holiday Inn in Sarajevo was the hangout of journalists who made (and lost) their careers reporting the war. Bosnia's war was fertile soil, seeded by misery, for many foreigners. Enough has been written about this war to fill a small library; it remains to be seen how "ethnic cleansing" fares as a policy outcome. If one looks at Bosnia now, more than two decades later, the most "ethnically clean" areas tend to have lower incomes and are poorer than more ethnically diverse areas. The Balkans have been truly Balkanized. Ethnicity is a fetid backwater of the human imagination.

Bosniaks and Croats both relayed stories about the war; not once did I hear a Serb discuss the war. There seemed to be a collective denial by Serbs that they could have perpetrated deeds so horrible. One Croat I worked with grew up in Banja Luka. When the war started he fled but returned to look after his mother when he learned she couldn't leave. He was interred in a Serbian labor camp, essentially as a slave. He spent the war doing hard manual labor, repairing broken infrastructure. A soft-spoken, well-read and gentle soul, his mind was broken, and he spent the ensuing post-war years trying to repair himself. I doubted that he would fully succeed. Bosniak friends told stories about the front lines. Particularly harrowing were stories about the Sarajevo airport and deeds done there to bring in goods and people or to get them out. One friend was shot in the back. He described how he thought he was dying as he lost consciousness, and the sensation of regaining consciousness afterwards. The war gave birth to deep-seated cynicism on all sides as many people concluded that it was mainly about money.

Some people gained considerably from others' wretchedness; a general condition of war. One person in Tuzla related how a leading businessman made his fortune by controlling food aid. A lot of food that is supposed to reach hungry people sadly gets diverted into the warehouses of those whose sole concern is to make money. Such rapacious opportunists do very well out of wars. Famished people will surrender all that they have of value just to get a few scraps for their children to eat. When food aid is brought to a place such as Bosnia was during the war, it must be transported somehow and stored somewhere. The people who transport and store it don't necessarily act from charity. In Bosnia, one can often spot the people who did well out of the war; they have nice houses, have invested in hotels and otherwise laundered their money into more legitimate activities such as retailing. Of course, many continue to be involved in illicit activities, too, as evidenced by continuing smuggling and prostitution. Such activities receive western help. One notorious occasion, hushed-up, involved the staff of an aid project. The person in question used project vehicles, bought with taxpayers' money, to chauffer prostitutes from trick to trick; it was a nice little side business until he got caught. Of course, being a foreigner, he didn't go to jail, and there was nothing to try him for. As with the flood of food, so with the flood of money, millions of donated dollars went missing in the immediate post-war period when donors were trying to restart Balkan financial systems. The banks and their armies of loan officers were involved in every type of scam. The amounts of money involved were staggering, as if throwing money at a problem would make it go away. Throwing too much money at problems usually makes them worse and leads to other, unanticipated, negative effects.

As home office manager of a project, I monitored implementation progress and provided occasional technical support. The project kicked off in September and I found myself in and out – mostly in – Sarajevo for the next two months. Project start-up on an international aid project can be intense, the only edification being that if the project starts properly it can make a positive difference in some people's lives. Fortunately, the Chief of Party, or project manager, and I clicked, as did most of the project team. He was first rate. When starting an international aid project, the donor wants to see immediate results, yet the project staff needs to arrange their lives, move households internationally, find somewhere to live, get families settled in, arrange domestic help, etc. etc. There is very little sympathy from the donor or beneficiaries that these two requirements aren't compatible. Somehow everyone manages to get settled in, though it may take six months before a real routine is established. Sometimes staff don't make the grade, or clash, and are let go. A well-run project staffed by smart people can accomplish much.

During the 1984 Winter Olympics, I wasn't anywhere near a television and didn't see the beautiful shots of Sarajevo nor get to watch the sporting events. On the mountains outside of Sarajevo, the venues where these events took place still stand – or don't. At the time of this writing, the bobsled run at Trebevic, a grim Olympic reminder, stands on steel girders above the snow; any sled that ventured onto it now would fly into a pile of twisted metal midway through the run, and might even trip a landmine. Sarajevo was described at the time as "magical." Sarajevo's magic lives on, in the hearts of the Bosniak people. One way of gauging economic growth in a city is by the number of cranes along the skyline. On my first visit to Sarajevo there were few cranes to be seen. The place looked cloistered and shell-shocked. When last in Sarajevo in the spring of 2006, I saw many cranes being used to rebuild at least a dozen buildings just between the airport and the Center. The Bosniak people impressed me as dynamic, artistic and, post-war, tenacious.

Sarajevo, venturing a prediction, will one day be the most visited Balkan destination, though maybe not for another half century. By then many of its artists could be feted as Europe's avant guard. Certainly, if one visits Sarajevo today they will be surprised by the scope and vigor of the artistic talent on display: from paintings to metal ware to jewelry, not to mention the performing and culinary arts, Sarajevo is bursting with creativity. The culinary arts are especially satisfying. The Karuzo is one exemplar where there is hardly space for a dozen and one is advised to try the *plat de jour*.

Mostar is already a highly-touristed Bosnia destination. There is simply too much to see. Besides its location near Medugorje, Mostar is a half-day's pleasant drive from Dubrovnik, and further along the road on the Croatian coast are the pretty towns of Ston and Mali Ston. At Medugorje, a Catholic pilgrimage destination, though not recognized as such officially by the Church, there were sightings of the Virgin Mary. I've heard that such religious "sightings" increase in frequency before a cataclysm; if so, Medugorje is an example of such clairvoyance. Also near Mostar is Blagaj where, as the tourist literature says: "It is the finest example of an underground karst river. It flows out of a 200m cliff wall and single-handedly creates the Buna River. Unsurprisingly, the Ottoman sultan was impressed and ordered a tekija to be built right next to it. This 16th century house/monastery was built for the Dervish cults and is still one of the most mystical places in all of Bosnia and Herzegovina." Flanking the summit on the opposing side are the ruins of a medieval castle. At the heart of Mostar is Stari Most – the old bridge. A world heritage site, the original bridge was another victim of the war. The bridge appears simultaneously delicate yet sturdy. During the war Mostar's streets were divided between Croat and Bosniak forces. The dividing line was drawn starkly down the middle of the street. Driving through Mostar I commented to the Croat driver that it looked like people on one side of the street were blasting away at people in the buildings on the opposite side of the street. His rejoinder was that not only did it look that way it was that way. He described what life was like there, on the front line, where he spent part of the war. One striking comment was how he found himself on opposing sides, shooting at his former classmates. Mostar is being rebuilt; its local government is a mess; yet despite such challenges, Mostar will prosper.

The tales told of the Bosnia conflict, of the gang rapes, mass murders, enforced slavery, systematic torture, are etched on the landscape and in the faces of many of the people who lived through the events. Atrocities were committed by all sides, yet disproportionately by one side. (Begging the question of what a proportionate atrocity is.) The Bosniaks and Croats seem to have come to terms with the horrors perpetrated, but the Serbs have acted as though they were hard done by. Yet the atrocities mentioned were not all that was done; the Serbs seemed bent on a policy of spite. Why else bomb the old town of Dubrovnik? Why destroy all of the orchards before withdrawing from an area? Why kill the animals? Why blast so many architectural treasures? Why publish photos of the ethnically cleansed? The old library in Sarajevo Center had a showing of pictures taken during the war.

Viewing the photos in that bombed-out shell of a building that had once been a stunning example of Austro-Hungarian architecture, I was moved to tears by what humanity (or is it inhumanity?) is capable of. Film footage of concentration camps has similarly moved me, but the immediacy of the display in those surroundings made that atrocity real in a new way and brought to life other atrocities of the twentieth, nineteenth, and so on, centuries to the first massacres by one people of another. There are at least two humanities, one evolving and the other devolving; one that creates and another that is capable only of destruction. One is "human" and the other a thinking – though thoughtless – beast, driven by its appetites, a creature motivated by little more than utilitarian considerations of pleasure and pain.

CHAPTER 6

MOST PEOPLE, THANKFULLY, HAVE LITTLE idea what it means to go through a jury trial for a murder case. Their notions are shaped by the media news and television courtroom dramas. It is altogether different to be in the courtroom following the procedures, observing and being observed by the jury, and riding the rollercoaster of starts and stops, of lawyers' motions, clarifications, documentation and presentation of evidence. Generally unfamiliar to the public is the extensive trial apparatus that exists to coordinate witnesses and to support victims. The Prosecuting Attorney's Office in Boise has many staff who are dedicated to these matters. The parade of witnesses that passes through a trial each has to be tracked down, depositioned, scheduled, interviewed and dismissed per courtroom procedure. The Victim Administrators' jobs are particularly difficult. Two were assigned to Lynn's case. As the months after her murder grinded into years, they would contact us occasionally to give us news or updates. These updates tended to be discouraging, as they usually involved information about some likely suspect whose DNA sample had been taken and sent to the national lab in Maryland for analysis. Then we would learn the test results and find out that they were negative. I don't recall the number of such instances, but 156 samples were taken over 2½ years.

The day came when Erick Hall murdered his next victim. Lynn's case Detective predicted this would happen; that the murderer would be driven to kill again and eventually would slip up. There were strong similarities between the evidence in the Hanlon case and in Lynn's. We now know what that evidence was. The usual process happened: we got a promising phone call, DNA was sent to the lab, test results were slow in coming, but this time the results returned positive. However, just to be sure that there weren't any mistakes, the DNA was re-tested. It was a relief to have a suspect; during the time between Lynn's death and the trial my parents suffered greatly. My Mom was the victim of her own constant conspiratorializing, while my Dad endured her scenario building and vain imaginings, though we all had to abide them. As a distraught mother she couldn't help herself. The wear and tear has had lasting effect. Then came the wait for a trial date; the defense raised motions that delayed the trial's start. The trial wouldn't happen for a year and a half after Hall's capture – so much for rapid justice. My parents, sister, Walt and I attended the trial, Laura's husband joining us part way through. Not wanting my wife or kids to go through the experience, I flew to Boise alone and was met by the hotel van. While riding to the hotel, the driver asked me what brought me to town; when I told her the Lynn Henneman trial she assumed I was from the media. I got there on a Sunday, and on Monday morning, we all went to the Prosecuting Attorney's office. The Victim Administrators and Attorneys debriefed us on how the trial would proceed, on some of the evidence that would be presented, and cautioned us how unpleasant some of it would be. When there was going to be particularly graphic testimony they would let us know so that we could leave if we wanted to. My Mom would spend almost half of the trial outside of the courtroom. We had all kinds of questions that they patiently answered. As the trial took shape the Victim Administrators became increasingly important logistical and emotional touchstones for us. They would prepare us each morning for the testimony we would hear that day and they would meet us at day's end to go over logistics for the day to come. They were our guides. I don't know how these dedicated people can do such emotionally wearing work day after day. The despair, hatred, and confusion that they constantly must deal with would become depressing to all but the sturdiest souls.

As the trial started the morning of October 12th, the Prosecuting Attorney opened with some key observations:

- There would be 12 jurors and three alternates, 10 women and five men, no one under 30.

- There were three charges in the case - murder, kidnapping, and rape.

- Hall had a very troubled childhood and this would be a factor for the defense. By 10 or 11 he was on the street; there were reports of Hall biting himself in class in first grade.

- During her brutalization, Lynn was "hogtied," her arms and legs tied up behind her back and bound together by her clothes, which were cut by a knife and then used to strangle her to death.

- Hall's girlfriend worked in a fast food restaurant near the place where Lynn's wallet was found, partially burned.

- Lynn had a capped tooth, which was important evidence in confirming the identity of the body.

- After all her years of living in New York, Lynn still had a Montana driver's license.

- A woman on a bicycle saw Lynn twice on the Greenbelt that evening, passing Lynn once on her way to meet a friend and again on her return, and observed a man on a bicycle talking to her.

The next day, Wednesday, October 13, witnesses' testimony began. The first person to testify was the flight Pilot who discovered that Lynn was not in her room. He described events about which we knew much already: When Lynn didn't show up in the Reception area to catch the van to the airport the Pilot went to her room. When she didn't answer his knock, he asked the hotel staff to open her door. Inside they found the television on; Lynn turned it on when she left the room to deter potential thieves. They found her uniform on a hanger, and everything in order. The hotel door is keyed into the main computer, so the hotel staff knew that the door was last opened around 3:30 the preceding afternoon. Both pilots had gone out to dinner the night before and were on the Boise River Bridge at sunset, about 10 minutes before Lynn's estimated time of death. They didn't recognize Erick Hall from his mug shots and they hadn't noticed anything amiss during their return to the hotel. The flight to Denver that morning was canceled because the plane was short of a crewmember and they had to fly a replacement Flight Attendant to Boise to cover for Lynn. One of the other Flight Attendants gave testimony. She mentioned that Lynn worked hard, finishing her tasks and then asking the other Flight Attendants how she could help. The crew spent the day in Boise in anguish as they waited for Lynn's replacement. A hotel staff testified that the room's door was linked to the computer system, establishing with certainty the time Lynn left the room.

The hard, wooden benches, like church pews, were already becoming uncomfortable, and this was just the first day of testimony. The presentation of evidence continued. The next witnesses established where Lynn was and when she was there, putting her on the bridge just after sunset. As we already knew, Lynn had gone to the Museum and bought a present for her niece in Idaho Falls, whose birthday was coming soon. This present was in a shopping bag with the Museum's logo; inside the bag was a credit card receipt showing the time of the transaction. This receipt matched the Museum's own receipt. The bag was found at the crime scene. Next the waitress from the brewpub where Lynn ate dinner testified. She remembered Lynn, partly because Lynn left a 20 percent tip; her many years of waitressing made Lynn a sympathetic customer, and she always left at least 20 percent. The restaurant receipt showed that she had a salad and a beer for dinner; the receipt also showed that Lynn left the restaurant near 7:00. The sun set that night at 7:38 - 7:39.

The witness who passed Lynn on her bicycle gave testimony. She remembered where she passed Lynn the first time. She said that there was a guy on a bike next to Lynn. She recounted how she looked at Lynn, who smiled back with an "it's okay" look. The witness continued on her way to meet her friend who didn't show up, so she returned and passed Lynn again. The guy was now walking next to Lynn pushing his bike; upon seeing the witness he got back on his bike to pursue her, leaving Lynn. Eventually the guy caught up to the witness and, as she expressed it, tried to hit on her. He then gave up on her and took off on his bike. The witness said that in the coming days when she saw Lynn's photo on the "Missing Person" bulletins she came forward with her information. She said that she has not been on the Greenbelt since that day. The guy on the bike, Chris, was the next witness. Chris said that he stopped to talk to Lynn when he saw her. For a long time, many people suspected that Chris was somehow involved in the murder, although his DNA did not match. Chris was a tall, ruggedly handsome, muscular, troubled looking man, probably in his early 30s. He had been in and out of the penal system and his record showed that he had difficulty holding down a job. Chris's testimony and his answers to questions were scattered; he spoke in a staccato voice, obviously having trouble expressing himself. His delivery was short and abrupt, given with attitude. He did not impress me as a murderer, although I would not have been surprised to learn he could be abusive. His thought process was twisted, believing he could pick up girls who were walking on the Greenbelt. I guessed that he had consumed vast quantities of drink and drugs over the years. He was a sad case. He mentioned that in his conversation with Lynn she told him "marriage was the only way to go," saying it in such a way that we knew he was repeating what Lynn had said. Chris then mentioned meeting John and Walt when they brought the Missing Person flyer to the restaurant where he was working. He told them, quite honestly, about his encounter with Lynn on the Greenbelt.

Leaving the witnesses, the trial turned to the available physical evidence. Lynn's wallet had been found partially burned on school grounds behind a fast food chain. At that time a girl who worked at the restaurant was seeing Hall. A picture of the wallet and articles pulled out of it was shown on a projector, and I felt like I had been hit with a body blow. On top of the small pile of articles was a picture of my daughter, partly burned, smiling at the courtroom. My son's picture, off to one side, was blackened. No useable fingerprints were found on any of the items. The detectives who gave testimony established the various items that Lynn had with her including the Museum bag, a small shoulder bag that she carried, a New York Times newspaper dated September 24, and specific articles of clothing that she wore. One detective described the Garden City Police's massive search, which reminded me of Keystone Cops. They had no map of the river showing where the search was conducted, no record of the times that different areas were searched or by whom, which would anger me later when photo evidence was presented of where Lynn's stuff was found.

Thursday, October 14, introduced the police task force that had been assembled to work on Lynn's case. Within days the force included the Garden City Police, the Boise Police, the County Police and the FBI. The police did not immediately assume that Lynn's disappearance was foul play. After evidence was found along the riverbank on October 9th and the body was found a few days later, there was no doubt of foul play. The articles found on the 9th included the articles mentioned, which were scattered in the brush on the riverbank, and Lynn's shoulder bag, which was partially submerged in the water, a sandal that was flung some distance, a knife and a bookmark. There had been just a little light rain during these days. They tried doing a spectral analysis of the site for signs of blood but none showed up, suggesting to me that Hall dragged Lynn into the water, leaving no trace of the blood that must have been flowing from her head wounds. Photos were shown of each of the items. Sitting on the courtroom bench looking at the photo evidence I vividly remembered my wife pointing to where the evidence was later found, and my reminding her that the police said they had scoured the whole area. When she said it, we were standing on the bridge directly above the place where, I guessed, Hall killed Lynn.

The fisherman who spotted her body noticed that it was caught in tree branches dragged there by the river's current, held by Lynn's long hair. A recovery team could not easily retrieve the body from the river on the Garden City side because of the density of underbrush. They had to salvage the body from the eastern shore. Fortuitously, this moved the crime scene to the jurisdiction of the Boise Police. The body had no face, as it had been ground off by river rock. Many crime scene pictures were shown, and I averted my eyes to the floor. The water's cold temperature preserved for 13 days the semen in the vagina, despite the body's underwater submersion, and the sample that the Police recovered, though very fragile, was sufficient for DNA analysis. The Crime Unit had to obtain dental records to make a positive identification. The autopsy was done on Sunday, October 18, twelve hours after the Forensic Pathologist finished cleaning the body of river debris. An "Evidence Technician" manages all of the evidence collected during a case, accepting, storing, and releasing evidence as may be required, and logging all use in a computer database. The police do not have unrestricted access to evidence.

While the term "lividity patterns" may be familiar to people who watch crime dramas, the term was new to me. After the heart stops, the blood, which is no longer being pumped, settles in pools in the body. Examining the pooling patterns, the Forensic Pathologist could determine Lynn's position after death; she was on her stomach, wrists and ankles bound behind her back above her body. Most likely Hall tied her up because, the evidence showed, she struggled. Why he would tie her up like an animal is also suggestive of his mental state. She had to be laying on a hard surface for at least twelve hours for the lividity patterns to be so pronounced, in a position tilted toward the upper body. She had received multiple blows to the head from a blunt object from different angles, indicating that she may have put up a fight; one blow wasn't enough. While the blows would have stunned her, they didn't kill her. The Forensic Pathologist could tell that she was still alive because there was evidence of bruising around the wounds, so the heart must have been beating. When she was found, she still had a knotted sweater tied around three of her limbs, one of her arms having slipped out of the knot. The autopsy showed that Lynn's upper arm had been broken, probably when Hall, realizing that daybreak was approaching, picked the body up – being hogtied made it easy – and threw it into the river. Autopsy photos showed the contents of Lynn's stomach – salad – and since the dinner had barely been digested it was possible to put her death between 8:00 and 9:00 p.m. The Pathologist showed three photographs that the

Defense argued stridently were prejudicial to Hall's case; these photos showed the Pathologist's reenactment of Lynn's position. The Prosecution countered that the photographs were germane to the case, and the judge overruled the Defense's objection. The County Coroner – a self-important official – gave testimony after the Forensic Pathologist; why elect a Coroner?

In the time since Lynn's death, I have glimpsed periodic flashes, snippets, of what happened to her that night, too real and unwanted for me to dismiss them as imagination. Lynn's anguish seemed to be transmitted precisely because of its powerful emotional charge. In these flashes, Lynn was walking across the bridge when Hall passes; she's already a little bit uneasy having just seen off Chris's unwelcome advances. Hall scares her; he sees the expression on her face and misreads it as contempt. He's a drugged-out low-life; no wonder she was scared. There is a moment of terror, an urgent desire to hurry. She speeds up. Hall gives chase. He reaches her, grabs her. There's a struggle and then blistering, searing pain, and the ultimate humiliation; at the end of consciousness there is an emotion – death – death is an emotion.

During the trial, I usually sat on the same side of the courtroom as Hall, whose table was angled towards the judge. From there, I was able at times to see his face and watch his expressions. A bit less than 6 feet tall with a solid build, he doesn't have an imposing presence. Dark-haired, with moderately refined features, some might consider him handsome. He sat through most of the trial passively, avoiding eye contact with the jury and being well mannered to the judge. Hall spent much of the trial scribbling notes and drawing, though once he lost his composure. He was always in the courtroom when the doors opened to let observers in, and he was always led out in shackles and chains at the end of the day with his back to the room. On this occasion, we stayed in the room during a break to talk to the attorneys. The guards brought Hall in and we watched as he was led to his chair and seated. Being on display like that in front of us clearly agitated him; his nostrils flared and eyes flashed. That was the only time we glimpsed his temper. Undoubtedly Hall is a psychopath. Because there was solid DNA evidence, we had no doubt of his guilt; the evidence was especially compelling, as the genetic analysis revealed that one of his genes was rare and perfectly matched his DNA profile. This information came to light because of a question posed to the DNA specialist by the Defense Attorney. Moreover, it was clear to all that Hall was the murderer. At times in the courtroom I was overwhelmed by anger at the senselessness and brutality of what he had done.

I watched his expressions when different witnesses testified or when photographs were shown on the projector. He could not bring himself to look at most of the films or pictures, seemingly disassociating himself from the evidence. At one point during the trial, I'm not sure when, I developed a biting reflex, which unfortunately I still have though it has diminished. Supposedly this reflex is a defensive response of the reptilian brain when threatened, but research on the psychology of this reflex is sparse and, despite being aware of the mechanism involved.

A United Airlines Flight Attendant who lived in Boise took it upon herself to show professional solidarity with my sister during the trial. She came to the trial several days, one day in uniform with flowers and a card for my Mom; she touched our hearts. She was there on one of the days when there was particularly graphic evidence and broke down afterwards. Several female witnesses gave testimony about Hall's abusive tendencies. When he was arrested Hall was homeless, living in a tent on churchyard grounds with his pregnant girlfriend. They were both into the meth scene. Sometime after Hall was arrested but before the trial, she was found floating dead in one of the many small pools on the edge of the Greenbelt; an autopsy showed she had been tripping on meth but could not determine the exact cause or circumstances of death. Her mother came to the trial; she was guardian of their child. Hall was all smiles for his "Mother-in-Law" when she showed up, but she looked morose. At no time during the trial did Hall demonstrate any sign that he comprehended the gravity of his crime or the heartbreak that he had brought to others.

On Friday, October 16, the prosecution showed a lengthy video of Hall's deposition, which he gave following his arrest. During this deposition Hall confessed to using "speed balls," a mixture of heroin and methamphetamine. On Friday late, the judge gave the jurors a long weekend to spend with their families and to recuperate from the draining week that they had just been through. My parents left town, thankfully; they needed to get away. They stayed with the parents of one of the other women who had been murdered on the Greenbelt the year before. This poor girl's father had reached out to my parents, my Dad especially, to console him and to offer friendship and understanding. This turned out to be a great emotional support to my Dad and their friendship continues. These two men share a loss that haunts them both; they are Christian men, in the most respectful sense, and have supported each other during some difficult times of trials, appeals, and retrials. I went with my sister to Idaho Falls and spent the weekend with her family. Walt stayed in Boise.

The trial resumed on Monday continuing the Hall videotape. While never admitting to guilt, among Hall's comments, caught on tape during the deposition, were: "it was all about anger versus sex," "when opportunity knocks," "because of the look she gave me." He talked about a rushing sound in his ears and that he thought she was still alive when he raped her. When some months later he remembered what happened, he saw "a person without a face," saying "it never should have happened." Apparently, he tried to block the whole thing from his mind. He said he had nightmares triggered by what happened "to this woman." On the tape, when the police left him alone in the room there was a whiteboard on the wall with a marker in the tray. On the whiteboard Hall wrote:

Anger
Rage
Honesty
Confusion
Fear of self – loss of control
5 levels or chapters of Erick

The police asked Hall if he would like to write a letter to the family. The letter was read in court, after which one of the jurors wept.

Tuesday, October 19 more evidence was presented – Lynn's clothes. The left front seam of her shorts was cut open and the right hem torn. One of Hall's former girlfriends testified next, she couldn't even bring herself to look at him to identify him. At the time of the murder Hall was living in a trailer house. The condition of the place was so bad that the landlord took pictures of it in order to get him evicted. These photos later appeared in the Boise news. The rest of that day's and Wednesday's evidence presented the DNA results and the "chain of custody" that definitively linked the semen sample taken from Lynn to Hall. The DNA specialist who gave testimony did her best to simplify what is an immensely complex subject. Among the things she described, there are 9 million genes, each differing one from the other. The DNA test examines 13 loci on a chromosome plus 1 for sex. The tests have become so sophisticated that it is now possible to use just a few cells and multiply them in the laboratory to get testable sample sizes.

The "sex crime kit" was admitted as a result of this testimony. The Prosecution's closing arguments were made powerfully and dramatically. In a moving delivery, the lead Prosecutor placed Hall in the situation where he had just raped Lynn. He put a 3-minute hourglass on the table and mimicked what could have gone on in Hall's mind: "Now what? What should I do next? This woman is lying here," the Prosecutor held his hands up in the air as if he is choking someone's neck with a sweater. He turned the three-minute timepiece over and, as the sand was draining away, he speculated what could have been going on in Hall's mind: "I'm choking her, should I let her go? She's still breathing – not dead. But I'm mad, angry, I hate, hate, hate, but if I let her go she lives," and so on. The point was made that at any time while he was choking Lynn, Hall could have stopped, he did not have to kill her, but he was in such a great rage that he couldn't bring himself to stop and let her live. The sand ran out, Hall didn't stop choking her, and now the woman was dead. The Defense's closing arguments were given on Thursday in a PowerPoint presentation that tied together all of the facts, "what we know" and "what we don't know." The Defense acceded to the rape charge but tried to blame Lynn's killing on the river, her sweater getting all tangled up around her neck as the water pulled her along. Both sides rested their cases on Thursday afternoon.

The feeling a crime victim has while waiting for a jury to decide a case is indescribable; a combination of anguish, anticipation and impatience. No decision was forthcoming on Thursday although it seemed to us, the family, that the evidence was overwhelming. Friday morning, too, we waited; finally, at 11:00 the call came that the jury had reached a verdict. The courtroom reconvened at noon and the jury foreman read the verdict: guilty on all three counts. Nowadays it sounds cliché to say that Hall sat there emotionless, yet he didn't show any emotion; he just sat there, eyes lowered. Next came the Penalty Phase when the jury decided Hall's sentence. Having established Hall's guilt, witnesses would be admitted during the sentencing phase who were not admissible before, although evidence from the Hanlon case could not be heard, in deference to the Defense. The Penalty Phase began at 3:30 on Friday afternoon and, at the request of the jury, would continue through Saturday with the judge's consent. Hall's prior criminal record now became a matter of court record. In summary, it was given as:

1991 – Convicted of grand theft in spring.
1991 – Aggravated rape in December.

1994 – Attempted escape from minimum-security prison.

1999 – Released from prison in December.

2000 – Murdered Lynn Henneman in September; and not admitted to the trial

2003 – Murdered Cheryl Hanlon in March.

As a juvenile, Hall had spent time incarcerated as well.

On Friday night, there was a dramatic testimony. Hall's first rape victim gave a highly charged account of her tragedy. The victim was mentally and emotionally frail and impressed upon me that this might be the most difficult thing she had ever done and was forcing herself, with all of her strength, to put Hall away. Maybe there was an element of revenge, but it seemed that as she testified she was exercising demons that had plagued her for years. She was flown in from somewhere down South to testify and right up to the minute she took the stand the Prosecution was afraid that she would back out. When Hall raped her, she was 17; she had been a troubled youth and even then may have suffered from bipolar disorder. She met Hall and one of his friends in a bar in Garden City. The friend invited her to stay the night with them in a trailer where they lived. She described how she started to feel scared but curled up in the corner and went to sleep. During the night, Hall grabbed her and dragged her out of the camper to a shed in back. There he forced himself on her despite her pleas to leave her alone; she can't recall what happened next. He had "shredded" off all of her clothes. When he finished having his way he threatened to bash her head in "with a hammer and throw her in the river." Sound familiar? She couldn't remember much after that. Within days she was institutionalized, and they discovered she was a recent rape victim. Everyone in the room was deeply moved by her testimony; many of the jurors were crying, men and women. One of the jurors was later quoted as saying that her testimony was a key consideration in giving Hall the death sentence. As a family, we sat there in stunned silence. How could someone like Hall have been considered as rehabilitated? How could he have been set loose again on society? It should have been clear that it would just be a matter of time before his demented craving would get the best of him. Lynn just happened to be there when it did. After the court was dismissed that night the victim came and gave my Mom a hug and they cried together. It seemed that a great burden had been lifted from her. Later I heard that after the trial she was reunited with her family, which she had not seen in years.

On Saturday morning the Prosecution wrapped up the case of Hall's (so far as is known) first rape victim, though she was not there. They showed pictures of the victim's injuries. The Defense recalled Hall's testimony at the time: "What have I done?" trying to leave the impression that he had a twinge of conscience. Next, one of Hall's former girlfriends gave testimony about their life together, how Hall mowed lawns to make money, how they relied on food banks for meals, and how Hall started "having an anger problem." Another former girlfriend gave testimony, the whole time staring at Hall sympathetically. She described a very violent relationship, on both sides, recalling how once Hall came after her screaming so loudly that he upset their neighbors. He pulled her through the car window where she sat and bit her on the cheek. The neighbors called the police to break up their fight. Twice he choked her while they were in bed; one can imagine what they were doing at the time. They were meth buddies; she would inject him with the drug so that he would not have to inject himself. Neighbors gave testimony of how Hall had threatened them with their lives. A friend of Hall's, who was serving time for forgery, was brought to court to describe the visible marks of abuse that Hall had left on his girlfriend, how she confided that Hall would force himself on her regularly, and how he would shoplift, presumably to support their drug habit. She said that sometimes Hall would follow people around "hit 'em over the head and take their money," but that he was always helpful to her and her family.

My sister and I gave our Victim Impact statements that morning. Mine was:

Lynn had a very special place in our family as a close friend, confidante and primary caregiver to our children, Meghan and Nathan. Lynn and I were just 20 months apart; we grew up together.

My wife, Diane, is an American Airlines Flight Attendant. Because of this, Lynn and Diane were especially close. When Diane and I had to travel for work, Lynn would arrange her schedule so that she could watch her niece and nephew. Lynn was part of our family. Losing her has been crushing; among the impacts are:

As a family, we can no longer rely on Lynn's loving care for the children when we are away. Because of both of our professions, this has sometimes left our children without a trusted adult family member.

Diane had to take six months of leave of absence for counseling to cope with her anguish at flying. She also had to overcome feelings of guilt. She felt responsible for Lynn becoming a Flight Attendant with her encouragement.

Ever since the day that we scattered Lynn's ashes our son has had difficulty coping. Emotionally, he has been unable to process this painful experience, despite therapy. This loss has affected his ability to handle stress.

For myself, I've lost my best friend.

My daughter, Meghan, tells of her loss in her own words. She wrote the following piece for a school assignment last year when she was in 5th grade. Her burned picture was in Lynn's wallet that was found behind the school.

Always in Your Heart

A few years ago, when I was seven, I found something out that changed my life forever. It was a quiet evening. I was up playing in my room and my brother Nathan was in the basement watching TV. Well, it just happened to be 7:02 p.m., the time I always went downstairs to skid across the kitchen floor in my favorite socks. So I hurried down the stairs with glee as I thought about how fast I would slide across the kitchen floor, but when I got downstairs, something was different. Usually at this time of night, my dad would be sitting in a cozy living room chair quietly reading one of his favorite books, but this time, instead of reading a book, he was sitting down with his hands over his eyes as he cried. "What's wrong dad?" I asked him curiously. He slowly lifted his hands from his face. "Well sweetie, I know you probably won't be able to believe this, but Aunt Lynn died."

I couldn't believe what he had said. *"No."* I thought. *"She can't be dead, it's a lie!"* Although I knew it wasn't. I felt a funny feeling inside me, an empty feeling, as if someone had just stabbed me in the heart. "How'd she die dad?" I asked solemnly. "Well, I think the Boise police said that she had been choked to death. They found her body floating down a stream." said Dad. After that, I didn't skid across the kitchen floor, or eat any dessert. I couldn't sleep that night. I stayed up all night, wishing that I never had to hear the news that I heard earlier that evening. After a few hours of lying in my bed and quietly crying and thinking of the nightmare come true, I finally couldn't take it. I cried myself to sleep with nobody to comfort me.

The next morning, I woke up, hoping that what happened the night before was just a dream, but when I reached up to rub my eyes, I felt a tiny tear course down my cheek. I then knew that it wasn't just a dream, or my imagination, I had actually found out that Aunt Lynn was dead. *"Why?"* I thought. *"Why does this have to be real?"* I sat up in bed very slowly. Nathan was already eating breakfast by the time I got to the kitchen. "What do you want to eat sweetie?" asked my mom. She sounded as if I had just cut myself and needed a Band-Aid. "Nothing," I said as though I had been crying forever. "I don't want to eat anything ever again." Then I curled up in a ball on the couch and thought, *"Why did this have to happen to me?"* I wondered. *"Why am I having so many bad things happen to me?"* Then my mom sat down next to me and hugged me. I felt a little tingle of comfort run through me. It helped me to know that my parents would always be there to comfort me.

A week later, my family and I traveled out to Montana for Aunt Lynn's memorial service. Everybody there seemed to be as depressed as I was, many of them said nice things about my Aunt Lynn, which really made me feel a lot better. Although everyone was crying and blowing their noses, I wasn't. I felt very sad, but no tears came. Why wasn't I crying? Then, it hit me. Aunt Lynn always hated to see me cry. So it would probably make her feel better to see that I wasn't crying.

A couple days after the service, my whole family (which includes my Nana, Papa, Aunt Laura, Uncle Mark, and their four kids Josh, Missy, Tyler, and Jessie.) went to sprinkle Aunt Lynn's ashes. We all gathered at her favorite place in the world, a place with a beautiful lake, waterfall, and plenty of beautiful hiking trails, a place called Fairy Lake. Everyone got pretty carnations to throw into Fairy Lake. We all lined up in a row. As we threw our flowers at the lake, I felt as if I was giving a special gift to Aunt Lynn, even though she was gone.

While the grown-ups went to sprinkle her ashes, the kids went to make a snow fort. As I lay down in the snow, I felt the warm rays of sunshine fall onto my face, as if Aunt Lynn was smiling at me from Heaven. In that moment, I learned something. If you save a little place in your heart for someone you love, even if they are dead, they're still alive within your heart. Ever since that day at Fairy Lake, I have remembered this. So whenever I feel lost or lonely, I remember that little place in my heart, where I keep my little piece of Aunt Lynn. Within me, I have a special angel that is always with me when I need her. I will always remember that if you love somebody, they will always remain with you, in your heart.

After giving my Impact Statement, I returned to my seat. I noticed that Hall had drawn a smiley face on his Styrofoam water cup and set the face towards us. I assume that, if he did this consciously, it was his way of communicating that he approved what he had heard. After my Impact Statement, my sister gave hers. Many jurors were in tears when we were finished.

Hall's background was tragic, as one report describes:

Hall's sisters testified that the family, with as many as six children, many half-siblings, bounced from home to home with no parental supervision, often experiencing a culture of violence. The sisters said the kids often subsisted on bread or were not given food at all. They were taught by their father to shoplift to get clothes and food; occasionally ate dog food for sustenance. They said they were victims of emotional neglect and physical abuse by Hall's parents, oldest brother, and later his mother's boyfriend. The women testified that they were sexually molested by the oldest brother. One sister said she was later sexually assaulted by Hall's mother's boyfriend.

Hall's mother left the oldest brother, when Hall was in his early teens, in charge of the younger kids. They said this brother would tease and punish them when he wasn't ignoring them. They said he was particularly abusive toward Erick Hall, beating and mercilessly berating him about his appearance, clothes, and "loner" nature until Hall blew up in anger. The older kids often ganged up against Erick, who was at least two years younger. The brother would make it a game... to pick on him, call him names. It was like 'let's gang up on Erick.'

Hall was very much a loner, with a lot of imagination and a lot of made up friends. Hall also was regularly beaten by his father and witnessed several fights between his parents in which they choked and pummeled each other. Because of the trauma at home, Hall and his brothers wet the bed for much of their childhood. The boy's mother used to wave the urine-stained sheets out the bedroom window to humiliate Hall when the school bus came. Hall barely looked at his sisters as they testified Monday, mostly holding his chin in his hand and looking down.

But people have tragic backgrounds without becoming murderers. Hall's two brothers are also in prison, one for murder. It would seem that propensity to murder is a social disease that can run in families.

Hall's trial was the first time an Idaho jury had the power to decide if a defendant should receive the death sentence, and it was the longest time an Idaho jury had been sequestered. The case against Erick Hall finally rested as summarized by the Boise press below.

Erick Hall – white, age 29

Sentenced to death in County, Idaho

By: A jury

Date of crime: 9/24/2000

Prosecution's case/defense response: Hall kidnapped and raped Lynn Henneman before strangling her with her own sweater. Hall's DNA was found on Henneman's body. The defense contested premeditation by arguing that if Hall killed Henneman it was out of panic or rage. In the penalty phase, witnesses for the prosecution included a woman who was raped by Hall in 1991 and two women who were previously assaulted by Hall. Hall had an extensive criminal history, had previously tried to escape from prison, and had been released from prison 10 months before killing Henneman. The defense presented evidence of Hall's abusive childhood and drug use. Although not presented at trial, Hall is facing charges for the rape and murder of Cheryl Hanlon in March of 2003, which DNA evidence linked him to as well.

Some of the jurors sent us letters after the trial; they had been as traumatized by the experience as we were. It matters to me not at all that Hall got the death sentence and is still alive. The Victim Administrators described to us what Hall's life would be like on Death Row. He would be in a small cage from which he could access an exercise cage once a day. He would be surrounded by other Death Row inmates and would have little privacy. I envision Hall waking up each morning and opening his eyes to see metal bars, and as it dawns on him where he is, he will remember why he is there and will know that there will never be anything different, and that this will be his lot in life until he dies, which may or may not be at the hands of the State. My view of capital punishment has changed. I now think that the choice of punishment ought to be up to the victims. One can argue this would make for uneven and unfair application of justice, but then the perpetrator wasn't being even or fair in committing the murder. My concern about meting out such justice is that disagreements about sentencing among the victims could spoil their relationships with each other. In the literature justifications for the death penalty tend toward the sentence as punishment or the sentence as a deterrent. I subscribe to neither argument but strongly advocate society's right to dispose of people such as Hall to protect its own citizens. How to "dispose of" such individuals is a matter for those who take it upon themselves to protect the public, so long as the public is protected.

When I returned to Vermont from Boise, I was mentally overwhelmed. I found no sympathy at home; my family had none to give, my children were uncomprehending, and we had been traumatized once already. Colleagues avoided the subject, either out of discomfort or because they thought it would be inappropriately nosey. This avoidance behavior by people who are acquaintances of victims of violent crimes is sadly common. I saw a news piece on this subject once and realized that though I may suffer, this same suffering is shared every day by thousands of other families whose friends don't know how to express sympathy. At least one friend went out of her way to be helpful. A "medicine woman," in previous centuries she would have been burned alive as a witch. Vermont seems to attract segments of the New Age crowd, and among this crowd are some unusually gifted people. When she saw me, she could "see" that I was "splotchy and gray." If this is how I looked, it was certainly how I felt. She offered to do some "cleansing and healing" work on me. I had never been subject to such a ritual before. Twice she performed a cleansing ritual using crystals and sounds. After the first ritual I noticed that my level of anxiety and stress decreased and the pain in my chest, unrelated to my heart, went away. The second episode was striking in its effect. Clearly, she was a gifted healer and I could feel her power "smooth over" my splotchy and gray self. An explanation might go something like: We all have "electrical bodies," so called because our nervous systems carry electrical impulses. Magnetism is a feature of electrical systems. During these rituals I felt a "magnetic reversal," which is as near as I can come to an explanation. Of course, this is not scientific, but then science can only explain what it can measure and dismisses – without probable cause – "data" that doesn't fit into its models.

CHAPTER 7

ALL PEOPLES CELEBRATE SOME OCCASIONS, whether the changing of the seasons, remembrance of important events, or religious observances. Is any culture so poor that it cannot afford to throw a party? Is any culture so rich that it can afford not to? Has there ever been a culture that judged every day to be of equal value? Will such a society ever exist?

Anglo-American by birth and culture, we mark our years by our holidays: New Years, St. Valentine's, Easter, Independence Day, Labor Day, Halloween, Thanksgiving, Christmas. A new place can mean a new calendar, and the Hindu calendar is very different from the US calendar. Nepal's calendar differs from India's by observances of the State, which are not religious: memorials to independence, historical personages, and government affairs. I am interested in how visitors and immigrants to the US view our holiday traditions and share my observances of Hindu festivals.

As described in basic tourist guidebooks, the Nepalese festival of "Dashain" is: "the longest and the most auspicious festival in the Nepalese annual calendar, celebrated by Nepalese of all caste and creed throughout the country. Throughout Nepal the Goddess Durga in all her manifestations are worshiped with innumerable pujas, abundant offerings and thousands of animal sacrifices for the ritual holy bathing, drenching the Goddess in blood for days." In general, Hindus across the Subcontinent observe ten days of ceremonies, rituals, fasts and feasts in honor of the supreme Mother Goddess. The festival begins with the fast of "Navaratri," and ends with the festivities of "Dusshera" and "Vijayadashami." Of the two great festivals, Dashain is most important in Nepal. Tihar, or Diwali in India, the Festival of Lights, is second of the great festivals. Together, these festivals would be the Western equivalent of Christmas and New Year's. I didn't get into Dashain; the blood ethos was too much. I "celebrated" my first Deshain shortly after starting Peace Corps training. Most of our language instructors had gone to be with their families for the festival's final days, and the PCVs remained in Godawari. We were hanging around the compound enjoying one of a few slack days. There were several goats tied up nearby and they were bleating out their strong dislike of their circumstances. That something was about to happen could be felt in the air. In late morning the compound's owner parked several Lories there. Soon his family and workers were on hand to watch, with us joining them. The owner and his sons picked out one of the goats, all of which were now in a panic, and, holding it up and pulling back its head by its short horns, took a kukri knife and slit its throat from ear to ear, aiming the animal's spouting blood at the Lorie, so that it would get a good dowsing. They circled the truck with the animal, its blood spurting out until, like a squirt gun that is slowly running out of water, the blood was eventually drained out and all that was left was a light burbling redness, seeping out of the gash matting the surrounding hair. The men's arms and clothes were splattered. After the first goat, they repeated the rite for each truck, one goat per truck. When finished they brought the carcasses to the house where, over the next few hours, the women dressed and cooked them into a feast. This scene was repeated in every city, town and hamlet in the country (except the Buddhist north), right across much of the Subcontinent. And who can say how many goats were sacrificed that day to the Goddess for her blessing? I had seen enough, but for those with greater fortitude, a jeep took them to Kathmandu to watch the sacrifices at Hanuman's Dhoka and other temples in Durbar Margh. There Gurkha soldiers sacrificed water buffalo. Their aim, as described, was to slice the head off in one blow of their super-sized kukris. They said of the scene that blood was flowing in the streets as deep as their shoe tops, thousands of people lining up for the Gurkhas to sacrifice their animals.

The next Dashain, I decided that I would rather be in Buddhist territory, where I wouldn't have to see the sacrifices. I went to Langtang Himalaya. On my way there I stopped to visit one of the women volunteers who lived in the area. She and her "family" convinced me to spend the evening. I tried to get out the next morning before the killing started, but in their politest, customary Nepali way, they made it impossible for me to leave until after the ceremonies were over, killing me with kindness; the animals fared worse. The highlight of the morning was being served a dish of hot goats' blood. I couldn't finish it, and nearly threw up. Fortunately, the hosts could see that it wasn't my cup of tea, err blood. One other time I got caught in Hindu country during Dashain, though just briefly, in the early morning as I made my way out of town. I was in Thamel, the tourist center of Kathmandu, to catch my ride; the early morning fog was thick. Two guys carrying a headless goat on a pole, with the pole's ends slung over their shoulders, passed by me and vanished back into the fog. That was all I wanted to see and was soon on my way.

Dewali/Tihar is an altogether different festival. Animals are sacrificed, yes, but not on the same scale as Dashain. As one guidebook has it: "This festival celebrates Laxmi, the Goddess of wealth. During the festival all the houses in the cities and villages are decorated with lit oil lamps. Thus, during the night, the entire village or city looks like a sparkling diamond. This festival is celebrated in five days starting from the thirteenth day of the waning moon in October. The festival is also known as 'Panchak Yama', which literally means 'the five days of the underworld lord'. 'Yamaraj' is worshiped in different forms in these five days. The festival is meant to bring life and prosperity."

Tihar is essentially a harvest festival, following the rice harvest; a time of plenty. The weather in Nepal's hills in this season is delightful. Now the warm days are over and the cooler days of the cold season approach. A perfect balance is reached. My first Tihar was justly a celebration of Laxmi Puja. Our Nepali language instructors and the PCV trainees played cards and drank heavily all night. We dispensed with the traditional rituals and got right to the hard stuff; on Tihar gambling is not illegal. During the evening, girls came by to sing songs of praise of the goddess.

Unfortunately for my partners, I had the hot hand that night. Volunteers describing Tihar celebrations in their villages relayed their experiences. One Terai volunteer was returning on his bicycle to his village late after visiting farmers and could see the way by following the lights of thousands of candles. In the remoter hills, Nepal's traditional heartland, the celebration can be more beautiful and mysterious. One year I was guiding a trek in the region north of Gorkha and saw that the villagers had made a small river float and placed a statue of Laxmi on it, wreathed in garlands, tika-ed and powdered with vermillion; the statue seemed alive. When night fell, a large crowd came to the river's edge carrying bowls made from tree leaves. In each bowl was set a lighted candle. The candles were placed in the water and set adrift on the river, and then the float with the statue was set in the water, now alighted with candles too, and let go. Standing downstream a short distance, the sight was breathtaking as a hundred lighted candles co-mingled on the waters, multiplied by their many reflections, rising and falling in their little bowls on the lightly cresting waves with the float, now in full flame, casting a very bright light. Drops of water, splashing gently under a thin moon, would catch a glint of candlelight from behind to make a prism effect and sparkle like diamonds as they danced in the air. Laxmi must have been pleased.

TIHAR CELEBRATIONS

The last day of Tihar is "Bhai Tika," when older sisters put a rice tika on their younger brothers' foreheads. This is a day of gatherings of family and friends. Nepalese are, or at least were, very welcoming and I always had an invitation to Bhai Tika and was given tikas by older "sisters." It is a day for warm relations and enjoyment, unless you happened to be a woman working in the kitchen. But the women were as enthusiastic for Bhai Tika as the men.

"Holi" is a three-day festival celebrated throughout India and Nepal. Its origins go back centuries. It is unlikely though, that it was celebrated in the past the way it is celebrated now. The second and third days are raucous. I was not prepared for what was to happen during my first Holi on the subcontinent. I was in Kathmandu and was able to watch from the sidelines. My second Holi I stayed in the village where I was posted. Peter, a fellow PCV, was visiting because Bahadurgunj had a large Madeshi population. He expected that the Indians would celebrate Holi more festively than would Nepalese. The first day of Holi is marked by the availability of "bhang" in the local bazaar. Vendors with pushcarts were selling frozen "bhang" popsicles, colored dark green by cannabis, potato cakes and other assorted green snacks. The villagers partook modestly, even the children sharing in these festivities; some of them were no more than five or six years old.

The next day began quietly enough; after all, the second day was women's Holi. Morning dal baat came and went. My Bauju had eaten some bhang just before the meal, she informed us. Our impression was that the women celebrated Holi at home. We returned to my dhera and were talking when, quite unexpectedly, we heard loud screams. We looked out my windows onto the town's main street below but couldn't see anything. The clamor suggested that the women's Holi celebration was going to get wild; their yells and screams bordered on hysteria. Finally, we spotted them coming down the street. They were covered in vermilion powder of every color of the rainbow. They had been dousing each other with it for the past half hour, and it was difficult to tell what colors their clothes actually were. They caught sight of Peter's and my heads peering down at them from the window and they let out a simultaneous scream "Mark!" and dashed for my building armed with vermilion powder and water. I ran to the next room and locked the door knowing that if they had a chance they would trash the place. Seconds after I locked the door there must have been a dozen bhang-crazed women trying to break it down. It took all of Peter's and my strength pushing against our side of the door to keep the deadbolt from snapping and breaking. All the while the women were threatening us from the other side. These women, normally conservative Hindu women, persisted in their intoxicated effort to break into my place for a quarter hour. When they finally gave up we collapsed. Sadly, that was the only time I have been chased by a bunch of women.

The third day of Holi was the men's turn. We started earlier than the women had. At 9:00 a.m. they were already gathering at the temple. I put on the worst clothes that I had in my chest. I could never tell whether Peter was wearing grubby clothes or not, they all appeared equally grubby. Minutes after reaching the temple the showers of vermilion started to fly: red, purple, blue, green, and yellow, getting into our ears, noses, throats, down our necks, in our hair; no place was left uncolored. It gave new meaning to the expression "powdered." But this was just the start. The men circumnavigated the town, throwing vermilion to the winds and at each other and any hapless victim along the way. At one point dirt was thrown and oil and grease. I could only watch with pity as a bus passed us on the road. The passengers who were too slow to shut their windows got dusted. The pictures that we took at the end of the parade suggest our condition.

Later, after we had bathed and scrubbed (the colors didn't fade completely for weeks), we began a visitation ritual. Prakash, Bhuvan, Peter and I were treated to bhang everywhere we stopped. Every item of food and drink had bhang. We visited the mayor, elderly and respectable gentleman that he was, and found him celebrating Holi in the prescribed manner. By the end of the day my judgment, and much else, was fully impaired.

In rural communities Hindu weddings must be attended with the utmost fortitude. They are marathon events that can drain away every last bit of one's energy. I was invited to my first Hindu wedding, ostensibly as a friend of the groom, but equally because I was a would-be photographer with a ready camera. He bought the film, locally, days before the ceremony. On the day of the wedding a tractor pulling a flatbed drove into town to pick up all of the invitees and take us to the wedding. It reminded me of a hayride – minus the hay and in broad daylight – slowly advancing to our destination with lots of camaraderie along the way. The tractor ride was an occasion itself; we stopped at many places along the way to pick up other guests and for tea. Fortunately, it was not yet the hot season. The tractor drove 25 kilometers on paved roads before diverting onto a dirt road. At that point the ride became more thrilling as we negotiated deep ruts and forded small rivulets that were, literally, a pain in the ass. Along the way we passed a small "refugee" community where I learned that these "refugees" had been resettled from Rara Lake when that region was made a National Park and protected area. The entire community had been relocated from the beautiful, cool high hills of

Rara to the burning Terai on the Indian border. It was too much for most of the refugees, who either fled the resettlement camp or became sick there and died. The soulless brick buildings to which they were relocated, and the surrounding barbed wire were a grim legacy. The tractor ploughed on its way. Eventually we reached the farm where the wedding was to be held. It was still daylight when we arrived and were served tea and a snack. We sat and visited for a long while, eventually the bride's entourage showed up and the party, slowly, wound up. I didn't see the ceremony itself, which was performed inside by the Brahmin. Being a Westerner made me an object of attention, mostly for the family on the bride's side; I was "old hat" to the groom's side. Meanwhile, I was taking pictures of people and wedding activities. Much later, after the ceremony was over, food was served. By then it was late, very late, but the party was now warming up. Dancing followed dinner, and what dancing! It lasted nearly until dawn. Because this was a caste Hindu wedding there wasn't alcohol, and there didn't need to be. The revelers had a wild time without it. I didn't often dance at local parties; the few times I had made it so much harder to say 'no' the next time. It was easier to just say 'I don't dance' and excuse myself. Not at a wedding, though. Everyone danced. I was not very good at dancing South Asian style, but that was OK, they played Michael Jackson; "Thriller" was a worldwide phenomenon. The seasonal favorites were from a recent Bollywood release "Disco Dancer." So, everyone – by this I mean all of the men – danced with fury to the sound of "I am a Disco Dancer…" These Bollywood feel-good movies often trade off of Western trends, such as disco. For a time in the 1980s they took to using English words for titles, 'Hero' for example, or "One." These titles usually reflected some Bollywood director's sense of the meaning of the specific word, at least in their bobtailed notions. Finally, at around dawn, the party died down, except for the hard cores. I wasn't one of them and found a corner and a mat and curled up and slept for an hour or two. Being a rural village, at sunrise the cocks crowed, and the cattle lowed, incessantly; so much for sleep. Naasta (sort of a light breakfast) was served. There is nothing like puri and jalebee (pronounced 'juh-lay-bee') to get one going in the morning. Puri is fried rice bread that puffs up into something like hollow donuts, though not so sweet and is typically served with curried vegetables call sambar. It's an acquired taste for Westerners used to eating cereal or eggs for breakfast, but really quite good and definitely filling. Jalebee look like orange colored pretzels, but that is as far as the similarity goes. Jalebees are corn syrup goo, fried in oil and only palatable when served hot. If hot, they drip out sickeningly sweet syrup, if served cold the syrup is even more sickening and oozes instead of drips. Two jalebees are enough for a morning-long sugar buzz. They are not recommended for diabetics. After naasta we hung out until the tractor left late in the morning. The party continued on the flatbed the whole way back to the village; I don't know where people found the energy reserves, unless they had more jalebees than I could swallow. I was a basket case by the time I got to my dhera, collapsing into bed. I've since seen a full Hindu wedding ceremony, and came to appreciate that they are tedious, like most wedding ceremonies anywhere. The fun happens at the other events that are not part of the ceremony. The ceremony so differs from Western weddings where everyone sits nicely in church pews. It is much more congenial to hang out nearby visiting friends. Eventually I brought the wedding film to be developed. Not one picture turned out. The groom had been ripped off; the film was inferior quality, manufactured god knows where. I felt really bad about the pictures but appreciated his invitation.

Shiva Ratri (a night consecrated to Lord Shiva) is another notable Hindu festival. Shiva, the Destroyer of Evil, is praised and worshipped on this night in the thousands of idols and monuments that glorify his name, the most common form being the Lingam or the phallus of Shiva that represents him. Shiva's Lingam is the symbol of pro-creation, the beginning of everything. Shiva Raatri is the night of Lord Shiva, when Brahma created him. One of the premier worship locations for this festival on the Subcontinent is Pashupatinath temple, located north of Kathmandu on the banks of the holy Bagmati River. Pashupati, which literally means 'Lord of animals," is one of Shiva's many forms. He is the guardian deity, protector of Nepal, thus Shiva Raatri is one of the major festivals. Pilgrims from all over the Subcontinent flock to Pashupatinath to worship and pray to the deity on his day and wash away their sins. Only Hindus are allowed inside the temple; I was not allowed entry and so observed the festival from across the Bagmati River. There was still plenty to do and see. A couple of friends visited the temple, which held a swarming mass of people. Outside of the temple on the surrounding low hills there were also throngs. Saddhus were there in force, fitting every description imaginable but almost all with long dreads. Many people think that the fashion for dreads started with Jamaican Rastafarians, but the Rastafarians took the practice from the Subcontinent's saddhus. Most saddhus worship Shiva and this is their night. Their garments ranged from loincloths to the simple, white linen wrap of the Milk Baba; from the cleanly to the filthy; male and female; high and straight. There were many bands of musicians playing songs around their campfires. Saddhus, like the fakirs of legend, could be seen doing many amazing things: driving nails through their tongues, standing motionless on one leg for hours (8 to be exact), standing on their heads, walking on hot coals, and performing other feats of human endurance that would impress circus crowds in the West. In some grottos saddhus and yohinis (the female equivalent) could be observed in sexual ritual, building their shakti, or energy. Of course, one wouldn't see this in a Western circus. Ganja was abundant. Most amusing were the various Western tourists who were trying to go local, imitating the dress and demeanor of the native culture. If they stopped and thought about it, they would have realized that one must be born Hindu to fit in. We were there until past the wee hours when, eventually, even hardcore Shiva worshipers' enthusiasm waned.

PHOTO-WISE SADDHU

Westerners can never be Hindus. We might be Hari Krishnas, Theosophists or whatever, but not real, pakha Hindus. There is a passage in the Laws of Manu that says that outsiders (non-Hindus) should be judged by their actions, which is more than might be said for Caste Hindus. I have met many low-caste Hindus and "untouchables" who, if judged by their actions, would have merited the title "Brahmin," and I have met quite a few Brahmins who hardly deserved the distinction.

Even among the educated classes the attitudes of the higher castes could be quite remarkable. Once at a meal with an educated, fairly liberal, Brahmin family we got to talking about the English language. The father was concerned that his children should learn to speak at least some English. He told the kids the English names of some things; "I" he said, pointing to himself, "you" pointing to his child, "he" pointing to me, "it" pointing to the low caste kitchen boy. The boy (in his mid-teens) wasn't even recognized as a person but belonged instead to a non-human category. This incident helped to clarify "Hindu-ness" for me, which up to that point I had often found baffling. (The boy eventually ran off and joined the army as soon as he was old enough; there he could get more respect.) While the low-castes are denigrated they can at the same time be integrated into the higher caste families. It is hard to conceive without seeing for oneself how the lower castes can be taken in by the higher castes, notably the "kaam garnes" or workmen. These workers will herd the animals and plow the fields of the upper and more affluent castes. In exchange they are fed, clothed and given roofs over their heads. But the exchange is not purely economic; they look after the children, are storytell-ers, jokers and clowns; they are integral to the lives of many upper caste families. Someone might point out that a near-approximation would be the historical place of black slaves on the Southern US plantations. My observation is that the lower castes are similarly integral to upper caste home life, as was the case in the South, and mostly they are not slaves.

Saddhus are, perhaps unsurprisingly, very ritualistic. Hinduism is a religion of rituals, and ritual occasions are led by Brahmins. As far as I could ever learn, saddhus, regardless of their caste, are responsible for conducting their own rituals, and there are rituals for everything: for purification, making a fire, smoking ganja, getting up in the morning, bathing (or not), soliciting, etc. Ritual governs much of their life. Sitting in a teashop one day I accidentally flashed the sole of my foot at the local saddhu's fire and he became most agitated and upset with me. He had to begin again his "lighting up" ritual, which he was in the middle of when I unceremoniously polluted the affair. He deconstructed his fire; rebuilt it and reheated the hemp that he would set on top of his chillum to light the ganja underneath. It took quite a bit of time and trouble to go through the ritual again. I was not so clumsy around saddhus thereafter. Westerners who play at being saddhus don't generally have a clue about the complex and ritualistic life that they try to emulate; familiarity with Rastafarian culture doesn't adequately prepare them. Moreover, true saddhus lead lives of deprivation, unfamiliar to Westerners. Diogenes the Cynic might have found them agreeable company.

On Christmas Day in 1982, my Dad found my (maternal) grandpa lying dead in the garage outside his house. Christmas Dinner was ready, and he was late. That my Dad went to fetch him was unusual since such a responsibility would normally have fallen to me or one of my sisters. Dad said later that he knew right away he was dead, and called an ambulance, which came and hauled the body away. No one felt like celebrating afterwards. A spirit inhabits every festive occasion, as Dickens observed, and can be squashed by individual circumstance. My Grandpa was a strange man, an idiot savant. Maybe he was undiagnosed with mild autism; we'll never know. His social IQ was low, but he was mathematically gifted. He could sum up a long column of numbers almost instantly. I was young, so I never came to appreciate this gift firsthand but my Dad, not given to exaggeration, was impressed. Besides skill with numbers, Grandpa could play almost any musical instrument he picked up and could also draw well. He made a career out of his math skills, working for the railroad all his life in the accounting department. Today computers would do this work. Reflecting on this fact, I wonder how others like him, alive today, make their way in a world where such unique skills have diminished value. In middle age he had a nervous breakdown from work-related stress after being promoted. He was good with numbers, not people. His inattentiveness and self-centeredness kept him from seeking help for my Grandmother when she was having a massive stroke. She never recovered and spent the rest of her days – nearly a decade – with the mental faculties of a child. This man never accepted his own mortality and didn't prepare for the inevitable. That night my Mom and youngest sister, sleeping on different levels of our house, were accosted by his specter. The next morning, they both described a desperate, maligned, and confused force intent upon them. If each person's life is summed up by a single sign at its end, would his have been a minus? But we each must one day be our own judge. What is my life's signature, and shall it be worth the living? It is already signed and again! And so, all celebrations end in this final celebration, and we exit the world as we entered it, but not with nothing to show. The chord of our relationships, the tone of our being, echo in worlds visible and invisible.

CHAPTER 8

IN THIS ERA OF THE 21st century, people have a complex relationship with food. Even for this era, my relationship with food has been outside the norm. Eating is a biological necessity – all creatures get hungry. What's become unnatural is the amount and frequency of Homo sapiens' eating. For many people, their eating habits get tangled up with other reflexes, which combine into destructive behaviors. For example, certain emotions drive some people to eat. When I was a kid my mother encouraged me to overeat, and I did. She wanted a "funny, fat, fuzzy-top," so that's what I became. I was obese until high school, and then lost a lot of weight. At twelve I weighed 180 pounds; at one point during my time in the Peace Corps, I was 145 pounds. Half of the graduating class at my thirty-year high school reunion was overweight and, ironically for me, I wasn't. Besides needing food for sustenance, I sustain myself through food as an agriculture professional. My work is to improve the food security for the rural poor by helping farmers in low-income countries grow and sell more food.

Our palates are suited to certain foods, though many foods are palatable. Taste buds are culturally distinctive, even if stomachs aren't. Their food makes some cultures distinctive. The Thai population in the US is very small, for example, but most Americans recognize Thai food, even if they know next to nothing else about Thai culture. For better and for worse, I have sampled many of their fares. Some suited to my palate and some not so much.

One of the least pleasant foods I've sampled was monkey, on the Indonesian island of Flores. I was there to analyze an investment in a small, juice-processing operation. We were looking at the raw material supply, in this case tomatoes, the power supply and ancillary investments. While we were scoping out the locale a villager carrying a dead monkey that he had just shot with an arrow walked by. The monkey's four limbs were bound to a stick that dangled over his shoulder. After talking to us for a few minutes, he continued on his way. We finished examining the site then followed him down, where we met with the villagers to gather some more information. They served us lunch: meat and potatoes. Taking a bite of the meat, I found its taste repugnant, not at all like chicken, or anything else that I could recognize. I tried a couple more bites, and then asked my colleague if we were eating the monkey the guy brought down earlier. He confirmed that we were, at which point my repugnance became nausea. I asked if the villagers would be insulted if I didn't finish my food and he said they would. Fortunately, there were a few dogs nearby and, wanting not to be noticed, I waited until a moment of pitched conversation when everyone was distracted and slipped them the meat. Serendipitously, the hunter had just captured this prey; otherwise, one of the villagers might have sacrificed a chicken or goat for us. My work often takes me to locations where there is serious poverty, and being their guest, people want to impress that they are good hosts. Often this means providing food, sometimes at considerable cost. So ironically, the many poor feed the few rich, making the metaphor literal.

Chinese prize birds' nest soup. Often, it is the priciest item on a menu. White-nest Swiftlets coat their nests with spittle, which is served in broth. This bird is native to Southeast Asia and its nests are exported throughout the region. I was part of a team visiting the tiny Indonesian island of Hansisi off the western tip of Timor Island, across a narrow strait from the city of Kupang, where there was a cave that had a White-nest Swiftlet nest guarded by watchmen. So valuable are these nests that they cover the costs of 24-hour security, of harvesting, packaging and shipment, and perhaps the luxurious setting in which the fine meal will be served – a very valuable value chain. Some foods are luxuries in the extreme and those supplying the fare have no concept why some people will pay exorbitant prices. Even cocoa and coffee farmers often have not tasted chocolate or a fresh brew, and don't understand what all the fuss is about, but appreciate the economic opportunities afforded.

Hansisi Island is a small, little-visited gem tucked away amongst Indonesia's thousands of islands. The shore is rimmed with a soft sandy beach and just offshore a marvelous coral reef. An excellent place to snorkel then, I fear that by now, at the rate things were going when I visited there in the mid-90s, the coral may all have been blasted away to catch a few fish, a fine example of the relatively poor impoverishing themselves further to cater to the relatively rich. Dynamite has replaced fishing nets in many parts of the world. On this visit to Hansisi, our group got stranded because the boat ran out of fuel. It was too late to send a boat back to Kupang to fetch some, so we were stranded there for the night. We slept on the beach. The only "food" available was very warm Guinness beer. Although a popular drink, Guinness is not thirst quenching and is a poor replacement for dinner. I haven't been able to drink Guinness since that night, although friends have assured me that I was in Paradise. Making the best of the situation, we were all in good humor, undoubtedly helped by the Guinness, we joked and laughed until the moon passed over the horizon, with the stars and our heads swirling. We went to sleep hungry and thirsty and found that our condition hadn't improved with waking. No one wanted another Guinness meal-replacement can. We had to scrounge for food in a small village on the island. When a boat finally showed up with fuel, we climbed in but couldn't resist snorkeling once more before heading back to Kupang. Only recently as a species have humans been able to watch fish in their own habitat. They seem to have no innate fear of human trespassers; we are alien to them and not pre-programmed into their nervous systems. But there is always a bigger fish.

Padang, at the opposite end of Indonesia on the island of Sumatra, is famous for its food and its chefs. Padang is a matriarchal society in which women have significant influence in the home and the community. As explained to us by a local woman, the men traditionally managed the home and, hence, much of the cooking. With their skills in the kitchen, and having abundant spices and other ingredients available, Padang men's reputations as chefs spread. Padang men can be found in the kitchens of many fine Jakarta hotels and restaurants. Unfortunately – or perhaps fortunately – for Padang's women, this meant that many of their menfolk had left. Bukitingi, north of Padang near the Lake Toba region, site of one of the world's most violent pre-historic volcanic explosions, has similarly explosive fare. A typical meal is inexpensive yet extravagant. On a small square table, the entire top is customarily filled with plates of every available dish. Diners can sample any of the sauces that come with the dishes but are charged if they eat the food. Exquisite sauces include coconut, pepper, tomato and other curries; dishes range from chicken to fish to tongue, brain, and yet more exotic cuisine. Gastronomic adventure!

Everyone enjoys a good meal, but how many really memorable meals have you had? Although I've sampled over 50 countries' cuisine only a few meals stand out. A great meal takes more than just a good chef and service. One's fellow diners must contribute to the experience. Excellent food and tense conversation may make a meal memorable, but not pleasant. Holidays usually afford both opportunities of memorable food and fellowship, but what of dining out?

One particular meal that stands out included superb company and over-abundant, though not so memorable, food, in the city of Bagan, in the then country of Burma. I was traveling with two other recently released PCVs. At that time, travelers to Burma were allowed just one week in the country, and they were allowed to bring one bottle of booze and one carton of cigarettes. We learned from tipsters in Nepal that the Burmese preferred Johnny Walker scotch and 555 cigarettes, so we bought one of each item to take with us. We sold the booze and cigarettes at exorbitant black-market prices, which almost covered the full cost of our stay. During the daytime, we went our separate ways, exploring areas that most interested us. At sunset, we met to watch the light fade under the eaves of one of the many ancient Buddhist temples, the world spinning into darkness and night. One night we hired a donkey-driven carriage to take us to a restaurant recommended by some locals. Wicker lanterns on the side of the carriage lighted the road and the donkeys trotted at the edge of their luminosity. The meal was served by candlelight and, for a few dollars at the exchange rate, we feasted like kings. All manner of curries and unfamiliar dishes were set on the table as we regaled ourselves with the day's explorations. Bagan, now a world heritage site, is not today what it was in 1986, so many of the temples have been lost for wont of upkeep. With a rented bicycle, one could ride to thousands of temples dotting the landscape, dodging the occasional cobra. In another unforgettable Burmese culinary encounter, I bought a packet of what I thought was dried shrimp at a train station for the trip to Rangoon, now Yangon. When I grew hungry, I pulled them out and began munching. To my disgust I realized that what I thought were prawns were instead dried and fried insects; their antennae stuck in my cheek and the roof of my mouth. Our best meal was at a hole-in-the-wall restaurant in Rangoon, where company and taste came perfectly together over giant Bengali prawns in curry prepared by a Rohingya chef – a truly memorable meal for all of the best reasons.

Some meals are memorable for reasons besides their taste or one's company. In Peru, shortly after the Government's devaluation of the currency in 1990, I paid 7 million Intis for a hamburger. There was nothing particularly memorable about the hamburgers but paying 7 million for a meal in any currency leaves one feeling impoverished. During one meal in Lima we were joined by the economist Hernando De Soto. At the time, he was the closest there was to a "development rock-star." So often is "business" a lunch companion. Lima then was a dangerous place, the Shining Path was still terrorizing the country and anyone notable was a likely target. There were armed security guards everywhere; we would have dined easier had we felt less exposed. A determined terrorist with an ax to grind and a gun could have found a good target simply by scoping out the restaurant that had the most security guards. De Soto was engaging, obviously brilliant and aware of it. Who knows? Perhaps one day he may win a Nobel Prize.

Occasionally there are foods prepared for purposes other than filling one's stomach. The island of Ko Samui, off Thailand's eastern coast, was a world traveler hotspot in the mid-1980s, becoming thoroughly overrun not long after by more affluent tourists. One local joint specialized in mushroom omelets. With a couple of companions, I reached Ko Samui and its liberating beaches two weeks after completing two years of Peace Corps service. In the uptight Hindu culture where I lived in Nepal, unmarried women were discouraged from socializing with unmarried men. The uptight culture spilled over into the Peace Corps culture, and relationships between male and female volunteers were mainly platonic. Flesh was generally concealed. Thai beaches were a stark contrast. We arrived in Ko Samui during a model shoot. International beauties posed for photographic shoots in newly-fashionable G-strings, many topless. What better entertainment for three hard-up ex-volunteers? In the two years and three months that I was in Nepal I'd had one liaison with a woman, more than a year earlier, and that was in a moment of drunken weakness with someone not quite to my taste. These models, mostly near my age or younger, uninhibitedly displaying their sexuality, made my month. We stayed at "Munchies" bungalows – for a dollar a night. "Mama Munchie" served special magic mushroom spaghetti or omelets. One night we indulged. We chatted for a long time after dinner, eventually getting pulled into a party. Later I found myself attracted to the beach and went down to the water's edge to watch the waves come ashore.

My brain was in a highly sensitive state, aware of everything. As time passed, I noticed that small clouds were forming by evapo-transpiration a short distance from each of the small groves of coconut trees that dotted the shoreline. My attention became completely rapt in watching this process of cloud formation. I walked to one of the small groves and sat down to watch as the clouds form just above the coconut trees overhead. While watching a small cloud take shape just above the grove, it began to descend towards me; either that or my consciousness was rising to it. Whatever was happening, suddenly my body jumped up to its feet and fled. This happened so fast that I was already some distance away when my thoughts caught up with my body. I became aware that my heart was pounding, my body shaking as though in terror. I'm still not sure what frightened me that night. Later I described this experience to an Aussie sailor friend who was acquainted with Southeast Asia sailor lore. He recounted tales of sailors who were found dead in coconut groves, for no apparent cause. Hallucination? On an earlier mushroom adventure at a lakeside hotel in Pokhara I spent the evening with great pleasure conversing with local children, as the sun set to the west behind the Annapurnas, and a new vantage point.

Foods may be culturally distinctive, pricey, memorable, remunerative – and deadly. A Pizza Hut anchovy pizza gave me my first experience of food poisoning. When we started to eat it I noticed an off smell, but didn't pay heed. This is survival rule number one: if you have doubt about the food you are eating then stop. Our senses often pick up subtle danger signs. The next morning, instead of skiing, I found myself paying homage to the toilet bowl, the "porcelain god" as we called it. After spilling my guts, we smoked a bowl, taking the edge off my nausea, and headed up to the slopes. Chemotherapy patients and others who smoke ganja medicinally to ease their nausea have my full sympathy. I have first-hand experience of its benefits. Lest there be misunderstandings, taking any mind-altering substance has a long-term effect, though not one normally discussed: such drugs diminish one's sense of pleasure over time and deaden one's sense of pain. Pleasure and pain are not equated here with emotions. Young people find it easy to abuse substances if the consequences are delayed. Youth is flippant; age is severe.

My first serious case of food poisoning nearly killed me. Dale and I had just finished trekking the Annapurna Circuit. We'd had breakfast in Pokhara at one of the westernized Lakeside restaurants. Pokhara, like Kathmandu, made good business of providing Western-style cuisine to tourists. Some of the restaurants were quite good. Before returning to my Peace Corps post, I decided to enjoy a piece of pie, since I wouldn't get another chance for months; so, I stopped at one of the specialty pie shops and bought a piece of lemon meringue. After I ate it I walked to the bus station and caught a bus to Butwal. While I was waiting at the bus stand, I bought some pineapple. Since I was one of the first to board the bus I sat in a rear window seat. The road from Pokhara to Butwal is a truly long and winding road – one of the windiest roads in the world. The hills are so huge that one can look from one point on the road to another point on the road, a short distance as the crow flies, and find that getting from point to point takes an hour. The road follows the contours of the hills that drop back out of view, winding and twisting deep into mountain recesses to meet the next hill and then slowly wend its way back to within view of the first point. The road continues like this all the way down to the Terai. The bus had been on the road for a couple of hours when it started to get crowded and I had two young passengers sharing the bench I was on. The bus was a "local" bus, meaning it stopped for everyone and everything that needed a lift. "Everything" could include goats, chickens, appliances, kerosene containers, and whatever else somebody decided they wanted to bring with them. That day it had gotten progressively hotter and as the bus continued south, more oppressive. It was one of those really sunny, hot and humid, intra-monsoon days that made everyone feel very uncomfortable – even before getting on the bus. The young passengers next to me were a couple of Brahman kids with chips on their shoulders. The one kid told me to move so he could sit next to the window, I didn't bother to answer. I was starting to feel sick and needed to be near it.

As time went by, and stops became starts and then more stops, I felt sicker and sicker, until the bus stopped in one village and I could hold back no longer. It must have been a sad sight. We pulled up to the bus stop; a wedding party was there waiting for the bus and people were dressed in their finest clothes. When the bus braked to a stop, I projectile-vomited out of the window, where it hit the pavement, ricocheted and sprayed the wedding party. There were looks of horror and disgust from people in the wedding party, now glowering at the pale, white face drooping limply out of the window. That was the beginning. The vomiting continued for hours. Once when the bus stopped I had to dash out into the rice field – both ends at the same time. The driver and his crew urged me to go to the hospital when we reached the town of Tansen, where there were expatriate doctors. However, just a few months before one of my friends had nearly died in that hospital from maltreatment and I wanted nothing to do with the place. By the time I'd been on the bus for six or seven hours, having suffered through one flat tire and I don't remember what else, there was nothing in me except violent spasms in my stomach, which was completely empty, and I was exhausted. I was also thoroughly dehydrated; there was nothing to drink and none on offer. Finally, I was laid on the backbench, taking up space that could have seated several people, and passed out. I must have been unconscious for several hours. When the bus reached Butwal, it was nightfall.

Fortunately, there was an Italian couple who had gotten on the bus at one of its many stops, probably in Tansen. I had not noticed them before. I wasn't aware of it, but they had been keeping an eye on me. As the bus was unloading they offered to help me. I was hardly aware of their aid. They took me with them, gave me liquids, and got a hotel room with an extra bed. I don't remember much except waking up the next morning and feeling bad, but better than the night before, and noted that the couple was looking after me. In many ways they were my guardian angels and may very well have saved my life. Once I felt good enough to leave, they helped me get to the bus station. They were bound for the Indian border so we got on the bus together. When we reached Tutipiple, I said goodbye and never saw them again. It took the better part of a week to recover.

The next bout of food poisoning was courtesy of "the friendly skies" of United Airlines. I was returning from a work assignment in the Philippines via Tokyo, then on to Chicago and Washington, DC. The flight left Manila early in the morning with a four-hour flying time to Tokyo. *En route* to Tokyo we were served the "Japanese Lunchbox," which had some wonderful delicacies including raw fish. What I later guessed was that those lunchboxes had been sitting on the tarmac in Manila too long and the fish had started to spoil. The plane offloaded in Tokyo and we waited for the flight to Chicago. About 45 minutes after leaving Tokyo it hit— that sick feeling of nausea when your innards seem like they are going to heave themselves out. For the next eight hours of the 12-hour flight I was continuously in the toilet. My stomach muscles started to contract painfully to rid my body of the tainted morsel. These contractions reached a point where they seemed timed to make me throw-up every half minute. At one point I wasn't even able to get up from my seat; I was just passing puke bags to the flight attendants, who were not pleased by the situation.

Flight attendants are supposed to be on board for passenger safety and to provide first aid. I didn't get much aid. By the time the plane landed in Chicago I was over the worst of it, but I must have looked like hell. Since it was an international flight I had to clear Customs before I could go on to Washington, DC. Customs officials are not generally known for their bedside manners, yet the Customs officials in Chicago actually escorted me through. They wanted to call an ambulance to take me to the hospital but by then there was no need. I had to wait in Chicago O'Hare for several hours before the flight to DC left, so I found some carpeting that I could lie on. I stopped at the United Airlines Helpdesk to let them know that they needed to monitor their food more carefully; they denied any culpability and argued that it must have been something else that I had eaten. This could not have been the case, however; since the flight left Manila so early in the morning I had had no chance to eat breakfast. While I was lying on the floor a United Flight Attendant took notice of me and offered to help in any way that she could. I gratefully accepted her offer for water. Eventually when my travel agent heard about the incident she got a $200-off travel voucher from United – big deal. Other Manila passengers also became sick, one of them a young girl. I was miserable for several days afterwards, even suffering a relapse. So, beware of airline food!

The third incident of food-borne illness occurred shortly after I returned from a work assignment in Bangladesh; this time with typhoid. I went to Bangladesh to start a new project that, ironically enough, was supposed to develop the country's agri-food sector including food safety. There were only two possible places that I could have contracted it: at an Indian restaurant that a friend took me to or from the Ministry of Agriculture where I had carelessly drunk some of their tea. I suspect it was the restaurant but noted that in the Ministry's offices washing tubs were used to wash the tableware. The glasses were washed in one tub of soapy water and then transferred to another tub for rinsing. I doubt that the water in the rinse tub had been boiled or treated to make it potable. I was in country for a couple of weeks and then returned to the US. I had to come back for a couple of weeks due to a prior commitment, and then I was scheduled to return. As my departure date approached, I started to feel a flu coming on.

The day before my flight, I had to call the airline and reschedule my trip to the next week because, as I thought, I had gotten the flu and needed a few days to recuperate, after which I would be ready to travel. Well, a few days turned into a few more days. I was progressively getting sicker. When the fever started, I could get up and around and still eat. As time progressed I could only lie in bed and lost all appetite. A couple of weeks went by and then the chills started; they were so violent that my body shook the entire bed. I knew at that point that I didn't have a normal case of the flu and I was thinking that maybe I had picked up malaria. In my diminished mental state, I was struck by how the fever was cyclical, going up to 104° and then dropping down again. I did not take into account that my temperature spiked just before taking acetaminophen to ease the pain, but acetaminophen also lowers a fever's temperature.

By the second week of fever, my wife was very concerned. She called the doctor and, after examining me, he arranged for me to go to Georgetown Medical Hospital, supposedly one of the premier hospitals in the area. After running a battery of tests on me, Georgetown emergency room's cowboys sent me home, concluding that whatever I had was not that serious. The next day my wife called the doctor and told him what had happened; he told her that I should lay off all medication and see what temperature my fever would reach. By this time, I was delirious; the fever reached 107° and the doctor had my wife get me to the hospital – not the one in Georgetown. They were going to send an ambulance, but I didn't think it was necessary. Hospital waiting rooms are hardly fit places for the healthy, let alone for the sick. It seemed to take forever for the staff to "process" me into a hospital bed. I had to lie on the waiting room floor because I was too dizzy to sit upright.

Once I was in a room, a nurse got me into a hospital gown and then sent me downstairs for tests. At that point I was hallucinating. I felt completely lucid yet euphoric, but I knew that the sensation had more to do with the fever than with a general improvement in my condition. This feeling of euphoria lasted a long time. I described the sensation to the doctor and my wife as I was experiencing it, explaining that I was aware it was a hallucination. Knowing that one is hallucinating does not make the hallucination go away. Most uncomfortably, the fever made my head feel like a metal band was wrapped around it being squeezed tightly, vice-like. I was given intravenous ciprofloxacin, a harsh treatment that left me feeling toxic. After several more days of delirium I finally started to feel better. I was in the hospital for a week before being discharged, and after being discharged I was still recuperating for several months. I returned to Bangladesh and contracted a bad case of dysentery. Typhoid—that was the diagnosis—kills many poor people in less developed countries, and now I understand why. I was strong and healthy, and it decimated me. For people in poverty who are not so strong or healthy, it is often lethal. Typhoid can also lead to further health complications. I was to suffer from a condition called "pyro-calcium phosphate deficiency" a couple of months later; the condition is similar to gout, but my ureic acid level was normal. My big toe was painful for several weeks and would flare up on occasion for the next year.

Typhoid is a silent killer. Poor people are among the main victims. Simple hygienic practices would lower its incidence. The dissemination of hygienic practices takes education, which takes money, which is in too short a supply for this killer. Typhoid has disappeared in developed countries thanks to filtered water, sewer systems, and simple ingrained habits such as washing one's hands after using the toilet. These systems cost money, but good hygienic habits are cheap yet ignorance of them persists. In the United States about 400 cases of typhoid are reported each year, and overseas travelers contract 70 percent of these cases. Typhoid fever is still common in the developing world, where it affects an estimated 12.5 million persons each year. As pointed out in medical journals Salmonella Typhi lives only in humans. Persons with typhoid fever carry the bacteria in their bloodstream and intestinal tract. In addition, a small number of persons are carriers who recover from typhoid fever but continue to carry the bacteria, viz. Typhoid Mary. Both ill persons and carriers shed S. typhi in their feces. Once S. typhi bacteria are eaten or drunk, they multiply and spread into the bloodstream. The body reacts with fever and other symptoms. The ancillary danger of typhoid is that it can so weaken a person that even if the disease doesn't kill them a simple malady such as a cold may, if the victim has been weakened enough. More readily preventable than, say, malaria or HIV, typhoid gets remarkably little attention from either the development or medical communities.

Food may also be valuable in its absence, for instance through fasting or more extreme forms of immolation. Fasting can have psychological value. Twice I've experimented with fasting for over a week, during strenuous physical exertion. Call it a "spiritual" quest, or at least an attempt at self-discovery. Noted teachers have observed that fasting at high altitude can bring interesting results. Traditionally, fasting has been used for physical and spiritual cleansing. Combining prolonged fasting and high altitude, I was able to observe the physiological and psychological effects. I chose Tilicho Lake as the site for this trial. To reach Tilicho Lake, one must turn south from the main Annapurna Circuit trail just west of Manang to the village of Khangsha. Khangsha is the last outpost on the way to Jomsom over the Tilicho Pass, or the first one returning by the same route. From Khangsha to Tilicho Lake was for me a strenuous two-day trek. I brought a tent since there was no place to stay, although I've read that now there is a trekker lodge midway, providing nominal accommodations. Khangsha is a Manangi village, which could be in Tibet. As is typical of such towns, on the outskirts are large numbers of prayer (Mani) stones piled together, prayer wheels adorn the path to the town's entrance, and one is greeted by fluttering white flags on rooftops sending "Om Mani Padme Hum" prayers to the heavens. I stayed there one night; fortunately, the matron spoke Nepali and we discussed the quality of the trail to the Lake. The map showed the trail following the river, but it was the monsoon and runoff from snowmelt had raised the water level. She suggested that the high trail would be safer.

MANI STONES

My map didn't show a high trail and as I walked along the river that morning I didn't notice the trails split. After hiking a few hours, the going got rougher because the water got higher, encroaching on the path, until I reached a point where the trail was completely impassable. My backpack held a tent, sleeping bag, clothes, and a few books; fortunately, I wasn't burdened with the weight of food or cooking equipment. To reach the high trail I had two choices: retrace my steps to Khangsha or go straight up. I chose the latter route. This was nearly a fatal mistake. The climb up started out steep, but not too steep. However, I couldn't see more than a couple hundred feet above me; had I been able to see farther I might have gone back. I climbed up several hundred feet until I found myself in cliffs, which couldn't be seen from below. Eventually, I reached a point where going down was no longer an option, and I could only go up. At this point I became scared and shaky. Some of the rock was loose, jettisoning downward when disturbed, handgrips were uncertain, and I was alone. I realized that if I made a mistake it could be my end. I continued up slowly, taking my time and being deliberate, and pushing down the panic that occasionally crept up on me. I wound my way through the cliffs until, at last, I reached an area that had some grass and the footing was a bit more certain. I continued up. Eventually after climbing a couple thousand feet I came across an animal trail or possibly a trail used by yak herders in the summer. I continued along this trail and eventually reached a high plateau. Across this plateau, I walked alongside a small streambed until I found myself entering a narrow mountain canyon. At this point I realized that I had taken another wrong turn. In 1987, the high trail was not very well defined, although I understand that now it is clearer. This time, I retraced my steps until I found the right trail, marked by prayer flags, which I was able to see on my return descent. I spent the night in a closed-in but pleasant vale and continued to the lake the next day.

The trail to the lake is steep, in spots treacherous, and deceiving in its length. When the trail flattened out and then started to descend I knew that I was getting close. First one reaches a small, clear pond. This is where I decided to set up camp. There was a flattish area without too many rocks where I could lie down without great discomfort. After setting up my tent I went on to explore Tilicho Lake proper. In the preceding autumn, a trekking group was decimated at Tilicho by foul weather and some trekkers died. They were stranded in Tilicho for many days without any hope of rescue because a blizzard pinned them down. At that time I was trekking with a friend in the Everest region and saw firsthand how dangerous the storm was, but we were in the less remote Sherpa areas where there were lodges, although the storm still killed some people there. The people who died at Tilicho were buried in rocky mounds, which one could see from a distance.

The ground was too rocky for digging graves, and the group would not have had time to do so since a helicopter evacuated the survivors once the storm broke.

The mountains surrounding Tilicho, especially Nilgiri and Annapurna I to the south, are formidable; icy gods of the alpine world, they stand sentinel over the desolate wilds. Yes, I grew hungry, but the gnawing hunger was not hunger for food. The quiet solitude of such places has an effect on the brain, dispelling the polluting electrochemical smog that accumulates in "civilized" places. Such smog is thickest where human populations are densest. I spent my days exploring the area and "meditating," although meditation without an effort, without a directed will that looks for results. The quiet of that place filled my mind. The main noises were the blowing wind, an occasional avalanche or ice slab breaking off of a glacier and crashing into the lake. Even birds were largely absent. Wildflowers and sedges mingled in short grasses were the most abundant forms of life. After a week I decided that it was time to return. I had given up on the idea of crossing over Meso Kanto La since I had not found the trail. The northern edge of the lake terminated at a cliff wall. Anyone attempting to go up there would almost surely have failed. There was a possible westward way to Jomsom around the Lake's southern shore; however, this way too would have been dangerous because of the glacier field that ended at the Lake's edge. A mountaineer with proper equipment might have maneuvered between the glaciers and the water's edge; on inspection I thought that it would be a high-risk gambit. A trail over the Meso Kanto La exists, but one must turn north and hike upward. In 1987 there weren't any obvious trail markers. In any event, by the time I was ready to leave I didn't have the strength to go the western Annapurna Circuit route.

The morning I left Tilicho, the weather was very cold, and I got frostbite while packing up my gear; the aluminum tent poles froze my fingers, which lost their nimbleness and then their sensitivity. At that altitude, even July can be freezing. The way down proved to be much more difficult than I anticipated. The trail was made of rocky scree and would slide underneath my feet. With each step, I found myself sliding several feet down the mountainside. I tried slowing my pace but still slid with every step. The sliding continued until I had slid over a thousand feet to a point where I was just a short distance from the cliffs that tumbled off into the Khangsha Khang River. At that point, I stopped to consider my options. There were two choices: I could try to go even slower or I could make a mad dash across the scree to a distant outcropping. Since going slow hadn't been working very well, I decided to make a dash. The outcrop was about a quarter of a mile away and the ground there would certainly be stable. Before dashing I took some deep breaths to gather what energy I had, and then ran. I slid half the distance to the cliff's edge, but my speed carried me to the outcrop, just a short distance above the cliff. I followed the outcrop up until I was again on the trail. Soon after this close call I was overcome by nausea. After going without food for a fortnight, microorganisms in the stomach get out of balance and over-produce. I vomited, and it wasn't pretty. Eventually I was able to continue walking and reached the vale that I had camped in on my way up, still a day from food. The next day I made it to Khangsha village. I stopped at the same trekking lodge where I had stayed on the way up. The matron was surprised to see me. We discussed my adventure and talked about Dharma. "After dukha comes sukha," she said – after suffering comes reward. The next day I continued down to Manang village. On the high cliffs above the entrance to Khangsha Valley there is a perfectly round hole carved out of the rock by wind and rain, piercing the ridge. Through this circle, the blue sky of heaven rises endlessly above. A circle, the sign of eternity; there can be no more appropriate landmark to the entrance of this valley. Surrounded by prayer flags and roped off, this natural wonder stands testament to all that is divine on Earth.

My second prolonged fast was in Montana's backcountry, north of Yellowstone Park. Starting south of Bozeman I hiked to Mystic Lake and on to Hylight Peak. Crossing Hylight Peak, I went south and then east to Paradise Valley, across to Emigrant and into the mountains behind Old Chico. I returned to Bozeman via Trail Creek and Three Bears Lake. My object in doing this hike was to push the limits of my endurance under duress, and to gauge the effect. There were moments – or were they eternities? – when space and time merged, subsumed into a greater vastness. In this vastness there is no "here" or "there" and the thread of time, moving from the past through the present to the future, unwinds. Behind Old Chico one afternoon I sat on a rock watching the river flow, sunlight dancing on the sparkling waves; individual drops splashed into the air, turning on themselves for one shining moment and fell back into the water, merging immediately and imperceptibly into the flow. Glittering, shining, the light played upon the water. The sun dipped behind the mountains leaving them silhouetted in deepening dusk.

The evening sky became orange, red, and then purple, and slowly the stars began blinking in the twilight, awakening from their daytime slumber. Later the moon rose above the opposite ridge, casting its silvery light on the dark ground and the shimmering river. The foam on the river, lightly colored rocks and heavy boulders strewn along the banks appeared fluorescent against nighttime shadows and forest pines. The temperature cooled and sounds of river, insects, whispering pines, an occasional rock, crashing down the mountain, merged; sensations all blending together, losing yet keeping their distinctness. At times my pulse raced, my heart quivered, then pounded in my chest—my head dizzy and light, sharp and focused. Fatigued, I got up, went into the tent and crawled into the sleeping bag. I recalled that once at a summer cabin I passed a tree through which the breeze blew the leaves. The sound caught my attention. What causes the sound of leaves blowing on a tree? Before, I might have reasoned, "oh, well, it's probably the leaves tapping against each other when the wind blows them, and that makes the blowing sound." Wrong. I noticed that the leaves did not touch each other yet they still made noise – the distinct sound of a tree. Interestingly, different tree species make different sounds when blown by the wind. Each leaf flapping in the air makes its own sound – has its own voice; their distinctive shapes and sizes aerodynamically create their pitch and tone. A single tree can be an orchestra of sound, a grove a symphony; quaking aspens make a wonderful, happy noise, while pines whisper. The trees in this canyon play their music day and night, filling a space in nature with their leafy harmony. Who knows if this music is not the main function of a species, filling some chord in nature of which we are but dimly aware? In nature, without other people around, one's sense of personal identity wanes. This identity, wired into electro-chemical pathways in our brains, can short circuit. If our internal conversations with ourselves and with imaginary others can stop for but a little while we may glimpse beyond our "identity reflexes." If we stop "becoming" and "be," one moment can be the portal to the All of our life.

These advertent and inadvertent experiences with food, and working in agriculture, bring me to appreciate the importance of safe food. Safe food, however, comes at a price, a price that makes some products unaffordable to poorer consumers in the very countries where they are grown and processed.

The byproduct of our beastly existence is excrement. But what is waste for one species may be a feast for another. After hiking all morning on the Annapurna Circuit my friend and I were hungry so stopped to eat lunch at a small trekkers lodge. Since it was the off-season not every lodge served food, but we found a place that would feed us. The matron was a Manangi woman wearing traditional Tibetan garbs and chunky coral and turquoise jewelry. She had a small toddler who was scampering around the floor. There was also a small Lhaso Apso dog keeping watch. She gave us menus but unfortunately most of the items were unavailable this time of year, the middle of the monsoon season, and her cupboard was bare. She offered us Ramen noodles, adding the usual garnishes: hot peppers, potatoes, onions, and some greens (probably nettles). She served us, and we started to eat. While we were chomping down, the infant, squatting on the kitchen floor, took a shit – no diapers. The dog came and ate the pile, which is disgusting (to an American eye) but not unusual since dogs will eat shit. After the dog finished eating the mother picked up the child and held up its ass for the dog to lick clean. At that point we lost our appetites.

What, if anything, did I gain from my experience of prolonged fasts? One lesson at least became clear: our brains accumulate a certain amount of neuro-physiological dross over time, and a break from society provides space for dispelling this waste. This dross is the product of "undigested" perceptions, incoherent representations that we make to ourselves of the world. Away from society and without a constant supply of food, the body becomes more sensitive, and aware of this sensitivity. Behavioral reflexes that have become ingrained through repetition begin to weaken. "Proprioception" happens more naturally. This explanation uses words that intimate time and process, but the description is not the experience.

An ancient tradition holds that there are three types of food: cells for the stomach, air for the lungs, and light for eyes. Physical nourishment comes from nature, the cells of other beings – plants and animals; the respiratory system consumes air in the lungs, and the brain consumes impressions taken in as light through the eyes. Physical food – cells; emotional food – molecules; mental food – atoms. Some foods are easier to digest, and more nourishing, than others. Food can be healthy or make us sick. If it is true that peoples' eating habits have deteriorated worldwide in recent decades, what does this suggest about the most important food that we consume – the impressions we take in? What of the waste material from these different types of foods? The digestive system eliminates waste through the alimentary canal; the lungs eliminate waste upon exhale; and what of the waste from impressions? Some is eliminated through excess talk – diarrhea of the mouth, or is pent up inside, constipated, perhaps eventually to emerge as some insidious thought or belief. The digestive system is instinctive, and it is not something that an individual can easily control. The respiratory system is also instinctive but a person, properly trained, as are some yogis, can exert considerable control over their breathing. The brain's digestion of impressions is not so instinctive, though is highly reflexive, and is subject to control but mostly is governed by the power of suggestion. May this be food for thought.

Trying not to be preachy, we all have images of ourselves, believing "I am this, I have such and such tastes, this or that ability," comparing ourselves to others along these dimensions we identify ourselves with our beliefs about ourselves. The resulting self-image drives us to manipulate our environments to suit ourselves to our own advantages. The resulting "self-sense" impels our actions, though we are often unaware of its influence on our behavior. When I receive a complement, for instance, my self-sense reflexively puffs up, if I'm criticized my self-sense becomes defensive; I feel pleasure or pain. Ambition, vindictiveness, jealousy, even the satisfaction I experience sometimes when I look in the mirror, and all other emotions that have strong personal elements, are driven by this self-sense. Depriving oneself of food and being alone for extended periods can diminish this self-sense, or at least makes its operation plainer. The physicist David Bohm describes proprioception – a sense of awareness of one's neuro-physiological responses in action – that apprehends the impulsive self-sense. Proprioception can happen in conditions of voluntary deprivation. The self-sense seems to be connected to the system that produces endorphins. Krishnamurti points out, "thought creates the thinker" and once this image of the thinker is established in our neuro-circuitry it drives the system. The "thinker" in us divides our mental process in two – the observer (the subject or "I," the narrator) who watches what happens, comments on and manipulates it – and the observed (the object or "me") to which things happen. But the process is one, not two. Our feelings and senses follow where thought leads, responding to our self-sense. And this is the state of humanity; we live our lives indirectly, experiencing life through this filter of our self-sense. Many will argue that this is only natural – and so we find ourselves living in this messy world.

Two very different questions feed my inner life, as consuming interests: (1) "why do I do what I do?" and (2) "how can agriculture improve the lives of poor people?" These questions have sharpened in focus over time. Long ago I would have posed the first question as: "what does my life mean?" Or earlier: "who am I?" Experience and study of philosophy-neuro-psychology leads one to the general question "why do people do what they do?" and the particular question about oneself. Why am I interested in the second question about agriculture? This question I can't answer, or the answer I have is not satisfactory: when I was born Mars was in Taurus in the tenth house.

CHAPTER 9

THE GROWTH OF KATHMANDU'S FOOD service industry is an illustrative example of how development happens. Until the Maoist uprising, Kathmandu was something of a Mecca for hungry travelers journeying in South Asia. Restaurants specialize in Western, Indian, Chinese, Tibetan, Japanese and other international cuisines, as well as local fare. One can find pizza, quiche, flavored yogurts, English Breakfasts, Swiss rostis, and many other assorted foods. Through the 1970s – 1990s this diverse fare was driven by the trekking and tourist industries. However, Kathmandu's culinary trade began during the days of the Hippie Trail in the late 1960s, with the help of a former Peace Corps Volunteer in Nepal who spotted a chance to make some money. Marijuana and hashish stimulate a craving for sweets. Hippies craved sugar. Combining the two – drugs and sweets – into one business model, this former Volunteer opened Kathmandu's first pie shop on what was to become Freak Street. His restaurant was famous for selling cakes, pies, and other sweet things alongside an assortment of narcotics. This story dovetails neatly with recent theories of economic growth.

Research on economic development, for instance by William Easterly, emphasizes the role of "knowledge leaks" and "skills matching." The spread of knowledge has substantial spillover effects on an economy. Knowledge, according to the economist Paul Romer, produces increasing returns and more investment in knowledge brings higher payoffs. But knowledge leaks; it tends to get away from the possessors; in the vernacular, knowledge is a "non-rival good." Bangladesh's garment industry is the classic economic example cited in development literature on the importance of knowledge leaking. Going back to the pie shop, the former

Volunteer invested in training Nepalese as bakers so that he could focus on other parts of his business. The problem he faced was that after teaching the staff his recipes they would leave his employment and start pie shops of their own. It wasn't long before Freak Street was dotted with pie shops, all selling narcotics and sweets; one of the most famous of these was the Yin Yang. The pie shops outlasted the hippies. In this development model, the knowledge of pie recipes created value for many Nepali bakers, and eventually spawned a whole cottage industry serving tourists. The former volunteer was eventually forced out due to price competition among the pie shops. This example of economic development also emphasizes the role of skills matching. The pie shops differentiated themselves by location, with the better pie shops in the prime spots. The better pie shops had nicer ambience with trained, attentive waiters who spoke English, and the best desserts. Eventually pie making diversified into many types of cuisine. The people with the best skills matched up with similarly talented individuals to maximize the value of their skills. Unskilled people could destroy the value of the business, which is why it is so important for people of similar skill levels to work together – to match with each other. This example nicely depicts development at the micro level.

Besides "knowledge leaks" and "skills matching," other factors play crucial roles in accelerating and protecting economic growth. As Douglass North points out, "institutions matter." Michael Porter's musings on economic development resonate with direct observation. In Porter's proposition, economic growth moves economies along a spectrum from "factor-driven" to "investment-driven" to "innovation-driven" development. Many poor countries are stuck supplying factors, that is, raw materials such as agricultural goods, timber, minerals, or other extractive resources. Without investment, they will be merely suppliers to firms in other countries that add value to these raw materials. One of the crucial challenges for developing countries is their need to increase capacity to build wealth to keep pace with the leading edge of innovation. As technologies such as GIS, the Internet, and a slew of other devices, establish themselves in the marketplace, it becomes more and more difficult for countries on the opposite end of the innovation spectrum to be able to effectively deploy them. Not to say it can't be done; mobile phones are an excellent example of a readily adaptable technology that have been successfully transferred to most countries. The processes, databases and recordkeeping that accompany an innovation such as "smart tags" (RFID), though, are much more difficult to deploy.

In agriculture, better organization and farm management can go a long way to help improve the lives of small producers. Organizations, which aggregate the supply of farmers' produce for sale and the inputs they will buy, can give groups of producers more bargaining power in the markets. Farm management – planting, growing and harvesting – can be coordinated across a group of producers to even out income streams, share profits, and spread risks. Crucially, farm products must meet the specifications of particular buyers or markets.

Such approaches can be especially effective in countries that have large numbers of "emerging" small producers. As with Kathmandu's pie shops, the most productive producers in an area are the most likely to match up with each other to realize the potential returns to better organization.

Value chain analyses are one of the main tools of our trade, the objective being to identify constraints to growth and opportunities to increase productivity. On a typical assignment, a specialist will assess a range of agricultural sub-sectors (i.e., dairy products, beef, fresh produce, etc.), then look at competing value chains within these sub-sectors. Done properly, such an assessment will use quantitative and qualitative analysis of the chains vertically and of chain segments horizontally. Segments are examined in relation to constraints, and products analyzed for potential productivity improvements. Such an analysis might examine, for instance: credit, raw material quality, skills capacity, operations and maintenance, market entry requirements, processing facilities and equipment, market information, and other relevant factors. This analysis is usually followed by more targeted investigation with the objective of prescribing a set of activities to address the identified constraints or seize opportunities.

One development mantra is "do no harm," which isn't always observed by development organizations in their search to "do good" among many competing objectives. In one case, I was told to do a deal with a large multinational fruit company that would link nucleus and smallholder farmers to new export markets. Nucleus farms typically are large farmers with substantial production capabilities, surrounded by many smaller farms. Nucleus farmers can help the small farms to manage their production: crop management, harvesting, packing, shipping, etc. These can be "win-win" arrangements since nucleus farms may ship greater volumes and lower their unit costs. We worked with the multinational company to understand their requirements and communicate these to the farmers. The multinational had certain standards that farmers had to meet before it would do business. Many of these requirements involved product handling and use of the company's logo and related intellectual property. Some farmers took on debt – borrowing from local banks – to make the necessary equipment and other purchases. After these changes had been set in motion, the company added to the requirements by setting out more rigorous sanitary standards – higher standards and more debt for some of the farmers. At this point the farmers wanted to know in greater detail the company's payment terms. The company's terms were less generous than some of the farmers (the best ones) were already getting, but other farmers were desperate for an agreement, seeing the deal as their big chance. The company made yet another demand – all of the farmers had to get a "voluntary" third-party, environmental certification. Getting this certification would entail major investments for some farmers, others balked.

By now a number of the farmers had pledged substantial future revenues to banks and other investment partners to raise capital, meanwhile the company's interest cooled because the volumes it needed would not be met because some of the biggest farmers were backing out. As a development organization, we had invested in facilitating the deal, training, arranging loan guarantees, financial structuring, and food safety diagnostics – all to naught. By the end, some farmers had gone under, others were deep in debt, the multinational hadn't sold one container and a lot of money had been wasted. "Do no harm…" If this deal was made a case study, one lesson would be to get all of the deal requirements on the table at the very beginning, not dribbling them out one-by-one, and estimate up-front what the costs would be for farmers to meet these standards.

Lest large multinational corporations be singled out as uniquely sinister, governments are equally – or more – culpable of crass disregard for smallholder farmers. One fine example is the difficulty they have getting decent seeds. In Sub-Saharan Africa especially, farmers use seeds that they've saved from year-to-year, that they find in local markets (the informal sector), and – much less frequently – buy from agro-dealers. Mostly their saved seeds and seeds from local markets are of poor quality, growing into plants with very low yields. In the US, a maize farmer might get 10-12 tons/hectare, whereas in sub-Saharan Africa they may get 1.5 tons/hectare. American farmers use almost exclusively improved hybrid varieties; the majority of African smallholders rarely use hybrids. Why? It's only partly to do with poverty. More often hybrids, or basic improved varieties, just aren't available because governments' regulations are overly burdensome and corrupt. Among the many reasons: varieties don't get released because of excessive or inconsistent data requirements on seed performance; prohibitions on private sector production of breeder and foundation seed that are needed to produce certified seed; lack of investment in research systems; onerous and costly seed inspection requirements, etc., etc. Each of these reasons are also accompanied by opportunities for graft by bureaucrats. Ghana, a lower-middle income country that should have a strong agriculture sector, deprives its poor farming households of access to better seeds by a rigged seed system that fails to deliver even modest yield increases, for example. Researchers have found that Ghana's so-called "improved varieties" are not even true-to-type, having low levels of genetic purity. No wonder farmers don't want to buy such seeds. The upshot is that Ghana has one of the less productive agricultural systems in the region.

There are many kinds of corruption, from self-dealing, which is usually illegal but ignored, to illicit. Kathmandu in the 80s had a dark side. Drugs had gotten harder: cocaine, heroin, and crack had infiltrated society. Women were at risk. Bicycling home one evening I saw a young woman flitting dangerously between the sidewalk and the street in an apparent daze. Traffic was moving swiftly, and she was chasing a butterfly between the cars. Her clothes and hair were disheveled. A small group gathered to watch her, concerned for her safety, but they didn't speak English and so couldn't help her. They stopped me and asked if I could get her to safety. I tried to convince her to come with me on my bike, hoping to get her off the street. She spoke with an Australian accent and, looking at her closely and having heard recent rumors, I guessed that she had been drugged, raped, and was let go or walked out in a daze. Some Nepali VIPs lived in the neighborhood. The group around us encouraged her to get on my bike – a few of them knew me – which she did momentarily, and then someone uttered the word "junkie," which offended her. She caught sight of another butterfly and chased it into the street. Trying to get her attention again was useless – she was oblivious. Such incidents of drug-related violence and abuse were becoming more frequent, eventually culminating in the murder of the royal family by the Crown Prince some years later.

Mostly, the "Big Men" get what they want despite laws and regulations, but not always. In 1987, not too long after the Chernobyl nuclear incident in the Ukraine, I went to my local grocer to buy some powdered milk. The storekeeper told me that it wasn't available, so I went to another shop and they didn't have any powdered milk either. I skipped it, returning to my favorite shop again a few days later. The storekeeper was still out of milk. So, I asked him "what gives?" He replied that he didn't expect to get powdered milk anytime soon, explaining that all of the local shops were boycotting the powdered milk brought into the country recently by a politically important importer. He said a large shipment of powdered milk had recently arrived in Kathmandu that had been condemned for human consumption in Poland. The milk was reported to have come from cows that were fed on grass growing in the nuclear fallout zone near Chernobyl and was condemned. There weren't any buyers until, that is, this Nepali importer came along. Word leaked out that radioactive powdered milk was being brought into the country. News spread by word of mouth since such news would never be published. Nepali consumers boycotted the effected brands of powdered milk and the shops that sold them. The boycott had the perverse yet predictable effect of getting the said importer to successfully lobby to ban the import of all other brands of powdered milk. (Predictable according to the "Logic of Collective Action," see Mancur Olson.) It wasn't long before all of the shelves in the city were emptied of powdered milk. In a country where news was tightly controlled, it was impossible to verify the story, at least without testing equipment. The situation lasted for a couple of months; I'm not sure what precipitated an end to the standoff, but I guess that the government had to climb down in the face of strong citizen opposition.

Being a "Big Man" is often a license to pillage. For instance, there is a statue of a respected former King in Bhaktapur. A curious thing about this statue is that it is frequented by a small flock of sparrows. These birds fly around the statue's hands, which are pressed together in the traditional sign of prayer, salutation and reverence. Some of the locals believe that the soul of the King resides in the sparrows because over the years the hands' position has moved, folding as it were. One night a Big Man showed up with a small crane to haul the statue away, no doubt to fence it to disreputable art dealers. The town's police chief was alerted to what was happening. When he tried to prevent the statue from being pilfered, the Big Man introduced himself, undoubtedly expecting the police chief to back off. By this time, a crowd had formed, and people were becoming very upset at the sight of their beloved statue getting ready to be hauled away. The police chief stood up to the Big Man, explaining that if he let the statue be taken the crowd would kill him that night, whereas if he stopped the theft he would at least have that night to put his affairs in order before being hauled away the next day. Fortunately, the statue is still there. The Big Men in Nepal are similar to Big Men elsewhere.

Such egregious stories are told of Big Men in Eastern Europe, Africa, and Latin America. The Big Men aren't always men, but usually they are.

International development professionals typically work hard, play hard, and shop hard. They are a committed bunch, especially those providing humanitarian assistance. However, foreign aid programs are as good as the consultants (and volunteers) who do the work, and these "specialists" are a mixed bag. International consulting is difficult to get into: one must have experience to get work but can't get the work because they don't have experience. Once they are in, too many consultants get recycled, way passed their "use by" dates. As a development professional, I've hired many consultants: most do their best, some don't do anything. There was one consultant who checked into the hotel then checked into the bar and didn't leave. His team members did his work for him, yet he had a contract, so he got paid (though not the full amount). Sometimes consultants will go on assignments when they have no business being out of range of a hospital, yet they have their medical clearance. I sent one guy to Egypt to work on agricultural information systems. After his assignment ended, he decided to do some sightseeing. A few days later he was found in his room dead from a heart attack. Technically, my employer wasn't liable for him since he was no longer on assignment, but we covered the cost of shipping the body home. I called his father to extend our condolences and let him know how we would manage the situation; it wasn't much of a consolation. One diabetic consultant brought the wrong medicine with him and couldn't focus on his work; we got garbage and the client got annoyed. There was one sad case of a guy who had a bad reaction to his malaria prophylaxis. One possible side effect of mefloquine is paranoia and his assignment ended with his institutionalization. If a job requires a team versus and individual there can be personality clashes. These consultants are thrown together because of their special qualifications, and often they are meeting for the first time. It can be a recipe for conflict. Just because a chef has all the right ingredients doesn't mean the meal will be good. Then there are the "take advantage" types, who see an international assignment as an opportunity for a family vacation. International development assignments are usually over-ambitious and require 12 plus hours a day commitment to get the job done. Bringing the family along is a sure way of not delivering on one's responsibilities.

Development professionals' salaries aren't commensurable with grand acquisitiveness, but there are opportunities for small purchases. There are also missed opportunities, to whit an assignment in Armenia. I was there not long after its independence from the USSR, when the economy verged on collapse. The crisis had leveled off, but unemployment was high, and many people were left impoverished. As an indication of how bad the situation had become, an English-speaking taxi driver told me that before the USSR imploded he had been a neurosurgeon but had given this job up because driving a taxi paid better. What a waste of talent when a neurosurgeon has to drive a cab because he can earn more money! Armenia is full of history, confirmed every day by the view of Mount Ararat, Time's nearby sentinel. Not far from the capital, Yerevan, are ancient Roman temple ruins and some of the oldest monasteries of Eastern Orthodoxy. One afternoon in Yerevan I passed a liquor store window. Armenia produces wine and brandy, much of it of dubious palatability. During my stay I tried a 12-year-old brandy and was not impressed; the 24-year-old brandy was better. The liquor store window displayed a 36-year-old brandy in an exquisite crystal globe decanter. In those days brandy was my preferred drink. I went in and asked the shopkeeper how much the bottle would cost. She quoted a price that converted to US$35 – a bargain. Before the trip I was instructed to bring plenty of cash because credit cards were not accepted in most places, although the hotel took American Express. When I checked in the hotel clerk confirmed that I could use my American Express. I decided to stop quickly at the liquor store on my way to the airport to buy the brandy. The decanter alone was worth the price. The clerk who checked me out, however, was not the same clerk who checked me in. He told me that the hotel would not accept American Express. Despite much arguing and complaining, I had to pay cash and could no longer afford the brandy. After paying airport tax, I left the country with seven dollars in my pocket.

Donor aid programs often have complicated objectives. Sometimes these objectives are aligned with the interests of a country but sometimes objectives conflict. There can be strings attached to the money. An example was a project to support increased sales in the US of gum Arabic from northern Nigeria. Gum Arabic is a tree resin with unique properties: it's an emulsifier that keeps foods like salad dressing from separating in the bottle, it keeps colors whole when they are mixed in drinks such as colas, and it is a natural adhesive that permits sugar coating to stick on pills. Nigeria was an important producer of gum Arabic in the 1960s but had since seen a long-term decline in market share relative to other countries. By the 2000s, most of the world's gum Arabic came from Sudan's Darfur region. Nigerian exporters had not shipped gum Arabic to US buyers for several seasons due to reasons of poor hygienic quality, adulteration and unreliable supply. Our project addressed these problems. As I learned later, the project was driven by considerations that had little to do with Nigeria. Sudan, as a sponsor of terrorism, was a pariah state, yet US companies were buying their gum supplies from there. The State Department wanted to put an end to this situation and tried leaning on the importers. These companies got smart and hired a lobbyist as well as contributed to congressional campaigns. The benefiting Congressmen then leaned on the State Department to give the buyers time to develop relationships with new suppliers outside of Sudan. The State Department backtracked and teamed up with the US Trade Representative's Office to find a solution and, because of one particular company and a Nigerian Governor who had good connections, northern Nigeria was identified as an alternative source of gum.

We were unaware of all of these machinations when we were awarded the contract and treated it like any other value chain project. We worked with the Nigerians to identify their priorities; we determined from the US importers their basis of competition and then put together a training module to address these issues. Because illiteracy in northern Nigeria is so high the training manual that accompanied the module was heavily illustrated with a minimum of words. It was during this process that interferences started coming from certain US importers, the lobbyists, and USTR. USAID, the agency administering the money for this project, had its hands tied in the directions it gave us. We managed to maneuver through the political minefields and in the end successfully introduced improved practices for harvesting, handling and sorting, drying and transporting, and tracing gum origin to the vicinity of specific villages. Within six months of the project's end, Nigerian exporters were once again shipping gum to US buyers.

The project helped finance the purchase of laboratory equipment. The US Embassy sent an entourage to Jigawa State in the dry north to inaugurate the laboratory for testing the quality of the gum Arabic harvested there. Whether this equipment was ever put to its intended use, or any use at all, is an open question.

The ceremony was reminiscent of a circus, especially the first night when we were treated to a dance drama and magic show. At the next day's inauguration, the US Ambassador said his tediums along with the other dignitaries and we returned to Kano late in the afternoon. This ceremony was my first exposure to "praise givers" – an acceptable occupation in Nigeria. "Praise givers" do exactly what the title implies, they shout – or scream – out praises of whichever dignitary they are being paid to honor. It struck me as extraordinarily egotistical, but was perfectly acceptable in the milieu, minus the disruption factor. The Embassy entourage included several large Chevrolet Suburbans, accompanied by a Nigerian security contingent. One very heavy, armor-plated Suburban belonged to the US Ambassador. The Ambassador left in a faster car as he was in a hurry to return to Kano. I ended up riding in the Suburban with one of the USAID staff. We were cruising down the highway at a more than respectable speed when one of the tires blew, shredding off of the wheel. The vehicle began careening toward the concrete divider on the left side of the road. As he was trying to regain control of the vehicle the driver began yelling at the top of his lungs, "Oh Jesus! Oh Jesus! Oh Jesus!" though Allah was god in that area. That frightened us. However, the Lord answered his prayer as he managed to avoid the divider and finally brought the Suburban to a stop. It happened so fast that there wasn't time to panic; it was only after stopping that my heart caught in my throat. The US Embassy in Nigeria has a rule that no Embassy vehicle can be on the road after dark, which is a wise precaution in Nigeria where drunk driving and highway robbery are endemic. We made it to Kano just a bit after dark but driving at more reasonable speeds. I tip my hat to the trainers in Langley for their drivers' safety training program. The Embassy driver was specially trained there to drive an armored vehicle; a worthwhile investment.

Nigeria is an interesting economic case; it's a country rich in oil money yet wracked by direst poverty. Instead of investing their money in their country, wealthy Nigerians shelter it abroad. This seems surprising since one might expect high returns from investments in a place so far from the technology frontier. Yet the reality belies the opportunities. People park their money in offshore accounts because they fear that they will not able to borrow or generally have access to their money when it is needed; better to save for a rainy day than make a risky investment now and face potential illiquidity. In emerging economies in general, as one economist explains: because people can't transfer purchasing power from the future to the present, they store it from the past. In Nigeria, however, the storing from the past has more of an asset stripping quality to it. This is manifest in the lack of money for repairs or basic operation and maintenance expenses. Many times I've heard Nigerians say that "we don't have a maintenance culture," yet expatriate Nigerians invest in maintenance and repairs in their overseas ventures. I once stayed in a government-run hotel in Maidugari in Borno State.

The hotel was built in 1978 but one would have thought it was twenty years older. The hotel's condition was deplorable. The furniture, what furniture there was, looked like the original stuff, broken and dilapidated. Walls hadn't been painted, ceiling tiles were hanging down or missing, air conditioning didn't work, and on and on. The first night I stayed there a pipe burst somewhere between the ground and second levels and water began dripping from the ceiling. The staff put out buckets to catch the drips, but all this did was keep the floor from getting slippery. The next morning when I went downstairs the ceiling was still dripping, though now a whole section of ceiling tile had crashed to the floor from the water's weight. My colleague explained that the leak might not be fixed for a while since the hotel staff would have to submit a requisition for the money to hire a plumber. Sure enough, at day's end we returned to the hotel and the water still falling – not just dripping – from the ceiling. We sidetracked around the lobby and went to the restaurant. The water was finding its way everywhere. As we sat in the restaurant one of the long fluorescent light bulbs exploded, shattering glass all over the tables and diners, followed by a rush of water. Then the electricity blew. The elevators weren't working anyway, but even if they had been I would have taken the stairs. If the leak had been fixed right away the cost and damage would have been minimal, as it was when I checked out the hotel water had been shut off completely and not one repairman was in sight. Such is the responsibility that people feel for government-owned assets. As my colleague explained, even with a requisition the repair would have been substandard; either the money would not have been enough, the repairman unqualified, the budget to cover emergency expenses non-existent, or there wouldn't be money in the account. I disagree with the statement that Nigeria lacks a maintenance culture. I observed how obsessively people took care of their personal computers, for instance. No problems with maintenance there. Any assets belonging to the State or fixed assets from which the revenue could not be secured, except for over the very short term, were not well maintained. This lack of investment security – the risk to investors – has cost Nigeria greatly as foreign investors, except for the oil majors, steer clear of the country.

An altogether sadder trip was to Rwanda, a year after the genocide. I was there to put together a bid to monetize US commodities in the local market to raise money for UN programs. My colleague and I stayed at the infamous Hotel Rwanda. It was surreal. My dilapidated room was decorated blood red: the curtains, bedspread, sofa and chairs were all the same unnerving red color. Whether the room was decorated before the genocide or not I don't know. During our stay it was an ever-present reminder of the tragic events that had played out across the country. The entire three days we were there the same Joe Cocker song played on infinite loop. At first it was irritating, but after a while became part of the background after realizing that no one was going to change it or turn it off, or perhaps no one knew how. And perhaps the oddest thing was that the restaurant served really good French cuisine, including some of the finest croissants I've had on the continent. Outside the hotel gates it was easy to spot which houses had belonged to Tutsi families. They were burnt out. There was a quiet gloom about the city; people spoke in, very un-African, hushed tones. We walked to the USAID Mission offices. Outside the Mission was a plaque with the names of the Mission staff who had lost their lives. We lost the bid. The company that won ended up cocking up the job and cost the Government a fair amount of money.

Is there more important work than the fighting poverty in this era? Half the world's population lives in poverty. But what is the value of just decreasing poverty? Should life improve in quantity (more money) or in quality (better opportunities)? Our quality of life is what we believe it is. If quality of life is better because of a new car and a big house, then that is what a good quality of life is – to the individual. We get what we focus on, more or less.

After basic needs are met – there is disagreement about what needs are really basic – what then? Societal issues of "fairness," equality of opportunity, persist. Despite the views of some people, research on other primate species suggests that a sense of "fairness" is innate. The involuntarily poor may not be satisfied, just like the voluntary rich. Wealth and poverty are relative terms. "Society," that is, an ordered community, demands a balance. A culture of "instant gratification" is unlikely to bring such a balance. Our individual concern for "status" tips the balance across society. High-status individuals should be taxed for their status, their conspicuous consumption, for certainly their high-status taxes those who have lower status. Delayed gratification, voluntary deprivation, and cooperation are desirable in a society if for no other reason than their contribution to more equitable social outcomes.

I'm fortunate to have done interesting work; I can't imagine any other kind. Starting with an internship that morphed into a position at USAID, I became involved in projects to develop African agriculture. The brilliant economist of political markets, Professor Mancur Olson, author of the "Logic of Collective Action," hired me to work for him at the University of Maryland. We studied how long it took on average to start a business in Nepal, hoping to lay the groundwork for regulatory reform. The findings from this research were picked up by U.S. News & World Report magazine, which reported how it took over 700 days to formally register a business. In development it is crucially important to make decisions based on sound evidence. To highlight why such evidence is important, consider one of the burning issues of the day: are genetically modified organisms better or worse for the environment? First, it is necessary to frame the question correctly: better in terms of habitat loss? In terms of soil or air, water or some other factor? Consider the evidence. The chart below suggests that when cereal yields (quantity produced on a unit of land) rise above 4 metric tons a hectare the amount of farmland needed to produce it declines.

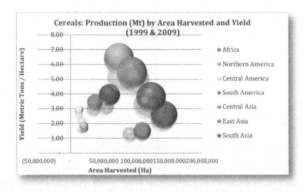

The transparent bubbles show 1999 production, the filled bubbles 2009. Increasing yields may be good for the habitat overall. But wait! What if we look at specific cereals crops, such as maize? Now we're not so sure. The chart below shows that despite increasing yields of maize the amount of land under production continues to increase. The reasons why this is the case ought to be looked at more closely, but famously include ethanol and other subsidies.

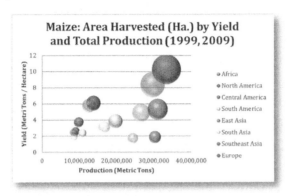

What about entirely different crops, not cereals? What relationship, if any, is there between increasing yields and the amount of land that farmers use? The chart below of roots and tubers (potatoes, cassava, etc.) suggests nothing. Yields haven't increased although the amount of land brought into production has increased considerably, especially in Africa. Still, the quantity of roots & tubers grown is small relative to cereals. Perhaps if Africans were to stop growing cassava and start growing maize and rice the fragile African habitat would be better off? This is a question that could be looked at and perhaps an experiment piloted, except that such piloting involves people's lives. There are no easy answers, and certainly there is no silver bullet for development.

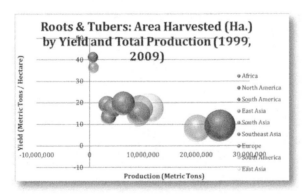

Arkansas, for the unfamiliar, is very rural and poverty in these areas is reminiscent of some developing countries. Small communities dot the landscape but in between are vast tracts of farm, forest and rangeland. Even the town centers appear impoverished, with so many shuttered storefronts. Wal-Mart has decimated the downtown districts of communities with sizeable populations. Morrilton, Arkansas, is an example. Wal-Mart moved in and drove most of the downtown stores out of business. I worked there at Winrock Foundation for a short time, which had its headquarters on nearby Petit Jean Mountain. This headquarters stands as a monument to the power of cash. Winthrop Rockefeller, one of the heirs to the Rockefeller fortune, built it to suit his fancy. On this remote mountaintop farm, he had two large barns built, a fishpond, boathouse, guest quarters, fitness center, and other assorted extravagances. The farmland blends into woodlands and wildlife is abundant. It was a pleasant place to stay. A small community of Winrock staff lived there in conditions resembling expatriate enclaves that one finds in cities in developing countries. The Mountain facilities have since been converted into a conference center. I was supporting the WIND Project, which was based in the Nusa Tengara Timor region of Indonesia. The project was installing wind-generators to pump water for irrigation and to power equipment for small enterprises. The work involved investment due diligence of citrus, berries, vegetables, agro-processing and fisheries value chains, which I modeled in detailed formulas on spreadsheets.

My faith in financial modeling of the type used for this project was shaken when the Asian financial crisis hit in 1998. Inflation and contingencies were calculated at the historical rate of increase of 15 percent annually. When the value of the Rupiyah plunged from 1,250 to 12,500 to the US dollar all of the built-in assumptions and projections became meaningless. There was no way that the investments would ever pay for themselves at the new exchange rate, and the sky-rocketing costs of parts for maintenance might mean the equipment would sit idle after the first need for repair. The Asian financial crisis should have served as a warning to financial planners of sub-prime mortgages, who likewise miscalculated their worst-case scenarios.

Circling back to earlier comments, life in multinational firms is seldom secure. Multinationals buy, merge, divest and close businesses so regularly that one loses track of what business lines they are in. People are transitory, but the firm goes on. Yet people work inordinately hard and are generally rewarded well for their efforts. Cold, hard calculations rule decision making; if they didn't there wouldn't be a business to employ anyone. Corporate cultures are unique and in multinationals as in much smaller firms there are strong bonds of camaraderie among employees and with the firm. In the multinational where I worked people would argue and, occasionally, fight with each other, even getting into shouting matches, but they were famously able to leave it behind at the office and go for a drink afterwards. There was even a culture of "leaving it behind." There the "development" issues, which had been my life, were turned upside down in the glare of investor interests. Developing countries were either "emerging markets" or little discussed. This perspective threw new light on why poor countries are poor, why China succeeds despite its lousy institutions, how to recognize opportunities, and the interrelationship between financial capital and political capital. For a multinational, scale is essential. With scale, new economies become possible. Profit rules and profitability does not have a distant horizon.

Fortune has seen me work for organizations to which my interests align. Now I find myself again in Washington, DC, working for an organization with a mission coinciding with my own. To do the work that one enjoys, you must have the vision – see the reality – know your interests. Circumstances will align, your relationships and networks will facilitate the necessary contacts, and the vision becomes reality. Look to yourself if your situation hasn't turn out as hoped. To know why, look to your thoughts, desires, fears, aspirations and habitual responses; they may be getting in the way. When you don't get your desired results, there is an underlying reason. The universe is made of responsive stuff; it rushes to fill a void. Most of us must work for a living, to support our loved ones and ourselves. I find my work interesting, but my profession is not who I am – not "me." People tire quickly of talking about their jobs or of listening to others discuss their careers. I've discussed my career to make a couple of points, first, about economic development generally and, second, that our interests and desires bring about our circumstances. Difficulties arise when our interests and desires have become routine, repetitive, and lead to circumstances with almost no volition on our parts. Without volition, being impelled, people find themselves in unwanted circumstances. We have all said, "but I didn't want that!" How we interpret our circumstances to ourselves will attract our experiences to us. There is a certain inevitability to our lives.

CHAPTER 10

"IDIOSYNCRATIC" MEANS A "PRIVATE MIXTURE." Whether we like to accept this reality or not, we are all a mixture of the ideas and beliefs that are in circulation in a society, trends of thought, tastes and preferences in fashion and music, etc., etc. What is private is how we personally mix these elements. We borrow and choose characteristics from the people we meet, or follow, the places we go and the things we come into contact with. "Thought" is a system common to all humanity and the notion of "mixture" should suggest that our thoughts are not our own, at least not originally, and then we mix them up – idiosyncratically. There are few original thoughts, and even fewer original ideas. Evidence suggests there are some traits to which we are genetically pre-disposed, such as a penchant towards violence or addiction, which may influence which currents in our environment most attract our attention. This is hardly an original observation, but for a coherent assessment of our real situation it is necessary to constantly be aware of this fact.

The Nepalese do not see themselves as Indian, Hindu yes, in the Terai and hills, but not Indian. The Nepali language, in certain respects, is a less modern language than Hindi, with its liberal sprinkling of Arabic and Englishisms. Linguists say that Nepali is closer to the ancient Sanskrit than Hindi. Nepalese are distinctive culturally and are proud of it. Formerly, the men wore the traditional hat – a "topi." A Nepali "topi" resembles the white and black hats that one sees Nehru wearing in pictures, but much more colorful. The colors and patterns can be downright outrageous, sporting large purple, orange and black diamond shapes, for instance. Sadly, topis have fallen out of style. Many Nepalese are derisive of Indians, although from the Indian perspective Nepal is a cultural backwater. One Nepali limerick goes: Dharma, karma, dhada ma / dhoti choina lardho ma. Translated very roughly this means: Cosmic order is in the hills / men don't cover their genitals with dhotis (a "dhoti" being the traditional white cotton cloth that Indian men tie around the waist). Nepalese laugh when they hear this limerick and say that a Nepali freak must have been made it up, which was the case. Nepalese distinguish themselves from Indians in other ways. They have a separate caste system; Newars, the ethnic group native to Kathmandu Valley, even have their own distinct caste system. Hill culture tribal influences are very strong, often inspired by Tibetan Buddhism and Lamaism. The hill tribes were once the strongest cultural element in Nepal and dominated the country, though none ever conquered it. The Hindu influence crept up slowly from the south into the hills over generations. A Japanese doctoral student wrote a dissertation on the spread of Indian influence in Nepal. His conclusion was that the Indians gained power – land – through credit. Caste Hindus from the south would arrive in a hill community, secure some land and open a shop, selling matches, utensils and other goods that hill tribes – Rais, Limbus, Thamangs, Gurungs, Maggars – found useful. These people didn't have cash to pay since a cash economy was largely absent. So, the shopkeepers would give them "credit" to pay for the goods. After this credit accumulated, or the debt depending on one's perspective, there came a day of reckoning when the shopkeeper would demand payment. The borrowers' main asset was land, which then became the payment. Eventually this method of obtaining land served to impoverish many hill peoples and entrench a Hindu caste aristocracy. While this dissertation's findings may be unknown to illiterate tribes-people, their animosity towards the Caste Hindus is not so obscure.

Some people are disenfranchised, while others have never been franchised. In my Peace Corps village was an idiot. He arrived one day, no one knew from where. What drew him to Bahadurgunj remained a mystery. His IQ was very low: he could speak in words but not in sentences, although he understood more than he could say. He may have been my age, in his early- to mid-twenties and was large by local standards but was afraid of almost everything. He was as quick to cry as he was to laugh. He had no place to stay and no one took him in. Instead, he found shelter on a porch across the street from where I lived, not far from the temple. In a more affluent, or more compassionate, place that had mental health facilities, he might have found some peace and belonging. The dark night, or dark nightmares, would cause him to scream for hours at a time, robbing neighbors of sleep. Thunder and lightning would bring terror and I thought he wouldn't survive to morning. He was often teased and sometimes beaten, mostly by people who seemed beaten down themselves. He had bad scars, suggesting an awful past. And then one day he was gone, same as he had come, no one knew where. People come and go, if not always so capriciously.

In a now bygone era, as dusk fell in Kathmandu, one could witness the nightly migration of gigantic fruit bats, with wingspans up to six feet. These fruit bats lived in the heart of the city, roosting in the trees around the royal palace, sleeping most of the day. Tourists stopped to gape at them from below, while watching their steps as the sidewalks were white with their droppings. At dusk they left their perches, circling the palace and its surroundings. As darkness deepened they began to fly south in squadrons. There are, or were, so many of them that one could watch them flying overhead for half-an-hour until they finally disappeared beyond the high hills surrounding the Kathmandu Valley. They would venture down to the lower hills and the Terai where they foraged on fruit and other batty delicacies before returning to their perches in Kathmandu again before dawn. Every now and then you could see one of these giants suspended from an electrical wire, fried. Stopping to rest, they found a permanent roost. The tightness of their death grip would keep them clinging for weeks until the skeletal carcass fell to the ground.

During the cold season in Kathmandu one might find Peace Corps Volunteers at Boudhanath Stupa where they would by sipping "thungbas." Boudhanath is a very large Tibetan Buddhist temple that was once on the outskirts of Kathmandu though now the suburbs surround it. On Saturdays especially, Boudha (for short) was a popular hangout for those in-the-know. Near the Stupa were many small shops that served food, sold trinkets, jewelry, and other goods. Boudha's picture appears on many Nepal postcards and in travelogues. Racks of prayer wheels surround the Stupa, with its giant rounded dome; pilgrims march by spinning the wheels as they circumnavigate the Stupa's perimeter. Tibetan pilgrims can be seen prostrating themselves on their course around the Stupa, resembling inchworms as their feet move into position where their hands had been when they lay prone. There are stories of Tibetan pilgrims crossing the length of Tibet in this manner to atone for some sin or to otherwise make their peace with higher powers. In back of one of the small shops was a little courtyard, paved in flagstone, with wooden benches lining the walls. A prayer flag stood in the middle of the courtyard. It was a pleasant place to sit and drink thungba for hours, chatting and casually whiling the day away. Thungba is unique. Millet, the main ingredient, is fermented in a special way, spread onto a mat several inches thick, hard yeast is crumbled then sprinkled on top of the mash. After drying awhile, the millet is packed away in a warm place for at least several days. The longer it ferments the stronger it becomes. Thungba is served traditionally in a large wooden mug and imbibed through a tall bamboo straw; the straws are plugged at one end and just above the plug there are three short slits on the sides. The slits allow the liquid to pass through the millet. The fermented red millet is packed into the mug to overflowing, and a few grains of rice sprinkled on the top (signifying something). When served, boiling hot water is poured over the millet and it must be allowed to steep for several minutes before it is consumed. Thungba's taste is somewhat reminiscent of a mix of warm beer and hot-spiced wine, but much more satisfying, especially on a cold day. When the millet is strongly fermented, three or four refills gives a nice buzz. Several thungbas can get you very drunk. As happens, tradition has sunk with time and cost. Instead of being served in large wooden mugs, most shops now serve thungba in plastic containers, detracting from the cultural experience though still good for its purpose. There were mornings when we went to Boudha for thungba and found that day had slipped into evening.

There are, or were, such hangouts tucked away all over Kathmandu, which tend to appeal to certain classes of customer. Some spots attracted mainly the mountaineer set, others harbored old beatniks and hippies, relics of a bygone era, many places catered to trekkers, some places attracted professional development types, not to mention the different places where Tibetans, hill Nepalese and Indians would frequent. Kathmandu's beatniks found their way there in the mid-60s before there was a hippie trail. Drugs were their thing. By the 1980s some of them (all men) had been in the subcontinent for over 20 years. Occasionally they would recite poetry or play music in the "Tea House." "Four-Finger Johnny" was a local favorite poet. Attending such events was a step back in time, hearkening to Alan Ginsberg circa 1960. One favorite hangout was the Pumpernickel Restaurant. The Pumpernickel attracted a diverse crowd from many different backgrounds, though "world traveler" types predominated. In late afternoon, about the time the bats would start their nightly journeys, a group of Pumpernickel regulars gathered. Some of my tightest bonds were with this group of disparate friends. There was Michi, a Hari Krishna refugee from West Germany, Indu, a physicist/astrologer/translator from Goa who came to Kathmandu to study ancient manuscripts, Jimmy, a Nepali who had struck it rich on Freak Street with a pie shop but now devoted his life to art, Willie, a Nepali keyboard player who was part of the local rock 'n roll scene, and many others who came and went.

Kathmandu was a "scene" in the 1980s populated by characters too unusual for fiction. The city was a South Asia magnet, drawing the intrepid, the religious, the concerned, the curious, the drug-addled, the shoppers and a host of others. When in Kathmandu I frequented the Pumpernickel, often going with Michi. We shared a house in what was then the northern outskirts of the city, in Maharajgunj near Ring Road, along with other West German transplants; I was the sole American. Michi was a creature of the Frankfurt "underground" who had drifted through Berlin, northern Italy and other hip cities in Western Europe. He survived as a chef – and a damn good one. As Michi explained, he was living a hard-edged lifestyle when one day in Italy he saw a group of Hari Krishnas parading down the street. He was so captivated that he joined them on the spot. He applied himself to learning about Krishna, absorbing the Bhagavad Gita, yoga and vegetarianism; he traveled to Kathmandu with them to reach the source, absorbing all he could of Hinduism. The Haris brought disillusionment, though not with Krishna to whom he became ever more devoted. The Haris were too regimented and Michi had an extraordinarily wild side, experimenting with hallucinogens and other mind-altering substances. He scraped by, picking up odd jobs as an electrician, chef, dobie, puppy-sitter. To save money, he cut his own hair; any time a strand looked too long or out of place he would simply chop it off with a knife. What he lacked in a keen intellect he compensated for with emotional sensitivity. Michi overstayed his Nepal visa by 2 years. When he finally decided to leave he had to pay a counterfeiter to a forge a visa so that Passport Control wouldn't arrest him on the way out. Because he was genuinely likeable but down-on-his-luck his friends were quite willing to help him out financially. Once he was puppy-sitting a couple of Lhaso Apsos for a friend who intended to smuggle them into Berlin where they would fetch a good price. He fed them some raw eggs – big mistake. They died of food poisoning the next day. This was Michi's nadir; he spun into darkness but not without light at tunnel's end. A German astrologer once predicted this low point and told him the approximate date his life would change. And what would you know? Within a couple of weeks, he met the woman who changed his life and returned to Germany.

Indu was a native of Goa, born into an English-speaking family; his father raised him in the classical Sanskrit tradition while his mother taught him Malayalam. According to Indu there are pockets in India where Sanskrit is still spoken. Indu graduated with a master's degree in physics, studying astronomy. But his astronomical studies introduced him to astrology, and he got hooked. He migrated to Kathmandu to study some ancient Sanskrit texts that he had learned about. Soon after arriving, he met his wife, a French sitar player who came to Kathmandu to master the instrument. Indu made a decent living translating rare Sanskrit texts into English. He said there were many private collections in Nepal with documents that had not been translated before. He combined this income with money earned from doing astrological readings. Indu told interesting stories about the predictive powers of Hindu astrology. He relayed an incident from his apprenticeship. As he described it, a man walked through the door and his guru told the man to sit down, then the master cast a chart. In Hindu astrology, each new event can be treated as a birth and a chart cast from that moment. His guru told the man that he had come to see him about a piece of missing jewelry and that he would find it in a particular location. The man went to search for the treasure, returning a short while later to thank the guru. Indu had no explanation for how this was possible, saying that it was basically "magic." Many trekkers came to Nepal seeking some kind of enlightenment and I often had inquiries from them about where they could meet a monk, yogi, astrologer, palmist or the like. I introduced some of them to Indu. Afterwards I would learn from them how uncannily accurate his psychological analysis was, as well as their personal histories. I met Indu in the same way; he did my Western and Indian horoscopes while I was in Peace Corps and we remained friends. That was a long time ago and since then many of his predictions have proven remarkably accurate.

Jimmy grew up in the KathmanduValley – a self-made man, Nepali style. He came from an impoverished background, growing up in a large household. Jimmy found his way to Kathmandu about the time the hippie trail was in full vogue. He found work in one of the small pie shops on Freak Street, starting as a cleaning boy and eventually becoming a manager. He picked up English. When he learned how to run a pie shop and satisfy customers he pooled together some money and started his own restaurant. The restaurant was a success, becoming a famous hash house and opium den at a time when drugs were still legal in Nepal. While running the restaurant he met a number of Western artists and fell in love with drawing and painting. When the public sale of drugs was prohibited he sold the restaurant for a tidy sum and took to art with a passion. As he described, he began with simple sketches and added to his technique, seeking advice when opportunity arose, until he became proficient. One day he had an epiphany and decided that he would chronicle, with ink and paper, life in Kathmandu. He began to draw scenes from the city including its temples, street life, and environs. The Kathmandu that he chronicled has long disappeared, vanishing with the arrival of democracy and Maoism. His drawings captured mundirs and stupas, many of which were destroyed by the earthquake or even earlier. Jimmy set out on a pilgrimage, continuing his mission as chronicler across the Nepali hills, an artistic epic that took him several years. All of his brushes, pencils and paper he loaded into his backpack. Because art supplies wouldn't be accessible he brought some small sketchbooks. He switched to watercolor as a more mobile medium. I caught up with Jimmy in Kathmandu not long after he finished his mission and saw his paintings. They were small renditions of Nepali hill life; a life both idyllic and destitute, and in many places a life that was to change with the Maoist insurgency.

JIMMY

These brief character sketches hopefully give a glimpse of Kathmandu's society in the 1980s. There were so many other characters. Gunther, a real German underground figure was making a new life for himself as a hotelier. Reiner, a news cameraman, had shot newsreel across the subcontinent and had gotten shot himself several times, with bullets, for his efforts. Mike, from one of the very first group of Peace Corps Volunteers in Nepal, had been in Kathmandu since the early 60s and had a restaurant. Baba, a certain type of saddhu, though he wasn't a real saddhu and Baba wasn't his real name, was a low intensity drug dealer who dressed in dreads and trekking gear. There were a dozen other trekking guides like me who hustled for a living, just because they liked life there better than anywhere else. This unusual time and place has been described in a few scattered magazines and newspaper articles, but the vitality is lacking. A society is made up of people and the material I've read was mostly written by journalists, generally don't get to know their subjects well.

World Travelers have time but no money; International Tourists have money but no time. These classifications were valid in the 1980s; working in the travel industry, I would hear marketing types discuss "segmentation strategies" for these classes of clients. Companies catered to each segment. The world traveler types traveled on local transportation with their backpacks, getting around as economically as possible, often with the objective of making their money last until want of it brought their adventure to an end. I left the Peace Corps as a world traveler with $3,000 in travelers' checks, making it through five countries in as many months before running out in Berkeley, California. Key to a world traveler's strategy is remaining in one place. Moving around, one spends more money; staying in one place and exploring it thoroughly is more economical. International tourists go with bags on wheels, stay in nicer hotels, move around a lot, and leave within a very short span, usually a week or two. These two travel segments have given way to a broader range of niche marketing segments. Now there are segments of outdoor adventure travelers, young families, backpackers, enthusiasts (birds, bikes, babes), indulgence, etc. Himalayan trekkers came in two varieties, now they come less frequently thanks to the politics. These two varieties were the pre-paid groups, who traveled with guides, tents, food, and everything else they might need; and the backpackers who carried what they brought and stayed in local trekkers' lodges. When asked, the locals said that they preferred the backpackers. Even though these world travelers didn't spend a lot, they spent at least some money in the villages along the route. Pre-paid groups often didn't spend any money locally. There are some economic studies of the effects of these two types of travelers on regional economic growth and in relation to sustainability. International tourists require lots of imported goods (food, fuel, furnishings) while world travelers make do with mainly locally available accruements. Sadly, the evidence for growth is on the side of the international tourists, except in the most remote areas where backpackers make a greater contribution to local economies.

But whether international tourists or world travelers, on trekking trails they can all fall prey to leeches. Wherever Hell is, it is full of them. In the West when someone calls another person a "leech" it is unlikely that they do so from actual experience, and so really cannot appreciate what the word "leech" truly means. Hungry for blood, they hide in damp and covered places, foliage, and ferns, near waters' edge, until they sense animal heat. Their sensors are at one end and they balance themselves on their other end, looking like little fingers in motion. A friend one time stepped off of the trail to take a dump, unwittingly walking into a leech field. I heard him scream and crashing out of the brush, his pants not yet all the way up, pulling at leeches that were inching up his body, hunting for flesh. They will attack an animal in the water. A leech infected one PCV when he went to the local borehole for some fresh water; it fixed itself to his ankle and gorged on his blood. During the monsoon especially they would wait around the borehole's edge. When they've gorged they will grow three or four times thicker from all of the blood they've sucked in. After ridding himself of the leech he staunched the wound for a long time to stop the bleeding; leeches excrete an anti-coagulant. Within days his wound became twice its normal size before eventually succumbing to antibiotics.

The most serious leech infection I saw was on an Australian who was trekking the Annapurna Circuit. He was very far from any medical help and the pain from the infection forced him to stay put. Seeing his leg made my stomach churn because the infection had turned into nasty colors. Where we met there was no sending for help. We gave him medicine and advised him to start back, no matter how painful it was. By the looks of his leg if he didn't get help sooner he wouldn't be able to later. However, he was committed to completing the Circuit. In a personal unpleasant experience while a guest in someone's house, during a night of unpleasant dreams, I awoke in the morning noticing that the hair on the back of my head felt unusual. Touching my hand to my head and bringing it to my eyes, I saw that it was covered in blood. Looking down at my sleeping bag, I saw a pool of blood and, lying in it, a fat leech. I washed the sleeping bag, but the bloodstain never came entirely clean.

And so, leeches are an apropos metaphor for a certain type of person who sucks their victims of money, empathy, or attention.

Do you recall what you were doing when you heard some piece of tragic news: where were you when you heard about 9/11? The Wall fell? John Lennon's assassination? Or Princess Diana's car crash? While these were landmark events in the West, other societies mark their lives by their own events. The day Nelson Mandela walked free from prison was such an event in South Africa, marking the lives of an entire continent. The day a lone man stood down a tank in China. The day Fidel Castro came to power in Cuba. The day Suharto fell from power in Indonesia. In South Asia, the day Indira Ghandi was assassinated by her Sikh bodyguards was such a day. Indira was one of the more spiritually attuned political figures of the Twentieth Century – a seeming contradiction – after lifting marshal law and suffering defeat at the polls she was re-elected later with the slogan "Indira is Indira." On the day she was murdered I was in the Nepal Terai town of Taulihawa. Taulihawa, the present-day site of the ancient kingdom of Kapilavastu, is more Indian than Nepali. The populace speaks a Hindi dialect, marriages tend to be across border, and societally the elites are much more influenced by what happens in India than they are by what happens in Nepal. In 1984, the main roads in and out of Taulihawa all connected to India to the south and during the monsoon season it was difficult to travel to the north, which was accomplished in a rickety wooden boat that was typically overburdened with people, animals and goods. I heard the news about Indira while I was walking from my boss's office to the bus stop a kilometer away; it was obvious that something was seriously amiss. There was an electric murmur buzzing through the streets, from shop to shop, radios were blaring out news and not playing Bollywood tunes. There was an occasional sound of wailing coming from disparate locations and teary-eyed, zombified people walking in shock on the streets. Within that one-kilometer I learned what had happened, but the details were all confused. It wasn't until I had reached my post in Bahadurgunj that I got a clearer story. As seems to be the case with such momentous events, there is a cacophony of news and speculation, then, as more information accumulates, the story emerges. This story sent shivers through this part of Nepal since a significant number of Sikhs lived there. The days after were filled with tension, as fear of bloody retaliation was high.

What would happen today if Muslims assassinated Modi? The scale of communal and revenge killing can hardly be imagined.

Human communication is so much more than words: it is the gesture, the tone, the glance, the look. Yet it is also the intimated meaning, even the atmosphere. Who hasn't walked into a room and noticed immediately the "tension in the air?" We sense, or intuit, others' intentions. I was having tea one day with another PCV in a local tea shop. The proprietor's daughter and her friend were teasing us. The girls were not more than four years old and could not speak Nepali, let alone understand English. We began to tease them back. The daughter, an unattractive but playful and intelligent girl, had been the most persistent. I looked at her and said teasingly in English, "you're ugly." With that she covered her face in her hands and ran away. My friend and I were flabbergasted; could she really have understood? The answer is yes, especially young and impressionable children. We can often sense what others are saying or thinking, though we don't understand the words; we have this capability, or intuition. Like any muscle that is not used, after a while the capability atrophies. Yet children are resilient, and in a largely rural, agrarian society their sense of power is qualitatively different than that of children in urban settings. I was once astonished to see a small boy, no more than three or four, with a slight stick in his hand, lead on a rope one of the largest water buffalo I have seen. With a flick of his great head the buffalo could have dashed the child lethally to the ground, yet the giant animal followed subserviently wherever the boy led. A ton of brute muscle bent to the child's will. A city kid would not be so emboldened. Nowadays city kids find their sense of power in the use of technology, though in this they are as dependent as they are empowered.

The "gods" of antiquity are still with us; now we might call them "higher consciousness." Our bodily organs are conscious: from the stomach's instinctive consciousness reminding us of mealtime, to the heart's heartaches and all too real pain when broken. We admit consciousness of cells, which demonstrate alertness, fatigue, memory, and adaptiveness. Yet, we – our scientists and specialists – won't admit the possibility of higher consciousness, except, perhaps, the Devil, who is of course in the details. If our instruments can't measure "higher consciousness" then they mustn't exist. Really? What instrument will measure such consciousness?

What will constitute proof? Some *places* are conscious in ways we can scarcely comprehend, though sensitive folks can feel their awareness. Ideas have a consciousness of their own and can possess a people, e.g., Nazism. Is this so strange? Our use of language admits this; "she was possessed by an idea." Groups of animals and plants have shared consciousness; a flock of birds or a swarm of gnats exhibit group consciousness in ways that differ from their individual consciousness. Groups of people are conscious, too, the whole of the group being greater than the sum of the individual parts: societies, companies, families, towns, streets. Nature is a conscious being, but her consciousness is so alien to our modes of perception that we aren't even aware of her awareness of us, through us.

The Earth is a higher consciousness, with an unimaginable immensity of awareness, with organs of perception beyond human understanding. The Sun is an aware being. The solar system may be one being in an ecosystem of like and unlike beings that comprise the galaxy. What we see in our astronomical photographs are snapshots of stars, moments in time, and we fail to appreciate that they hurtle through space at immense speeds, varying in their forms, colors, and – who has ears to hear? – sounds. Cannot the starry worlds form ecosystems richer and more diverse than our animal kingdom on Earth? "Higher consciousness" doesn't necessarily mean "better" but such consciousness is different, perceiving not through senses (as we know them) but through shared intuition or other organs of sense that we do not apprehend. These consciousnesses would seem as "gods" to peoples who had the capacity to be aware of them. The problem for many peoples, as always, was, and is, the tendency to anthropomorphize, ascribing human characteristics because the reality is incomprehensible. So begins the slippery slope to superstition and "intelligent design." We pray to GOD to intervene in the world on our behalf but let us suppose that there are intermediate consciousnesses between the God we pray to and us. While not suggesting that we pray to possible intermediaries, what do we have a right to expect? It may be that GOD, even if GOD wanted to, could not intervene in our lives directly but only through the conditions governing the world that GOD created.

We will attract to us that which we seek, a condition of God in our world, so that we do indeed create our own realities. Mostly, we create them in mechanical ways, out of habit of thought and action and reflex, which are stronger than hopes and prayers because they bear the weight of routine. Life's highly responsive conditions are thus rendered dead by our mundane ways of living.

We each, to come back to an earlier point, make our own realities, but we do so in ways that we often are hardly aware of. Each thought suggests the nature of our reality and shades our perceptions. The fleeting self-suggestion becomes habitual and persistent. And this brush colors all of life. Sometimes the results can be very specific in a most un-coincidental way. For instance, my wife used to say how she wanted to have twins, a boy and a girl and get it over with all at once. She got her wish, which I had predicted when we first met. Years earlier I took up palm reading, as much for conversation as for prognostication. We met when I was her trek guide, and, for fun, I read her palm. Besides predicting twins, I told her that she would meet the man of her dreams soon, if she hadn't already. Talk about a self-fulfilling prophecy! My interest in palmistry was sparked by a visit to a professional palmist in Kathmandu, whose character analysis and predictions of my future have proven uncanny. My wife always said she had to pay extra for an American guide, and twenty-five years later I was still working it off. The day we met, we toured the Tibetan refugee camp that was then in Kathmandu, stopping there to see Tibetan rugs being made. An attractive, young Tibetan woman was selling them at the tour's end. I stopped to look, and she asked if "my wife" would be interested in buying one. I replied that I didn't have a wife and that I had just met this woman that morning. The Tibetan woman corrected me, suggesting I was wrong – that she was my wife. I assured her, wrongly as it turned out, that this wasn't the case.

People, places and things exist for us in networks of relationships; people, places and things being tangible while relationships are intangible. Relationships are particular and general: there is this tree, and there are all of the trees that came before and those yet to come; trees that are here and those elsewhere. The point is that a single object has infinite relationships. We touch infinity at every moment. A simple Spirograph, a child's toy, can be an illustration. A Spirograph design has circles within circles, lines crossing lines, around a center point, and can be reduced to an algorithm. So also are the networks of relationships within which we live. That wise man, Krishnamurti, said, "To be is to be related." Networks of relationships, circling in Time as they do, might be depicted by a three-dimensional Spirograph: but what computer can decipher this algorithm?

The greatest mystery, Time, the physicist David Bohm described as the "order of succession." Time does not stretch out in an infinite line with the past in one direction and the future in the other. Our lives turn in circles; past, present and future turn upon themselves at every moment. The ancients often described the life in time as ascending or descending in spirals. From another perspective our lives in time resemble a Spirograph drawing, with recurring circles intersecting each other at many, many points. The 'you' that we see – *now* – is the window to your soul. Earlier I mentioned that our lives recur. We are born, and we die, birth and death being one event. There are some moments, similar to the experience of déjà vu (seeing again), that are not moments of seeing again; rather, the time is the same, the moment is the same. At these moments our recurring lives come together in one point; all these lives are simultaneously all accessible.

Such moments drift away, leaving us amazed, our minds not fleet enough to keep pace, nor able to grasp their import. But we are hard-wired sensually to the present. And so, at the age of 20 I find myself standing in front of the bamboo-screened closet, aware of the again-ness of the moment, or later in the Ukraine, as the cycles of recurrence momentarily converge, then separate. We are especially aware of recurring moments whenever we face choices that have significant consequences. We feel other probable realities. When recurrences converge in eternity they can be sensed physically, and the body can come to recognize these moments. The brain suddenly registers a moment when channels come together, as though the nerves carry separate signals that jump the same synapse all at once. At a molecular level, maybe our ears hear sounds, or our nose scents smells that stimulate an "action potential" that come from intersecting lives to a point on a single nerve. Normally we seem to perceive one time at a time, and our life is lived in successive moments. Now suppose that our lives, 70 or 80 years, are a single moment of perception for the Sun. Seen all at once from the Sun's perspective, our lives don't stretch out in time, they are a brief spark, the whole life perceptible in a single instant. But why suppose?

GOD is a concept, put together by our thoughts. GOD, as a concept, is very much alive as Allah, Brahma/Vishnu/Shiva, the Absolute, the One, etc. The Truth is that these concepts spring from the imagination. Yet, there is something, from which all emerges and to which everything returns, a ground from which springs a stream.

CHAPTER 11

CONSCIOUSNESS IS BOTH EXTRAORDINARILY SIMPLE and immensely complex. We can't control consciousness, it just happens. Yet there isn't an accepted scientific explanation for it. So, what is consciousness? The Economist magazine published a survey on the human brain, which sparked Letters to the Editor from scientists. One letter captured the issue nicely: "We don't know what consciousness is; there is not even an agreed definition. And then, how is consciousness to be studied? We don't know how. The scientific, reductionist approach is inadequate as consciousness may be an emergent property; consciousness may not be reducible to its component molecules."

Undoubtedly, science will try to explain consciousness – on its own terms. This explanation may be something to the effect that consciousness is "signal transduction of highly complex biochemical reactions." Seek and ye shall find. If in this pursuit of explanations scientists reach a grand theory of consciousness, science will face the foundation of its own claims. Science explains phenomena in terms of "time." But what if consciousness transcends time? Whatever science may "prove" about consciousness will apply only as a statement of cause and effect. However, if consciousness transcends time, it transcends cause and effect. Ultimately, this is the limitation of the scientific approach to the study of consciousness.

Any observant person can note that consciousness varies in its quality; it can be attentive and focused, vague and impressionistic, incisive, automatic, slow or accelerated. Particularly, we are all familiar with the automatic quality of consciousness, we spend so much of our lives in it; we say that we were "on autopilot." Autopilot is a very apropos description of a reflexive, conditioned quality of consciousness. Whether autopilot mode is an inevitable aspect of consciousness I don't know, but it exists. Autopilot mode is not necessarily harmful and, in fact, may be quite useful. We talk about going through our "morning routines" – we shower, eat breakfast, brush our teeth, dress – and the next thing we know we are out of doors and at work. When we are on "autopilot," we may drift off into imaginations or fantasies, all the while going through our routines. Such automatic behavior points to another feature of consciousness: that its quality can contract as well as expand. We use phrases such as "it felt like an eternity" or "the time flew," telling us not so much about time as about our perception of it. We know that these differences are differences in the quality of consciousness and not its quantity. Our clichés are marvelous indicators of our states of consciousness; we say, "I wasn't paying attention," "I lost my focus," "it was like I just woke up," and so on.

When we concentrate, focus, our consciousness contracts, narrows. In moments of insight and new understanding we are aware that it expands. Attention, consciousness's awareness of itself, or proprioception, to use the language of science, is the starting point. Attention is always NOW, not in the future or the past. "Thought" (linguistically a past participle), our whole system of thought, is the past meeting the future NOW. The "present" for us is seldom really present – it is the past. I'm not referring here to thinking; thinking is always active and in the present while thought is passive, originating from the past – a reflex. Through this system of thought we divide ourselves into two: into "I" and "me," object and subject. This "me" is put together through time by thought; "me" is whatever we have thought about ourselves. Internally, "I" observes what is happening to "me." By separating ourselves in this way, we divide into two (or more) what is one, whole consciousness process. And we extend this division through time, starting from a very young age and lasting a lifetime. The religious impulse is to expand consciousness, to unify it. Religion should be the science of the expansion of consciousness. Instead, what we see the world over is that religion is a narrowing, fragmenting factor within consciousness.

Kapilavastu was named for the Indian sage Kapila, who was an important figure in Shamkhya philosophy; Kapilavastu was also the ancient home of Śuddhodana, whose kingdom, named after the sage, was the birthplace of Siddhartha, the Buddha. I lived in Kapilavastu while I was in the Peace Corps. When I lived there, the District was still mostly forested, extensive clearing had begun only recently. Nepal's East-West Highway passed through it, though at that time the bridge at Butwal was still under construction and one normally had to cross over on foot; although, when the river was low enough, buses would drive through. The power lines were just being installed alongside the highway; otherwise, the only electricity in the District extended north into Nepal from the Indian grid. Kapilavastu is now a backwater and the people who live there are referred to as "Madeshis," being mostly of Indian origin, or else they are Tharu, the indigenous tribe. The Madeshis speak their own, difficult, local dialect. One of Nepal's few significant Muslim populations also resides in western Kapilavastu, near Bahadurgunj and Krishnanagar. The border at Krishnanagar is closed to tourists, but the locals, of whom I was accepted as one, crossed freely. The District capitol, Taulihawa, was cut off from the rest of the District by a river, except during the dry season when vehicles could cross. Because of Taulihawa's remoteness and the difficulty I had in reaching it, I saw my boss, the Agriculture District Officer, just a few times during my entire service.

The East-West Highway in Kapilavastu passes through some beautiful places where the ancient Terai forests reach up to the road's edge (or at least used to). The jungle was very dense in spots and one could sometimes see quite unusual animals. In one place the jungle opens out into an ancient streambed that has eroded remarkably. There is an indescribable quality to the place. The area's inhabitants sense it too; they will sometimes go there to spend pleasant hours, though there is nothing in particular to do or see.

Once on my way back to the village, I passed through this place when "it" happened the first time. I felt a strange sensation near my solar plexus. It felt like two electrical wires were brushing lightly against each other, giving off prickly shocks whenever they would touch. This sensation lasted for a few minutes, causing some minor discomfort and a slight sense of exultation. Then the sensation passed.

Some weeks later I was passing through the area again going in the other direction. I was mentally absorbed in the meaning of a passage in a book I had been reading. The electrical sensation near my solar plexus started and slowly intensified, increasing until I was overwhelmed by wave after wave of powerful emotion. Ecstasy is too hollow a word to describe the sensation, which was as physical as it was emotional. Heaven itself might have descended on me. These waves persisted until it seemed that physically I could no longer contain them and would soon burst. The people around me seemed unaware of what was happening. Gradually, the sensation passed, and I settled back to my 'normal' state of consciousness. Such exalted states of consciousness are not mental; instead the mental, the emotional and physical fuse together in a way that is impossible to describe. Thought is much too slow to function in such states of awareness, as are so-called normal emotions. Thought disrupts the rhythm. While in this state, the intellect was as if adrift, untethered, rocked by the waves, until eventually it found its bearing and anchored itself, and the sensation slowly ebbed away, though lingering for a while.

I experienced this dynamic state of consciousness one other time when I was again passing this place. But this time the sensation crept slowly, emerging into my awareness. The mild electric shocks that tingled my solar plexus were again transmuted into waves of ecstasy. This time the state was even more intense than the previous times and persisted. We touch eternity every moment and infinity envelops us. Life has infinite possibilities; consciousness cannot be separated from life yet goes much deeper. I am uncertain of the relationship between the states of consciousness that I here relate and Kapilavastu's physical environment. Though I cannot say with certainty, my strong impression is that there is an intrinsic energy in this place emanating from sources sown there over millennia, perhaps the echoes of Siddhartha or Kapila, their followers, or other consciousness not discernable by human cognition. For various reasons I was receptive to this energy, energy and consciousness being two sides of one phenomenon. It is not imagination to say there are fields of consciousness of which we know next to nothing and about which we should avoid drawing conclusions.

How do I value this experience? One friend used to say that "truth is the search for evidence," as if having enough facts will lead to the truth. There are millions of "facts," for instance, about the Arab/Israeli conflict, but not one true version. The challenge with evidence and facts is how we "value" them. And this is perhaps our great challenge as a thinking species: how we value what we all might agree on – given certain facts. Meaning is personal. Value is subjective. How can we agree? I have given facts about an extremely personal, mystical event, that I cannot explain but only roughly describe. My only recourse is to learn what others who have had such experiences say about them, and the experiences' value and meaning for themselves. Yet, our circumstances are different, and so the experience is unique. No traverse is ever the same. There is nothing, no facts, to weigh in the scale and no value to assign. However, the experience is true, beyond any measure.

Our ability to compare and measure subjective phenomena, such as individual perceptions, feelings and emotions, is a matter for statistics, or psychoanalysis. Such means are crude at best. We cannot measure an emotion as we can measure, say, the height of a tree or the time that it takes to get to the moon, as if an emotion can be to the left or to the right. In our daily lives we may be able to see that a person suffers or is in pain, but we can't feel the extent of their suffering. The terms we use to describe emotions can hardly be called precise: that I am "very happy," "joyful," or "ecstatic" communicates to another only approximately how I feel, in a relative sense, and is understood by that person only approximately based on their own experience. Our unit of measure of our emotional life is our own subjective experience. I can never be sure that my subjective assessment of conditions is equivalent to your own. There is a class of phenomena for which we have no observable standards, which are largely beyond our ability to compare and measure. Such phenomena can only be described. These phenomena play no small role in human life and include: pain, love, imagination and dreams, fantasy, moral sense, intuition, visions, clairvoyance, seemingly inexplicable events, and the so-called "after life." This realm of phenomena is only beginning to be explored in a systematic way; but scientific method is not yet adequate and may never be. Watching neurons fire in an MRI is unlikely to ever provide the researcher with evidence of intensity of any of these phenomena. Yet such phenomena have been one of the most enduring subjects of human interest, the source of religion, mysticism, superstition and "magic." Too often we are ready to discount such phenomena. Since such phenomena cannot be compared or measured they are ignored or explained away – as "coincidence," for instance. Language is inadequate to the task, comprising representations that rely on individual conditioning and understanding.

I've witnessed mind-opening experiences, which have encouraged me to be receptive to events outside the norm. This "norm" refers to events that are directly explainable by reasons of cause and effect. To those so inclined, no doubt there are immediately obvious explanations for incidents that are here recounted – and missing the point. But please, don't start from a conclusion; let your criticism come through self-discovery. The nature of writing, of language, is to distinguish between a perceiver and what is perceived – subject and object. A narrator's perspective still makes these distinctions. Thoughts are in words; they are representations that our brain makes through words. It is necessary to understand that such representations are a matter of expediency in communication, a utilitarian convenience. Examined systematically, the perceiver and what is perceived merge into a single movement, like momentary waves that rise from and fall back to the river.

In the months following these ecstatic experiences, several unusual events happened. During these months I was in an agitated state. I had several prophetic dreams, experienced visions, and witnessed the fulfillment of some predictions, not made by me. This period culminated in a single event that encapsulated my unsettled mental state.

Mani Rimdu is a harvest festival celebrating the powers of light and darkness. Tibetans and Sherpas celebrate this festival with an elaborate ceremony of costume and dance. Tengboché Monastery is the heart of the Sherpa culture and religion. The Monastery's living quarters surround a stone courtyard that lies in its center, and in the middle of this courtyard is a traditional tall pole. The outer sanctum is a place of worship, a place that leaves an overwhelming impression on visitors. Even the most casual visitor could not help but feel reverential. The floors were made of wood worn smooth by centuries of use. Strong, thick wooden beams buttressed the walls and ceiling. But what immediately impressed visitors were the religious relics that filled the room. There were sacred texts, some in the process of being copied by monks, religious paintings that draped the walls (called Thankaas), icons, robed Buddha statues and bodhisattvas, riots of color, the smell of incense mingling with scents of candle wax and smoke. The old Monastery, if it were better known, would have been a world heritage site. This was the original Monastery, which later burnt down and was rebuilt.

My friend Tom and I had been in the Everest region for almost two weeks. In Pheriche, we chanced to meet former President Jimmy Carter and his wife Rosalynn, and two worn-out Secret Service Agents, and had the opportunity to visit with them. Conversation with a former President could be exhausting. This meeting gave me a slight appreciation of what it might be like to report to the head of a powerful country. The President was very interested in going fishing while he was in Nepal and, since I had some experience with its fisheries, I was grilled—for want of a fish. Grilling subordinates is what Presidents must do – before chewing them up. The number of questions and the level of detail may vary by issue, but the point seemed to be to maximize information in a condensed timeframe as input into decision-making, a science of its own, and a large part of a President's job. Rosalynn Carter impressed me quite unexpectedly; she had a presence, an ineffable quality that is difficult to put my finger on. After leaving Pheriche, Tom and I continued our return journey to Lukla airport, from where we would fly back to Kathmandu. We stopped at Tengboché for a couple of days on the way down.

The day after we arrived, the Mani Rimdu festival was just beginning. When we realized how opportune our timing was, we decided to remain at the Monastery.

TENGBOCHE MONASTERY

The dance ceremony started in the morning with the archaic sound of Tibetan long horns. The horns themselves looked old, and really were long – three to four meters in length – the longest resting on a pad on the ground. The monks blasted very deep notes that rose and crashed up through the horn until the sound finally vibrated out of their horns' fluted ends. The dancers, all monks and apprentices, assembled and, slowly, the ceremony began. There were several major acts, each with different themes and dancers in varied costumes. I was struck by how well the dancers knew their parts; there were few noticeable mistakes. Each costumed dancer wore a mask signifying his role in the drama. Most of the masks resembled the panoply of gods and demons that one sees in Tibetan thaankas, such as the Wheel of Life motif. Each mask was itself a work of art, outrageous in aspect. The day began sunny, though the afternoon grew cloudy. The crisp, yet slightly damp air of the Himalayan autumn was chill, but not cold.

Late in the morning, between acts, under the watchfulness of the High Lama and fellow monks, a character dressed as a Bodhisattva came to entertain the audience. He played a few tricks and frightened a few children. Most unexpectedly, he then grabbed me out of the audience. The crowd laughed and thought it all in good fun.

I too thought it all in good fun. However, it became apparent that, while amusing the audience, there was something very purposeful occurring at the same time. The acolyte's actions were deliberate; he locked my arm in his and made me circle the center pole three times, each time passing before the High Lama. The acolyte stopped at a pedestal. He took a pair of heavy clappers and banged them together and placed them immediately before each of my body's orifices one at a time, so that the vibrations penetrated, further delighting the audience. He then showed me a series of very complicated hand and finger postures, making me repeat each one until I executed it properly. Next, he had me help him make tsampa using my right hand while he used his left (tsampa is the traditional food of millet flour mixed with water). The acolyte then returned me to the audience and with that the mock "rite" was over and the next act began. This episode left me exhilarated, confused and overwhelmed. I had imagined one day being "initiated." For a long time afterward, I took this event as symbolic of "my" spiritual journey. The spiritual quest, while coming from a worthy impulse, is a selfish response. Our real journey is to explore the stream of consciousness within the milieu from which it ever emerges.

Places have power, inexplicable but yet sensible, sensible to our inner sense, not our usual senses. Who hasn't felt the unusualness of some particular place? There are places that have peculiar powers, some enchanting and some darker. Such places abide in legends and fairy tales, and they are one of the surest things we know in our experience. Places have the power to play on our emotions, so that we might feel nauseous, dizzy or joyful, for instance. There are such places in the Himalayas and their foothills, places with natural springs, towering boulders and crumbling caves, which communicate their power to those who are attentive. Besides the events described in Kapilavastu, I've encountered powerful places on the Annapurna Circuit's western trail, also north of Namché Bazaar at Shyangboché where a magnetic force almost swept me away. Religious and holy sites often harbor such power, no place more so than Saint Peter's Basilica in Rome. There, on the stone floor in a certain historically significant but not central spot, one who is sensitive can feel a surge of energy. The word "surge" is an appropriate description of the force that suddenly blasts through the body, pervading the cellular structure from toe to head. I wasn't aware of the spot's historical significance until inquiring afterward. There is perhaps a dozen such places where I've felt this inherent magnetism, which can electrify one's whole body. In bygone eras in East Asia such places might have been described as having feng shui, the habitations of sprite or jinn, or other forces

– light and dark. One thing of which I am certain, such places are aware, though scientific instruments may never detect it. Their power is beyond imagination.

If one listens, through an inner ear one can hear the voice of some places. Taleju temple in Kathmandu's Durbar Square talks to passersby. She speaks of the deep wisdom of centuries; of the men who planned and built her, with their calculated design; those men, they knew, they brought her to life – conscious, aware, eternal. The crowds shuffle by, scarcely aware that she watches. She inhabits all of her time, dwelling in each part and the whole, from her creation to final destruction. Her senses are not those of an animal, yet she is sentient.

Humans, in contrast to other animals, use complex language that doesn't communicate as directly as Taleju. If animals had humans' capacity they would communicate with us directly, by the same means. Our first thoughts create an entity inside of us – the thinker or "I," the object in who these thoughts occur. We like to see this "I" as something constant; it isn't. This "I" is as subject to change and to becoming as the fleeting world that our senses perceive. We feel that the entity who we are is real, has substance, though it is as ephemeral as the clouds passing across the sky. This "I" rides on top of consciousness, like a brief wave, ever seeking futilely to guide and direct. "I" have seen the unreality of this "I" and have struggled to be rid of it, yet this "I" can't be disposed of so easily. It is enmeshed in the neuro-physiology of the brain, etched there as synapses and neuro-chemicals, glandular secretions and other "wetware." There is a structure, but a fluid and electrical one. This structure accretes, and one day may be discovered to be a cause of Alzheimer's and other related diseases of the brain. Attentiveness, proprioception, is key to untangling this neural web. One feels, senses, the unreality of this "I" that has literally thought itself into existence. As someone very wise once said, "who 'I' am is emerging constantly," out of the stream of consciousness.

Some experiences have no corollary to any of the five senses. Tal is a small village on the towering eastern slopes of the Annapurna Massif. "Tal" means Lake. Standing on the ridge overlooking the small valley in which Tal rests one can clearly see that the village lies in an old lakebed. The last time I passed through Tal I was returning from a sojourn to Tilicho Lake. Following prolonged fasting and intentional hardship, I still could not eat much, yet I was engaged in physically vigorous activity, trekking a difficult trail all day. My body's energy was in disequilibrium. Five years earlier when my friend Dale and I passed through Tal, we stayed in a young woman's house for a couple of days. Her husband was a trader and was away on business. I stayed with her again on my return from Tilicho, but instead of a house she now had a new lodge; I remembered her although she did not recognize me. Her husband was away on business again – or still. I took an upstairs room overlooking the valley and beyond to the lower flanks of Annapurna II. The sides of Annapurna II are remote and devoid of human presence, although on the map they do not appear to be far removed from settlements yet getting there would be very difficult. I sat on the balcony and watched the sunlight play through the clouds as it illumined one patch of land, then shifted to another, broke gloriously through and then moved swiftly away leaving gloom in its wake. With this view fresh in mind, I laid down to rest.

As I lay there, my consciousness accelerated, right out of my body high into space above. My consciousness rushed past the area that I had been watching just a short time before, soaring beyond. I'm not sure how long I lay there, though when I returned it was not yet dark; I was as if in a trance, not sleeping, but not awake – conscious of sensations never before experienced. The trance ended as my consciousness sped back to my body, leaving me gasping for breath; I felt as if I had just finished a marathon. This is not my sole out-of-body experience, but one that, now years later, is all the more remarkable. Other out-of-body experiences have happened while I slept and were unusual in that while outside my body I saw myself lying there. I found that I am susceptible to such experiences when during sleep my head tilts back at a certain angle, either affecting the flow of blood or air. I've been to a sleep disorder clinic and was diagnosed as having "positional apnea." Whether these others were really "out of body experiences" I cannot say, but the experience at Tal was unique.

Clairvoyance is seeing the future, whether in flashes of insight, trances or dreams, and can be classed with premonitions, déjà vu and synchronicity of events. I dreamed I was in a place that might have passed for 1920s America, driving down a narrow country road surrounded by fields. The car passed a gas station and went on to a small hamlet. We stopped at the hamlet and got out of the car, walking to the entryway of a house. The house had trellises loaded with bunches of grapes along the walkway and many fruit trees nearby. I remembered the dream. Some months later I was working in the Ukraine. We were traveling in the countryside near Odessa and visited one of the region's more successful farmers. We drove to our destination on the same country road, through the same small hamlet to see the same farmer. The sensation was freaky as I knew for nearly half-an-hour exactly what was going to happen, who I would see, where each person would sit or stand, what we would discuss and where we would go.

These incidences are outside of "normal" consciousness. There was, however, no intimation of "sacredness" in them. Consciousness has the capacity to roam in dimensions beyond the bounds of sequential time; the stream is all one at its source and its termination. On a walk through the neighborhood where I lived in Vermont, all my sense of self became suspended and there was a consciousness of "the ocean being compressed into a drop," as others have described this sensation; but the description is not the thing. In that state there is no division where "I" stop and where the world starts; all merges. An altogether other experience of consciousness happened when I was riding my bicycle one evening in the Terai. The sun was low in the sky; I had a sense of the merging of all life around me. It struck me at that moment that if I could spin around quickly, like a dervish, I would have 360° vision. With this thought, suddenly through some other sense I perceived the world around me in 360°: I saw the cars that passed behind me, the water buffalo fading from view, farmers in their fields. I was conscious of their presence though they were not within the range of my eyesight. This merging of all things has come on other occasions: watching the giant fruit bats fly over the dhera roof in Kathmandu, sitting by the Dredge watching the sunset across Paradise Valley in Montana, and walking along Trail Creek Road watching the wind blow through the trees, when time melted into eternity and I apprehended that forever in those moments would I watch those trees blow in that wind. But these sidis, as the Hindus call such powers, are not within my control.

One dreary November day I was driving my car; the sky was overcast, cold and threatening snow. Clouds hid Vermont's Green Mountains, making the terrain look flat and few leaves were left to dangle from bare tree limbs. I had been on the road since before dawn and the afternoon would soon turn into evening. I had jet lag from a recent trip to Africa and was going home for the holidays. Since Lynn died, the holidays seem hollow, though family and friends bring comfort. A shaft of sunlight broke weakly through the gloom, shining in through the car windshield, at once illuminating everything: Love gives potency to life and brings meaning. Forgive this poor attempt at expression, yet, love cannot come from outside of our consciousness. Love is not an intruder. It emerges from within and reaches out – ex-presses. To say "God loves us" is to miss the point; it separates "God" from "us." Like consciousness, and intelligence, love is emergent. Love is no more a property or quality of a thing or a relationship than is consciousness, rather the reverse. Things or relationships reveal themselves as regards consciousness, intelligence and love.

Altogether different, because the event seemed to originate externally, was my one ghostly experience. When I worked for a major multinational agribusiness, I frequently traveled to Cobham in the UK, just outside of London. Cobham, in Surrey, is a small town but is, as the locals say, a "horsey" district and upper income. In many respects Cobham is a London bedroom community, with beautiful houses, mostly in a neo-Tudor style. Reflecting Tudor times, there are properties in Cobham dating to that era. One such property is the Cedar House, which was built in the mid-1500s. My employer booked me there during one stay. The rooms then were decorated in a 1960s mod-deco style, a decade not remembered for comfort. Nevertheless, my room was comfortable enough. One particular evening I returned to Cedar House from a day of work. I went down to the restaurant for dinner, though the evening was just starting, the time was probably around 6:30 or 7:00. Earlier it had rained but the sun was starting to show from behind the clouds. I was the only person in the restaurant.

The waitress took my dinner order and went to the kitchen. As I read a magazine while waiting for the meal, someone walked across the old wood floor, through the hallway in front of the dining area. I heard the door open and then slam loudly shut; the door slammed so hard that the windows shook. The slamming door got my attention and I glanced out the window. I didn't see anyone and didn't think much more about it, except that it was strange that I hadn't seen anyone pass by outside because the window is right next to the door. I turned back to my magazine and continued reading. About 10 minutes later I heard the door open again and slam shut with such force that again the windows shook. Well, this time I was really curious. I looked up to see who had made so much noise but couldn't see anyone from where I was sitting. Thinking this strange, I got up to take a look. I went to the hallway and looked in both directions left and right but saw no one. There was a bar ahead toward the front of the house, so I thought that whoever made the commotion probably went there. I walked into the bar, but it was empty. The barroom curved toward the front of the house, so I went on to look and found the wall rounded to an abrupt end. There was no way out and no one there. I thought this was very strange. Returning to my table I went back to my magazine, a bit disconcerted.

Some minutes later, the waitress brought my meal. After dinner, she brought the check and I made a joke about "the house being haunted." Her response caught me off guard. She told me that the house was haunted with at least three ghosts. She said that they actually had a priest try to exercise a ghost in one room not long before. I told her what had just happened, and she wasn't at all surprised. She told me that she had seen one of the ghosts in the hallway, a woman apparition coming toward her reading a book. I found it all quite fascinating. When I went to bed that night, I wondered if I might have another haunting, but nothing else happened during the rest of my stay.

Cobham may have other ghosts, exuding as it does ages past. Many an old house has stories to divulge to those who can decipher them. When I was there I liked to go for long walks in the evenings through Cobham's neighborhoods and admire the houses. A house speaks volumes about its inhabitants—current, former, and perhaps future; houses echo their owners.

Similarly, I took long walks through Livingston, Montana, when living there and I became aware that houses, like people, have their own characters. The town's older houses are in the east side, though in age stripling compared to Cobham, many were built in the early 20th Century. Those houses could all but talk, betraying their inhabitants' characters: what they were like, whether they cared about anyone besides themselves, if they were organized, had a sense of pride, their social status – if they were aspirational, how their children were treated, and many other secrets as well.

Another inexplicable incident happened in Bahadurgunj. My dhai ("big brother" in Nepali) and his wife had two girls and she had just given birth to a baby boy. When the infant was about four months old, he became very sick. The illness lasted for several weeks and kept getting worse. The family took him to a doctor, who prescribed antibiotics, but the baby had nearly completed the course of medicine with no observable improvement. The family was deeply concerned; we discussed the baby's treatment and what might be done: drink plenty of water, keep warm, avoid over-stimulation, etc. But as weeks passed, the parents became desperate.

Early one evening I dropped by to check on them. My sister-in-law, or bauju, was there alone and we talked about the baby's health. After a few minutes a man from the village who I had tea with from time-to-time dropped by. As we were chatting, he began to take items out of his shoulder bag, which I recognized as being associated with some Hindu rituals; a small bell, an incense burner, an ash holder. My bauju and I watched as he began to prepare for what was obviously going to be a Brahmanic ritual. She had not mentioned that in their desperation they had sought the services of a Brahman, a special Brahman, an Aryuvedic healer. I watched with interest as he began the ritual, finding it curious that my presence (a foreigner) wasn't a problem. He walked over to the corner and rang the small bell – awakening the vital forces (gods). He repeated this action in each corner of the room, for each of the four cardinal directions, chanting a prayer all the while. When he finished with the bell he circled the room with the burning incense, its light smoke and sweet smell pervaded the air. I was surprised that this slight, youngish, inconspicuous man with whom I occasionally socialized was also a healer; he hadn't mentioned it. He looked so ordinary with his short, well-groomed hair, neatly trimmed mustache, cotton shirt and polyester pants; I would not have guessed that he had such an ability.

He continued to chant his prayers as he touched the baby's tongue with a small amount of ash. After performing a few more short rituals, we discussed what he had just done, then he left. Within 24 hours the baby began to show signs of improvement. Within 48 hours, he was definitely getting better. After three days he was nearly back to normal. I have since spoken to Western doctors about this incident and of the baby's recovery. They assured me that it just took a bit longer than usual for the antibiotics to take effect.

Then there are hallucinations, individually and *en masse*. When I was six or seven years old I had a different kind of encounter with – something. While sound asleep in the middle of the night, I abruptly awoke to a noise. Earlier that day I had been playing with some toys, which I stored in a brown paper bag. Usually I kept the bags of toys in the closet but on this night, I left the bag lying tipped over on the floor with the toys scattered around. I glanced sleepily across the room and spotted a small, humanoid creature bending over and peering into the bag. Surprised – I must have made a noise – the – whatever it was – looked at me and quickly darted out of the room, tearing off a piece from the bag as it fled. The thing was maybe a foot tall when it stood up. The monsters from *Monsters Inc.* would have been disappointed – I was too terrified to scream. I ducked under the covers and remained hidden, until sometime later I fell back to sleep. When I got up in the morning I checked the bag and noted the torn-off piece lying on the floor, which was not there when I went to bed. To me this was proof that the creature I saw the night before was real. The whole event, of course, could have been the active imagination of a young mind emerging from a dream, except for the torn bag and piece of paper, which I could never explain. For years afterward, if I woke up during the night, I would lay in bed frightened of what might be lurking in the shadows of my room. Get up to pee? No way! Background noise from the heater or the air conditioner would bring relief because I thought such noises would frighten any creatures that might be lurking. More than forty years later I can still recall this incident quite clearly. Apparently, this experience isn't unique and there are other people who have seen similar humanoid things. There is a fuzzy line between imagination and perception. Some researchers say that imagination and perception involve the same mental processes, that they spring from the same source in the brain.

Then there are haunting experiences that are completely imagined but they leave a lasting impression anyway. In South Asia, there is wide acceptance of metempsychosis. Metempsychosis is the belief that the spirits of dead people can inhabit the bodies of animals, though there are variations on the theme. The Tibetan Book of the Dead recounts that a person's unsatiated appetites can lead them to an animal or other form of existence that will help to expunge the obsession. One can imagine the gluttonous reborn as pigs, the rapacious reborn as vultures, the sexually insatiable reborn as bitches, and so on. On two occasions such imagination seemed plausible to me. The first time was associated with one of the most wretched animals I've ever seen. I was living in a small, Nepalese village east of Itahari, on the East-West Highway during Peace Corps training. The village was named Khorsani, which translates as 'hot pepper'. The family with whom I stayed was a high caste Brahman family, ruled by an elderly matriarch. Almost every night I woke to agonized moaning. The nearest description of the sound would be what one hears in a hospital emergency room after there has been a terrible trauma and the victim is in dire straits. The moans would start low and gradually grow louder until reaching an agonized pitch, as though death was just a single moan away. The sound seemed possessed: the spirit inside expressing the embodied suffering of the creature it inhabited.

When I first heard the moan, I thought it must have been the matriarch, who was clearly tubercular. She often woke up everyone in the house with severe coughing spasms every morning before dawn. One night the moaning became so unbearable that someone finally did something about it, that's when I realized a dog was the source. I had no idea that a dog could make such a sound, although I have heard a rabbit in its extremity sound like a screaming infant. The dog was a pathetic creature, missing half a front leg and a very bad case of mange. Its skin was studded with open sores and scarred from its constant scratching and biting with almost no hair left. The bitch had obviously had many litters of puppies, probably one too many, as one could guess that she passed the mange on to her most recent litters. We used to joke about the "lifecycle of the Terai hairless, ending under a bus," but this poor animal wasn't humorous. I've never seen a living being in such constant misery. It made me squirm to see her. One night during her serenade the thought took hold, for whatever reason, that this had once been some poor wretch of a person. That thought lingered. I expected the animal to die at any time during my two months in the village, but it didn't. Yet I could not shake the image that some wanton, human desire may have expiated itself in this poor creature.

In the second instance of imagined metempsychosis I mistook the dragging legs of an old bull for the shuffling feet of an old man. One night I woke from a sound sleep while in my dhera in Bahadurgunj. Through the open-air windows that overlooked the main street below, came the sound of dragging and shuffling. The noise reminded me of an old man limping with a cane in one hand and leaning against another person for support, walking slowly together. When I woke up I had the distinct impression, which I could not shake, of a particular person pacing back and forth down the street. Over some weeks this sound woke me up, until one night I got up to see who was pacing the village streets at such an hour. When I looked, limping slowly down the street was an old bull, a large animal that must have served his purpose and finally been turned loose to die. The impression the animal left was of an aging man.

So, what's the point of these anecdotes about some unusual experiences? To cast seeds of doubt, to make us question our certainties, to suggest there are many things we don't know – and can't know. There are domains that science and technology can't reach, where there are no causes or effects and explanations are bound to be partial or false.

Time is no more than the slimmest of realities, separating the present moment from the future and past, though this sounds cliché. The present – NOW – is all there is and all that we'll ever know. Yet probable pasts and intimations of possible futures intrude on this present, which is hard- and soft-wired in our neuro-physiology and biology. Prophetic dreams, premonitions, déjà vu, "ghosts," may be shades of future, past or "probable" presents. There are bleed-throughs from different times into our present; and every being's present is uniquely its own. From this perspective, a thousand years ago may be as close as yesterday, and tomorrow may be impossibly distant. Some spaces – places – psychological states – have unusual properties in relation to Time and some events imprint themselves in space. Time turns back on itself; we feel like we have been here before because we have been here before, in this exact place and time, and our time recurs, and we confront our choices again. Does this seem strange? The evidence is ever before us.

I have an image of myself; it has been conditioned into me almost from birth. I identify with this image – why, it's just me! Over life's course I came to accept, believe, in this image. I think about it, nurture and protect it, and become attached to, nay, inseparable from, this image. At the most basic level this self-image is an electro-biochemical network of neurons and hormonal secretions, wired into my psyche. Fuzzy though this image is, when I'm praised I feel good because of the image. If I am criticized, I'm pained because this image is pricked. Maybe I react: lashing out or retreating. The image sparks fear and insecurity if I find it threatened. We all know people who obsessively feed their images of themselves, constantly, as if they couldn't feel their existence without incessantly feeding it. Such are the myriad people who constantly need to be "stroked." They are right in a way, without constant stroking they won't exist, at least not as they imagine. Negative emotions signal that our self-image is disturbed. With good reason Buddhists warn of the dangers of attachment. A large share of human thought and emotion revolves around these images, these identities that we make for ourselves, wittingly or no. Much of the world's violence and wrongs originate with these images of ourselves and our tribes. And the image is always becoming – it never is. In the very end, the image is – imaginary.

Like the tarot hermit, I have always sought answers, ultimately for meaning. As most Christian kids brought up in evangelical American culture, I found wisdom in the Bible. But unlike my Christian cohorts, that wisdom just wet my appetite. "Something" was missing. I spent hours in bookstores exploring bookshelves, reading science, philosophy, psychology, and New Age books; and I did find what I was looking for. I consumed passages, digested ideas, as fast as I could shove them in, though they sometimes left a bad taste, returning to the most nourishing sources again and again, over many years, as the meanings slowly unfolded themselves, still finding new meaning in these sources. Oftentimes an author's meaning is quite in the open but the mind must be ready to receive. My companions have been classical and contemporary: Plato, Chuang Tse, the Bible, the Upanishads, the Mahavastu, Thoreau and Nietzsche, Krishnamurti, Gurdjieff, Ouspensky, Maurice Nicol, Rodney Collin, and the first book by "Seth." In particular, "Thought as a System," a dialogue with the physicist Professor David Bohm, offers a roadmap of the human psyche and is the well from which I've drawn the most. Years ago, I chanced upon a book by Edgar Cayce in which he predicted in the 1930s that a new teaching would one day bring hope to humanity, existing then in Russia; "*Tertium Organum*," by P.D. Ouspensky, is such a source and holds keys to many of life's great mysteries, and will lead to future discoveries and a more holistic science. More recently published research on neurobiology has turned out some excellent books that, wittingly or no, point to conclusions similar to the sages. Among the more accessible works are those of Robert Sapolsky. These teachers point to a life of discovery in every moment.

EPILOGUE

I FELT COMPELLED TO WRITE "Being Here: mylogs." Many years ago, I began to write them, stopping, then starting again. The future rushes to the past.

Some circumstances in our lives must necessarily recur. Committing the circumstances of my life to writing also commits them to fate. These writings reveal few regrets, though I have them. Yet I may aspire to other conditions in another recurrence of my life. Hopefully there is something useful here, for some reader someday, even though it be just one.

The Stoics believed in a divine, rational being. If the Stoics were neuroscientists they might instead have become Cynics. Beliefs frame our emotions while emotions guide our decisions, informing us of the choices we are making. Neuroscientists have learned that people who have damaged certain areas of their brains (the pre-frontal cortex) lose the power to choose. Desire must play a role in human affairs; without it, nothing would be done. We may desire a better world, but trouble starts with the desire to be a better person. I am this, but I will become that – self-improvement. Ideals of desire-less states notwithstanding, emotions help us to value, to weigh, our perceptions, to calibrate them with available choices. There is a state of mind that is undivided, and emotions are intelligent. However, trying to reach that state is its own hindrance. This approach cannot work.

What is intelligence, and is mental capability its highest form? Thought, as past knowledge meeting current circumstances, effects our perceptions. Where do we – humanity – go from here with our individual, communal, national and other aspirations colliding ever more frequently? With our knowledge we rush headlong; our technology drives us, yet we know not how to steer. What is the destination?

The upright animals that walked out of Africa's savannah grew in intelligence. Biologically, the story of *Homo sapiens* is the story of the development of the frontal cortex. We are fitted to screen and process vast amounts of information and knowledge. Our shared knowledge propels us and is not just something we use. We presume that each of us, individually, controls our knowledge, it is there passively in our brains to be used. But this is not so. Knowledge is always active, not passive, ever shaping our perceptions. Four states of attention are possible: sleep, unaware, divided, and undivided. The first three may blend together, undivided attention is distinct. Knowledge blocks undivided attention. Experiment—see for yourself if this is not the case.

Everywhere we see incoherence and fragmentation in human affairs, and with the constant addition of new knowledge, the situation has huge momentum, but momentum in what direction?

Life creates and destroys, brings joy and tragedy, well-being and misery, comprehension and incomprehensibility. We begin where we are.

INDEX

M

R

S

W

Y

Z

About the Author

∾

MARK HUISENGA GREW UP IN Livingston, Montana, in the shadow of Yellowstone National Park. After working as a volunteer extension agent, Huisenga went on to become a trekking guide in Nepal. For part of his time in Nepal, he lived in Kapilavastu, the kingdom of the Buddha's father.

Huisenga works as an agricultural market analyst, a job that has taken him to over fifty countries around the globe. His perspective on the American experience shifted dramatically following the murder of his sister, a flight attendant on layover in Boise, Idaho, in 2000. Huisenga continues to be involved with the country of Nepal and most recently worked as an advisor in the aftermath of the 2015 earthquake.

Huisenga currently works for an international development organization and lives in Arlington, Virginia.

Made in the USA
Middletown, DE
05 December 2022

17128365R00117

Mark Huisenga spent years as a trekking guide deep in the spectacular Himalayas and the country of Nepal. But it isn't until the brutal, mysterious murder of his sister that Huisenga truly begins to understand what it means to be alive on this earth.

Written with stunning emotional strength and breathless adventure, *Being Here: mylogs* is a sweeping look at the complexity of human existence. Huisenga welcomes readers into some of the most formidable chapters of his life with inspiring insight and grace, weaving together elements of travel epics and true-crime classics.

As Huisenga and his family grapple with the shattering aftermath of his sister's murder, he must also come to terms with what it means to be part of the human experience as a whole. *Being Here: mylogs* is an astounding story of emotional resilience that will leave you breathless with suspense.

ISBN 978-1-5406-4452-7

9 781540 644527 >